The Peace Puppy

The Peace Puppy

A Memoir of Caregiving and Canine Solace

SUSAN HARTZLER

DOGS IN OUR WORLD
Series Editor Brian Patrick Duggan

McFarland & Company, Inc., Publishers
Jefferson, North Carolina

ALSO BY SUSAN HARTZLER

I'm Not Single, I Have a Dog: Dating Tales from the Bark Side (McFarland, 2021)

ISBN (print) 978-1-4766-9482-5
ISBN (ebook) 978-1-4766-5332-7

LIBRARY OF CONGRESS AND BRITISH LIBRARY
CATALOGUING DATA ARE AVAILABLE

Library of Congress Control Number 2024028671

Front cover image: Author's collection

Printed in the United States of America

*McFarland & Company, Inc., Publishers
Box 611, Jefferson, North Carolina 28640
www.mcfarlandpub.com*

In loving memory
of Mom and Dad

Acknowledgments

I couldn't have completed this manuscript without the love and support of my chosen family: Kim Ostrovsky, Catherine Overturf, Maria Miereanu, Brenda Piccirillo, Emilie and Myron Rayman, Natasha Testa, Cade Overturf, Sharon Stone, Cathy Scribner, Laurie Winter, Elaine Stanley, Gene and Jimmy Naylor, Leslie Westbrook, Michael O'Shea, and Pam Marks.

A special thank you to my writing coach, Mandy Jackson-Beverly, for helping me get this story out of my head and to my friend, Maura Kruse-Noonan, for her edits, love and support. My unending gratitude goes to McFarland for giving me a chance, especially to my editor, Brian Patrick Duggan.

Finally, I'd like to acknowledge the dogs I've had the pleasure of sharing my life with, most of all Baldwin, who forever lives in my heart.

Table of Contents

Table of Contents

Preface

Step into my heartfelt memoir *The Peace Puppy* and embark on a transformative journey into the uncharted territory of caregiving and the extraordinary power of love, particularly puppy love. Through my personal account of caring for my ailing father in his final years, this memoir illuminates the immense challenges faced by adult children who selflessly dedicate their lives to the care of their parents and the dogs who help us along the way.

Startling statistics reveal a growing reality—more and more adult children find themselves in the role of caregiver for their aging parent(s). In today's fast-paced society, these brave individuals must navigate the complexities of balancing careers, personal lives, and the all-consuming task of caregiving. This delicate balancing act often leaves caretakers feeling overwhelmed, isolated, and emotionally drained.

Caretaking, or, in my case, overseeing a caretaker, takes an undeniable toll on those assuming the responsibility. Physical and mental exhaustion become constant companions, and the weight of responsibilities can seem insurmountable. Yet, within this struggle lies the potential for growth, resilience, and the discovery of the extraordinary capacity of the human spirit, especially for those of us lucky enough to have a dog like Baldwin by our side.

The Peace Puppy serves as a compassionate guide for those thrust into the role of caretaker, with invaluable insights, lessons learned, and even a bit of practical advice (get a dog). It goes beyond mere storytelling, providing an honest portrayal of the highs and lows that accompany the journey of caregiving a parent. It explores the rewards and disasters, revealing moments of profound connection, fulfillment, and joy.

For me, a beacon of hope emerged within the difficulties I faced—and that hope came in the form of my rescue dog, Baldwin. Within the pages of this memoir, you will witness how his unconditional love and

1

Preface

intuitive understanding became my solace and support. Ultimately, Baldwin turned into an unexpected lifeline, helping me sustain my role as overseer of dad's care through the toughest of times.

The Peace Puppy is more than a memoir; it's a testament to the transformative power of compassion. It pays tribute to all the selfless caregivers and serves as a gentle reminder that even in the face of adversity, healing, growth, and profound connections can emerge, especially when we open our hearts to the love of a rescue dog to help us along the way.

Introduction

My journey begins in 2000, the year Mom passed away, forever altering my life. She'd spent the last years of her life caring for Dad, who battled Parkinson's disease. After she died, my siblings and I were left with the weighty responsibility of deciding our dad's future. And amidst our grief, one thing remained resolute—Dad's steadfast desire to remain in the home he'd lived in for more than four decades. It was then that the pressing question arose: Who would step up to assist Dad?

Knowing that Dad couldn't manage on his own, all three of us acknowledged the need for assistance. From meal preparation, medication and getting to his numerous doctors' appointments to walking and even basic communication, he required support in every aspect of his daily life. It was I who volunteered to move back home. At 42, I was the youngest, unmarried, and unattached sibling unless, of course, you considered my dog, Baldwin, my loyal companion. I thought perhaps this selfless act of moving home to oversee Dad's care would finally put an end to the acrimony in the family caused by me, the rebel child.

That fluff ball face!

3

Introduction

In a relentless pursuit of approval, I desperately wanted to be a so-called "good girl," the person who I appeared to be to my dog. I believed that my volunteerism would lead to my redemption, but this would never be the case. Instead, I learned to focus on the positive relationships that I'd cultivated in my life, like the one I had with Baldwin and a few close friends who became my chosen family.

The Peace Puppy delves into my journey from seeking validation as a "good girl" to realizing that I was enough all along. It showcases how a small, black fluff ball named Baldwin helped me see the truth. Through the ups and downs, *The Peace Puppy* illuminates the power of self-discovery and the profound impact that a furry companion can have on our lives.

In the pages of *The Peace Puppy*, it is my sincere hope that you will find not only a memoir but also a testament to the indomitable spirit of caregivers along with the extraordinary bond between humans and their canine companions. It's a story of hope, healing, and the enduring power of love. May this memoir inspire and uplift, reminding us that the love of a rescue dog can guide us through the darkest of days.

1

Dog Gone It

The afternoon sun streamed through the windows of my humble one-bedroom Santa Monica apartment. It was more beach shack than comfy home, and its weathered exterior and dated interior gave it a sort of rustic charm. At least, that's what I tried to convince myself. This worn-out place was the only apartment I could find (and afford) after being unceremoniously evicted from the swanky Westside condo I'd rented. Plus, dogs were accepted, and I wasn't moving without my new fluffy companion, Baldwin.

That chilly weekday afternoon in January, I stood in the tiny bathroom and wiped the steam from the mirror. I was forty-two, and the reflection staring back at me was hardly familiar—my swollen, teary eyes appeared more red than hazel, and I didn't remember inviting crows to dance on my face while I napped.

"Damn, I look exhausted."

A furry paw on my leg alerted me to the watchful gaze of Baldwin. There's nothing quite like a rescue dog to make you feel loved. Reaching down, I tousled Baldwin's curly mop of hair that would soon turn into dreadlocks. Baldwin, the dog I'd adopted after losing my Blondie, had a Muppet-like face and a tiny stub of a tail. Blondie, in contrast, had lustrous golden fur, a fox-like face, and a feathered tail that gracefully swayed when she walked. Their appearances couldn't have been more different, but they each held a special place in my heart.

I couldn't help but smile at the sight of the six-month-old pup, a gift from Mom. Baldwin was a bundle of high-octane energy. Despite his mischievous antics and occasional accidents, I fell in love with him the moment I held him in my arms.

"Stress leave?" I asked my canine companion. "Do I look that bad?"

He barked and circled around my legs, herding me out of the bathroom through the narrow hallway that led to my bedroom.

My new curly-haired companion was more dog than I'd bargained for. Turned out, he was a Hungarian Puli, part of the herding family. I didn't yet understand that herding dogs required substantial time and training, along with a job to keep them occupied.

I looked at my soaking-wet self in the full-length mirror leaning against the blank white wall of my dark, gloomy bedroom.

"Was it that obvious?" Even I could see the weariness etched across my face.

I touched my flushed cheek. "Maybe it's just from the shower." I massaged my forehead, attempting to soften the deepened wrinkles.

"Woof," my canine sidekick responded.

"But there's no excuse for these dark circles under my eyes. Or the fact that I look like an old lady."

I heard my former boyfriend enter the apartment. My handsome ex-boyfriend, ten years my senior, had a striking appearance with his piercing blue eyes and Spanish sun-kissed olive skin. He could easily pass for half his age.

Although Jack and I had officially broken up, he was sleeping on my couch while searching for a place of his own. Our romantic relationship may have faded, but after a decade together, we'd become best friends.

"Why are you home, Dudan?" Jack's nickname for me was inspired by a three-year-old's adorable mispronunciation of my name.

Carefully stepping through the maze of piled-up moving boxes, Jack headed toward me. He didn't get very

Baldwin loved car rides, especially when Jack came along.

far before being intercepted by Baldwin, who wiggled his entire body to greet his second human.

"They sent me home on stress leave," I said. "Can you believe it?"

"I'm not surprised," Jack said, "considering everything you've been through in the last six months."

Jack bent down to pet Baldwin, but the fluff ball attacked him with big, wet, sloppy dog kisses—so enthusiastically that he knocked Jack off his feet.

"Okay, okay, buddy," Jack said. "I love you too."

Baldwin scurried back to me, as if proudly announcing Jack's arrival.

"I know," I told the fluffy ball of fur. "Jack's home!"

At the sound of Jack's name, Baldwin excitedly ran back to him and jumped onto his lap.

"Anyone would be stressed in your shoes," Jack said. "You work too much, lost your twenty-year-old dog a couple months ago, got robbed at gunpoint, got hit by a car in front of Starbucks, was forced to move, and we broke up."

"Broke up *again*," I corrected him. "Your bad luck must be rubbing off on me. Anyway, in all fairness, that car only grazed me, nothing like what happened to you last year. I didn't have to spend two weeks in the ICU with a brain bleed after being struck by a car."

"I wish my meditation practice would rub off on you," Jack counseled. "I told you. You need to meditate."

"I know, I know," I sighed. "I've tried reiki and yoga. You've got to give me a little credit for that."

"Well, at least your boss recognizes that you're only human," Jack said, embracing Baldwin tightly. "That last media FAM you led sounded like a complete nightmare."

I'd just returned from a media familiarization tour, or FAM for short—a trip designed to introduce important media representatives to a destination or property and, hopefully, write a glowing review of their experience afterward. Being a public relations agent in the travel arena meant dealing with demanding journalists accustomed to VIP treatment wherever they went.

Baldwin hopped off Jack's lap, his brown eyes barely visible through his soft black curls. He didn't say a word, but he didn't need to. I'd only had him for a few weeks, yet I couldn't imagine my life without him. Besides, Mom had bought him for me—a sort of peace offering in the form of a furry companion.

The Peace Puppy

Speaking of Mom, it was her birthday and I needed to get ready to head home to the San Fernando Valley where I grew up to celebrate that night. Standing at only five-foot-two, Mom reminded me of a cupcake with her frosted brown hair. We'd finally found common ground after clashing since my teenage years. Buying me that dog was a tribute to our newfound relationship.

I'd been living in my new place for a few weeks by then but hadn't unpacked a single thing. Cardboard boxes filled with my belongings were stacked against the walls of the small ground-floor one-bedroom unit, giving the space the appearance of a hoarder's den. Even my wardrobe sat crumpled in boxes on the floor crammed in my tiny bedroom.

I opened one in search of something to wear. I needed to get moving to avoid the dreaded crawl on the 405 freeway into the San Fernando Valley.

"I'm sorry you won't be joining us tonight," I pouted.

"Your mom called me earlier to make sure I knew I was invited," Jack replied, now standing. "I already have band practice, or I'd join you."

"She called you?" The news halted me in my tracks. It was another olive branch from Mom to me. "I didn't even know she had your phone number."

"Me neither," Jack said. "Tell her happy birthday, and let your parents know I'll visit them soon."

My heart sank. That's the kind of compassion that made me fall in love with Jack in the first place. Our relationship had always been unbalanced and tumultuous, with me taking on the provider role, especially financially. Over the years, we'd broken up and gotten back together repeatedly, leaving me drained from relationship cycling.

This time, I was determined to remain broken up. We could still be friends, but Jack and I had different hopes and dreams about the future. He didn't want to get married and have children while I craved a family of my own. More than a year had passed since we'd been intimate with each other.

I pulled a white cotton blouse from a box. "Does this look too wrinkled?"

"Dudan." Jack, the fashion guru, shook his head no and rummaged through another box, handing me my black cashmere sweater. "Wear this. It'll be cold in the Valley."

Accepting the sweater from his outstretched hand, I remarked, "I always imagine the San Fernando Valley as a hot punchbowl. As a kid, I despised that heat. And there was no escape since we were the only family in the neighborhood without central air or a swimming pool."

"We had both," Jack replied with a wry grin. Having grown up in the Valley, he too was well aware of the scorching summer days. "But then again, my mom attempted suicide every other day by throwing herself in the pool, so I guess it all balances out."

I raised an eyebrow at his dark humor before refocusing on getting ready.

Slipping into my favorite pair of jeans, I asked, "Do I really look that bad?"

"You look fine," Jack reassured me. "But you better hurry if you don't want to be late."

Grabbing Baldwin and the present I'd wrapped for Mom, I rushed out the door into the cool night air. As I opened my car door, it occurred to me that I'd forgotten something.

"We've got to go back," I told my canine sidekick just as he was about to jump into the passenger seat.

Baldwin gazed up at me with his sweet puppy eyes, wagging his stumpy tail in agreement. We hurried back along the narrow path and I impatiently unlocked the door.

"Back already?" Jack remarked. Baldwin darted over to him, as if they hadn't seen each other in ages.

"Forgot the gift receipt," I said grabbing the receipt I'd left by the door. "It's only a nightshirt and slippers but you never know."

"I don't understand why you bother giving her gifts in the first place. She returns everything."

"You're hardly one to criticize. When we first met, I thought you were a trust fund kid with all your designer clothes. Little did I know that you had a habit of buying things, wearing them, and then returning them."

"That was before grunge." Jack pulled a blue plaid flannel shirt over a tight-fitting white tee. "Anyway, have fun."

Baldwin and I headed back to my SUV and hit the road. With Baldwin riding shotgun, I spoke to him like a person, and I swear, he understood.

"I can't wait to show Mom how you roll over and show me your tummy." The fluff ball tilted his head in agreement.

His Beverly Hills trainer included tricks as part of her obedience curriculum. Through reward-based training, I learned to use a clicker to mark the behavior I wanted. He'd effortlessly mastered the basics—sitting, lying, staying—and easily grasped the handful of tricks she introduced.

I'll never forget his first high five. It happened in my Westside kitchen one evening before we moved.

"High five," I said, kneeling in front of him.

His eyes stared into mine with determination. I could see he was thinking hard about what I was asking him to do. Hesitantly, he lifted his paw and put it in my outstretched hand.

"Good boy," I said, clicking my approval.

In time, he learned to weave through my legs, roll over, play dead, twirl, and speak. I even got him to sneeze on command, which became what I called his signature trick.

I looked over at my canine sidekick now curled up in the passenger seat and pondered my current predicament.

"Should I tell them about being sent home from work on stress leave?"

Baldwin looked up at me, his red tongue hanging out of his mouth.

"Maybe not. Mom has enough to deal with taking care of Dad."

Dad's ongoing struggle with Parkinson's Disease not only affected him but also took a toll on Mom, both physically and emotionally. The debilitating disease confined him to a wheelchair, leaving my little cupcake of a mom to haul it—and him—around.

My brother Will and I did our best to help, but finding a suitable caregiver proved to be a constant struggle. The latest one we hired managed to last two days, which was an improvement over his short-lived predecessors.

"I don't want any stranger living here," Mom insisted. "They're only after our money, anyway."

Even the Meals on Wheels program couldn't meet Mom's expectations, barely lasting a week before she canceled the service.

"Wouldn't you know it, the day after I canceled, they served meals from Spago."

Mom, a first-grade teacher originally from a small town in Vermont, wore the pants in the family. Dad, born and raised in Kansas City, Missouri, worked as an engineer at Atomics International, which was later acquired by Rockwell International and known as Rocketdyne. He spent a lot of time away from us at work.

I pulled into the driveway of our family ranch-style track home. Nestled in the community of Northridge in the suburbs of Los Angeles, our neighborhood was originally surrounded by orange groves, and though they'd been replaced long ago by developments, a few resilient trees still stood tall, adding a certain fragrance to the entire area. Stepping out of the car, I took a deep breath, savoring the familiar fruity, sweet, and fresh scent.

Will, who looked like my twin with his blond hair, hazel eyes and fair skin, planned to meet us at the restaurant. Even though he lived in the Valley too, his newlywed status kept him too preoccupied with his wife to spend much time with Mom and Dad.

My older sister Erin, a natural beauty, had curly, flowing blonde hair that set her apart from Will and me, giving her a radiant and ethereal appearance. Her relocation to the suburbs of Northern California after tying the knot with her college love seemed fitting for someone with such a sunny and compassionate personality. She lived there with her husband and my two adorable nieces, giving up her impressive job working with marine wildlife in San Diego to raise her family.

Both of my siblings were engrossed in their own lives, leaving the responsibility of caring for Mom and Dad squarely on my shoulders. I didn't mind. Throughout my childhood, I'd always felt like the black sheep of the family. Besides being perfect (at least in my eyes), Erin and Will excelled academically, according to Mom. I'd hear her proudly bragging about their promising futures to anyone who'd listen.

Then came me—a strong-willed child. My third-grade teacher remarked that I marched to the beat of my own drum. When my teenage years unfolded, I became rebellious, a trait that persisted well into my twenties. So assuming the primary caregiving duties for our parents seemed to be the least I could offer as penitence for my wild youth.

Once I parked my SUV, Baldwin sprinted with sheer joy toward the back gate, eager to stretch his legs on the expansive quarter-acre backyard. The sight of it reminded me of my childhood dog, Siesta, who played with me for hours in the vast space. That backyard became our personal Eden where that little grey Chihuahua mix taught me invaluable lessons about love and acceptance.

Baldwin stopped in his tracks when I opened the back door, turning mid-stride to follow me inside. Before the door closed, the fluff ball shot past me heading straight to the den where Mom sat engrossed in her book.

With unbridled excitement, he leaped onto her lap, knocking the book from her hands. He then proceeded to shower her face with dog kisses.

"Well, hello there, mister," Mom said, clearly entertained by Baldwin's behavior.

"That's enough, Baldwin," I intervened, gently pulling him off Mom and placing him back on the floor.

"You really should have given him a different name," Mom remarked, reaching for a tissue to wipe the dog slobber off her face. "I don't like Baldwin."

"I know, you've mentioned that before," I replied, attempting to keep Baldwin from jumping on her again. "If only every dog owner sought your approval before naming their pets..."

Baldwin wriggled free from my grasp and made a beeline for Mom once again. This time, she was prepared. Mom scooped him up in her hands, holding him in front of her to examine his comical face.

"He looks like a Buster. You should call him Buster."

"His name is Baldwin," I grumbled. "I've made reservations at your favorite restaurant for six o'clock. We should get going."

Their dog, Molly the Collie, a pound mutt I gave them years ago, entered the room wagging her fluffy, white tail. Baldwin did his best to get her to play with him, but the elderly dog would have nothing to do with him. She turned away from my crazy puppy and walked toward the living room. Baldwin and I followed and found Dad there, asleep in his wheelchair.

I touched him gently. "Dad, it's birthday time."

"Hi, Suzie," he said, his voice weak.

Once the very definition of tall, dark and handsome, Dad was now fragile and frail, confined to a wheelchair. I hated to see him like that, but I had to accept the fact that he was no longer the strong, capable man who raised me.

He leaned forward and patted Baldwin on the head. "Hey, little guy."

"Do you have everything you need?" I asked, taking the brake off his wheelchair.

"For what?"

"It's Mom's birthday dinner, remember?"

I carefully maneuvered Dad's wheelchair around the dogs, pushing him toward the back door where Mom patiently waited. Once outside, I assisted Dad into my car, then struggled to lift his heavy wheelchair into the back of my SUV.

"How do you manage to lift this thing on your own?" I asked Mom.

"It's not a big deal," she replied, slipping into the back seat.

As I reversed out of the driveway, I stole a glance at Mom through the rear-view mirror. Her once-sparking brown eyes were now dull and empty. She appeared weary, as if the weight of caring for Dad had aged her exponentially.

"Mom," I began, taking a deep breath, "you need to let people help you."

"We're managing just fine," she responded, her gaze fixed outside the window.

"What about the church? You and Dad have been active members for years. Surely someone from the congregation could lend a hand."

Mom remained silent. I knew better than to push the conversation further. Mom was stubborn, and there was little I could say to change her mind. Like mother, like daughter. Still, I couldn't shake the worry that Dad's care was taking a toll on her.

2

Embarking
on a New Journey

After dinner, Mom asked for my help changing the sheets on Dad's bed.

"It's your bed too," I said, puzzled.

"Not anymore," she replied, avoiding my gaze. "Your father wets the bed. I sleep on the couch."

I couldn't believe what I was hearing. *Did she just say that Dad wets the bed?* On our way to the master bedroom, Mom handed me a package containing a new waterproof mattress cover.

"He keeps me up all night," she continued, her voice filled with exhaustion. "Claims there are squirrels in the bed."

"What?" My stomach churned as I unwrapped the vinyl cover and positioned myself on the opposite side of the bed. "Why didn't you tell me Dad's condition was this bad?"

With a distant look in her eyes, she confessed, "I've been considering moving him to the Veterans Administration hospital."

Dad's navy portrait.

"The VA?" I protested. "Mom, you can't do that."

"One of my friends from church has her husband there," she explained, avoiding my gaze. "And since Dad served in the navy, it's free. Besides, there's a new facility in the Valley, just five minutes away."

Mom and Dad's wedding photograph.

"I understand that you feel this is the best option, Mom, but can we at least talk about it? Please?"

She turned away from me and picked up a framed photo of her wedding day. I watched her head drop, her shoulders trembling. *Was she crying?* I'd never seen her shed a tear before.

I gave Mom a comforting hug, and to my surprise, she didn't resist. For the first time ever, Mom allowed me to embrace her fully—instead of giving me what I call her usual A-frame hug. You know, the kind where each person bends at the waist and hugs the other without actually touching?

"It's going to be okay, Mom," I murmured, trying to offer reassurance amidst the turmoil of my latest break-up and the revelation about Dad's health.

She pulled away from the hug, returning the photo to its place on the dresser, and stood up straight as if our vulnerable moment had never occurred.

"Listen, I know you're upset about your break-up with Jack," she began, her voice filled with a mixture of sympathy and understanding. "I've been through bad break-ups myself. Before I met your dad, I had a boyfriend..."

"You mean the one who could rip a phone book in half?"

"Yes, that's the one. There's something I've been wanting to tell you kids for a long time, but your dad convinced me not to."

Erin, Will, and I had always known there was something hidden in our mom's past—a secret—but it was never openly discussed. Still, I didn't know if I had the capacity for one more revelation that night. My head ached from trying to process too much information.

"Mom, I want to hear about it." I glanced toward the door. "But right now, I'm completely overwhelmed. Can we talk about it tomorrow?"

"Of course, honey," she replied, giving me one of her A-frame hugs. "Whenever you're ready."

On the way home, I tried to process everything I'd learned. I felt a bit guilty for not being more aware of their struggles. Then I remembered Mom's secret.

"What's wrong with me?" I held the steering wheel tight. "Mom wanted to tell me her big secret tonight. I could have picked a better time to set my boundaries."

I pulled into the parking lot of my Santa Monica apartment, surprised to see Jack's car already there. Excitedly, Baldwin jumped out of my car and tugged me toward the front door only to dash inside, headed straight for Jack.

"Whoa, boy," Jack exclaimed, rising from the couch where he'd been playing his guitar. After moving his instrument to a safe spot, Jack motioned for Baldwin to jump in his lap.

I put my purse down. "You're back already?"

"Yeah, Billy was a no-show," Jack remarked, stroking Baldwin, happily snugged in his lap. "It's true what they say about drummers."

I took off Baldwin's leash and draped it on the hook by the door, the only thing I'd hung since moving in. Jack gestured for me to take a seat beside him on the couch.

"How was the party?"

"Dinner was fine," I said, "but what happened afterward left me a wreck." I rubbed the back of my neck. "Dad's not doing well. No, that's an understatement. They don't even sleep together any longer. He pees in bed and fights invisible squirrels throughout the night. Mom's considering moving him to the VA hospital."

"That's too bad," Jack sympathized, his foot rhythmically bouncing to an internal beat in his head. "Your dad's a good guy."

"He is, but he's a lot sicker than I've been led to believe. Mom's been keeping the facts from me—from all of us."

"I had a feeling she was struggling," Jack said. "I could see it in her eyes."

"Really? Why didn't you tell me? You have more experience in this, taking care of your dad at the end of his life."

"I'm no expert, but it doesn't take Sherlock Holmes to see that your mom is in over her head. I figured you knew."

"I had no idea. At least she's not suffering from Parkinson's. Poor Dad. Forty years on the job and this is what he gets?"

"You should be concerned about your mom," Jack cautioned. "Wouldn't want her to have a stroke or something."

"Don't even say that."

"Well, it's the truth," he stated matter-of-factly.

"I feel bad for both of them. It's like I've let them down. But they never share the truth with me. I mean, they kept the death of Bonnie the bunny from me for my entire sophomore year in college. Dad accidentally dropped a broken sledgehammer on her. Who keeps a broken sledgehammer in their tool shed, anyway?"

"Hey, I hate to change the subject, but I found a place in Venice," Jack announced. "Just got the approval. I'll be moving in two weeks."

"Uh-oh," I responded, concern and uncertainty in my voice. "That a good thing?"

The Peace Puppy

Jack's gaze shifted to Baldwin, now peacefully asleep in his arms. "I'm worried about this little guy. I don't think you fully realize how much care and attention he requires. I won't be around to look after him while you're at work anymore. I mean, I can check in on him occasionally, but your dog nanny won't be available twenty-four-seven."

I looked at Baldwin and knew Jack was right. Caring for the energetic puppy demanded a significant commitment of time and energy. So did my job.

"I understand," I replied, my voice laced with sadness. "I love Baldwin, and I want what's best for him."

Jack nodded, gently moving the fluff ball off his lap to pick up his guitar again. He strummed softly as the weight of the situation settled between us. It became evident that tough decisions and changes were on the horizon.

Reaching out to ruffle Baldwin's curls, I managed a smile. "I'm glad you found a place."

"It's just a block from the beach. That bike you gave me for Christmas will come in handy."

"Glad to hear," I replied, trying to hold back my tears. "I'm exhausted. Time for bed."

Baldwin followed me as I made my way to the bedroom. After closing the door, I sat down on the bed, pulling Baldwin close and letting my tears fall onto his puppy curls.

"What would I do without you?" I whispered.

In response, Baldwin offered some big, wet, messy kisses. "You always know just what I need. Thanks for the kisses."

I reached for my Tarot card deck from the bedside table. Ever since my life went into free fall mode, I'd been studying the seventy-eight-card deck. I was desperately seeking insight into what the future held.

Since moving, I'd adopted a nightly ritual of drawing three cards. Each evening, I shuffled the deck and posed the question, "What do I need to know?"

That night when I pulled my first card, I didn't feel any better about my future.

"Shit!" I exclaimed, my heart racing as I held the Tower. The sight of it filled me with trepidation. "I really don't need any more upheaval, thank you very much. I'm already grappling with enough chaos."

I proceeded to draw the next card, which turned out to be the Seven of Swords. Consulting my trusty *Tarot Book for Beginners*, I discovered its meaning: deception, trickery, stealth, and strategic manipulation. Another wave of disappointment washed over me.

"Well, that sucks."

With a hint of unease, I drew the final card for the evening—the dreaded Death card. "Oh no," I muttered, my concern mounting. "I've never pulled this one before."

The card's imagery depicted a skeletal figure mounted on a white horse, clutching a black flag embellished with a single white flower. It immediately sent shivers down my spine. I looked up its interpretation, bracing myself for bad news.

I read aloud to my sleeping dog. "According to the book, the Death card should not be taken as a literal representation of physical death. Rather, it symbolizes transformation and change, often indicating the end of a phase in life."

I gently stroked Baldwin, now softly snoring. "I hope that doesn't mean us. I can't bear the thought of losing you. I'll find a way to keep us together."

I carefully moved my boy off my lap so I could change into my pajamas. Exhaustion weighed heavily on me, leaving me too drained to tend to my usual nightly routine like brushing my teeth or washing my face. I lay my head on my pillow and, like Baldwin, fell fast asleep.

The following morning, the phone shattered me awake. "What the hell?" I grumbled. "Leave me alone." I pulled the covers over my head. The phone rang again. "Who on Earth is calling me at six a.m.?" Finally, I answered. "Hello?" I said as I rubbed the sleep from my eyes.

"Sue," Will said, "Mom died."

I sat up in a panic. "You mean Dad, right?"

"No, Mom," Will confirmed, his voice quivering.

I'm sure my scream woke up the whole apartment building, maybe even the entire neighborhood. Jack ran full speed into the bedroom in his tighty-whities, his eyes adjusting to the early morning light.

"What's wrong?"

I fell back on my bed, my heart racing. "Not Mommy, not Mommy."

"What's wrong with your mom?"

"She's dead," I said through my tears.

"Oh, Dudan, I'm so sorry."

I jumped out of bed. "I've got to get home."

"Okay, okay," Jack said, clutching his hands behind his head. "Well, you're not driving anywhere in your current condition. I'll drive."

Baldwin looked up at me, his eyes wide, his ears pinned back. I swear, he looked as though he was about to cry too. I picked him up in my arms, inhaled his musky doggy scent and held him tight.

"Why don't you pack some essentials," Jack suggested. "You might want to stay awhile."

"Right," I said, shaking like a leaf.

He rolled my suitcase out from behind one of the boxes lining my bedroom. Since I frequently traveled for work, my toiletries were already packed inside. I threw in some undies, socks, jeans and a couple tee-shirts.

"Don't forget this." Jack added a bag of Baldwin's food and his bowls before zipping the suitcase closed.

I hurriedly left the house, clad only in my pajamas, holding onto Baldwin tightly. I didn't even notice that I'd forgotten to put my shoes on. Jack came after me, pulling my suitcase with one hand and carrying my tennis shoes in the other.

In the car, Baldwin nestled into my lap and tried to console me by licking away my tears. My mind kept replaying the conversation I'd had with Mom the previous night.

"She was going to tell me her secret," I murmured, burying my face in Baldwin's curls. "And now I'll never know."

Jack reached out and placed his hand on my shoulder. "Breathe, Dudan, breathe."

"What's going to happen to Dad?"

"Everything will work out, I promise."

"How will I live without her?"

"Give yourself time to grieve," Jack replied, his voice calm and reassuring. "You'll find your way, I promise."

The following afternoon, Erin, along with her husband Alan and their daughters, teenager Frankie (short for Frances, my middle name after Mom's childhood bestie) and ten-year-old Charlie (named after her paternal grandmother), flew down from Northern California. Will had driven over from his place in nearby Woodland Hills with his new wife, Charlotte, earlier that morning.

At sundown, Dad, Erin, Will, and I sat around Mom's fancy cherry wood dining table to plan a funeral and discuss Dad's future now that Mom was gone.

After we brainstormed plans for Mom's service, the conversation turned to Dad's living situation. Where would he live now that his primary caretaker was gone? Did he have enough money saved to move to a

Molly the Collie, what a sweet girl.

nursing home? Or should we move him to the nearby Sepulveda VA center like Mom planned?

So many questions, yet none of us wanted to be the one to let Dad know he wouldn't be able to live by himself at the family home.

Molly the Collie entered the room. Baldwin got up, barked in excitement, and ran puppy circles around her, trying his best to get her to play. But Molly wasn't having it. She laid down and closed her eyes for a nap.

"Come here, boy," I said. "She doesn't want to play." Baldwin listened to me for once in his short life and took his spot under the table at my feet. "We'll play frisbee soon," I promised.

"Your Mom, she loved this house." Dad smiled, taking my hand in his. "We used to sit in the backyard at night, looking at the stars."

Erin was the first to broach the elephant in the room. "You can't stay here alone."

The smile on Dad's face disappeared. "What do you mean?" He crossed his arms, defiant.

"I'm not moving to one of those old people homes."

"We'll figure something out," Will reassured him.

I remember thinking I could quit my job and move home. Maybe then I could finally prove to them that I am a good girl, not the rebellious delinquent I used to be. Dad would be able to stay at home like he wanted. Baldwin would have a huge backyard like he needed. But I would no longer have my mom.

3

Never Fur-get

I took a deep breath at the thought of moving back to the place where I grew up. I thought about the colorful, whimsical Alice in Wonderland wallpaper of my childhood bedroom. It was long gone, as were the stories I used to make up about the Queen of Hearts and the Cheshire Cat. I remembered my excitement when Mom told me I could redecorate my bedroom back in high school. My childhood quickly disappeared behind a façade of blue calico wallpaper, leaving Alice to her adventures and me to find my own.

Childhood memories got tangled up with my grief as our conversation continued. Baldwin was at my feet, reminding me of our family dog, Siesta, who used to sit under the dinner table waiting for me to give her scraps of my dinner. The grey Chihuahua mix never ate a bite of dog food her entire life, and she lived to the ripe old age of twenty. Instead, I shared my meal with her

Me and my Baldwin, a great caregiving team (photograph by Pamela Marks, https://pawprincestudios.com/).

Me and Siesta in our vast backyard.

every night, feeding her under the table, much to Dad's dismay, while Mom gave her bologna and donuts.

"I have a say in what happens to me," Dad announced. "And I don't want to move. This is my home."

24

3. Never Fur-get

"We know, Dad," I reassured him. "I can move home and help care for you," I offered. "I mean, Jack and I just broke up. I'm sure I can get out of my lease. Anyway, I never unpacked after my move so I'm ready to go."

"What about your job?" Erin asked.

"I can take a leave of absence. At least for now."

"Good plan, Sue," Will said. "We'll hire a caretaker to help. Sue, what was the name of the last guy Mom fired?"

"I think it was Jason."

"Jason, yes." Will picked up his cell phone and searched for Jason's number. "Got it," he said as he dialed.

Dad patted my hand. "You'll really take care of me?"

"Of course, I will."

Our conversation was cut short when we heard Will say into the phone, "We really need you here," then saw him nod. "Great. Can you come now?" Will hit the end button, then turned to us and said, "He's on his way."

We debated the next steps only to be interrupted by Baldwin who barked to let us all know someone was at the door.

"I've got it, boy." He followed me to the door to greet Jason, the caretaker Mom shooed out of the house months earlier.

Baldwin grabbed the leg of Jason's pants and pulled him inside.

"Baldwin, let go," I commanded. "Sorry about that."

"No worries," Jason said, dropping his overnight bag to pet Baldwin. "I like dogs."

The Filipino man's olive-toned complexion hinted at his heritage. He wasn't tall, but his well-defined biceps rippled beneath his t-shirt. I couldn't help but assume that his muscular arms would come in handy in his caretaker role. I could barely lift Dad by myself.

"Everyone's in the dining room."

Baldwin led the way, strutting as he walked. Will stood and shook Jason's hand.

"Thanks for coming on such short notice."

"Yes, we really appreciate it," Erin added.

"I'm happy to help," Jason replied, his eyes twinkling.

"Hello, sir," Jason greeted Dad with a salute then took a seat next to him at the dining room table. "Ready go to the Yangtze River?"

I looked at Will, confused, then turned to Jason and asked, "The Yankee what?"

"Your dad talked about his time in navy when he traveled down the Yangtze River."

25

The Peace Puppy

"He never told me about traveling down any river," I said.

Will added, "Yeah, Dad, what do you know about the Yangtze River?"

"I know it's the longest river in Asia," Dad replied. "Saw it during our tour of China back when I was in the navy."

"I remember dressing up in your uniform for Halloween," I mentioned, "but that's pretty much all I ever knew about your navy days. Did you ever ride in a submarine?"

"Sure did," he said.

Curiosity piqued, Erin leaned in and asked, "What was that like?"

"Claustrophobic," he replied. "Being in a submarine is no joke. The confined spaces can make you feel trapped."

"I can't even imagine," I said.

"My favorite part of being in the navy was the camaraderie among the crew."

His words resonated with me, and I wondered aloud, "Do you ever hear from anyone who served with you?"

Dad's expression softened. "Every now and then, I receive a letter or

Dad and his fellow navy seamen. Dad is in the second row from the top, the fourth from the right.

a call from an old navy buddy. It's always a pleasant surprise to catch up. Those bonds we formed back then, they're something special."

Will asked, "What was it like to fight in World War II?"

"I didn't see any combat," Dad said. "Unless you count the time I started a bar fight."

"What?" I asked. "You started a bar fight?"

Maybe I wasn't the only rebel in the family after all.

"Yeah," he said, closing his eyes as if trying to recall the memory. "We went out drinking one night in China. There were lots of girls at the bar. I remember they didn't look that pretty when we arrived, but they got better looking with every beer."

"You drank beer?" I interrupted.

"We all did."

"What happened next?" Will asked.

"That's about all I remember."

Will's eyes widened in surprise. "You blacked out?"

Dad shrugged, a hint of bemusement on his face. "I guess so. It's one of those moments that slipped away in a haze of alcohol."

Who is this person? The dad I knew didn't even cuss.

"We all nursed hangovers the next day, and I noticed one of my buddies had a black eye, so I asked him what happened. He told me he got it in a brawl that I started when I threw an ashtray at a Marine who was bothering one of the ladies."

"Oh my God, Dad, that's quite a story," Erin said, shaking her head in disbelief.

"I learned my lesson," he chuckled. "Never drank again."

"Let's get back on topic," Will said.

"Sue will stay here for now," Erin said, "and I'll look into assisted living homes near me. We can revisit this topic in a few months."

After providing a month's notice on my place in Santa Monica, I moved back home to Northridge. Fortunately, my understanding landlord allowed me to terminate the lease early, without any penalties. Meanwhile, Jack stayed at my apartment until the end of the month while he waited for his new place in Venice to become available.

With the help of a friend of Will's and his truck, I moved my belongings. Since I decided to leave my furniture for Jack to take with him, there wasn't a significant amount of stuff to transport. We managed to complete the entire move within a single afternoon.

The problem? Where to put my stuff. Mom, a true fashionista, had filled every closet in the house with her extensive wardrobe. Unfortunately, her clothes were tailored for her petite frame. None of it quite fit my five-foot-seven stature, so I moved her clothes to Will's old room, leaving it for Erin and her daughters to go through before donating whatever was left to Goodwill.

"I started going through Mom's stuff," I told Will the next afternoon. "Boy, does she have a lot of clothes."

"Yeah, she did like to shop."

"Look at what I found." I handed Will a picture of Mom and Dad on their honeymoon in 1954. The image captured them on their cross-country drive from New York to Los Angeles where Dad's job as an engineer awaited.

In the image, Mom's gaze was filled with love and adoration as she looked at her husband, who stood with a sense of pride before their brand-new Chevy. Her eyes reflected a profound hope for the future ahead of them.

"I remember that car," Will said. "They kept it until I graduated high school. The brakes didn't even work but Mom still drove that thing."

"And look at this." I handed him a large scrapbook brimming with recipes Mom had meticulously cut out of newspapers and magazines in the 1960s. "It doesn't quite add up. I mean, she was an amazing cook, but she hated the kitchen."

"Yeah, she was a mystery."

"Did you know she wrote poetry?"

"What?" He leaned in closer to read the poem I held in my hand.

"*Night,*" he read the title out loud.

"*Night seems to steal in on us,*" he continued. "*Like a cat steals upon a mouse / Slow, still steps / Till at last it catches us / And holds us in its folds.*"

"She wrote this?"

"She did. And there's more," I replied, spreading out pages of her poems. "Why didn't she share this with me? I'm a writer."

"I'll never understand her," Will said, his voice trembling. In that moment, I felt the weight of his sorrow. Our mother, now a memory.

28

3. Never Fur-get

Jack remained a constant presence in my life, often spending time in the Valley with me. He claimed his visits were to help me with Dad, but I suspected he also missed Baldwin. Who wouldn't?

One gloomy afternoon shortly before Mom's funeral, Jack came over and found me still in bed, cuddled up with Baldwin.

"Dudan, it's already noon," he announced. "You can't sleep all day."

Baldwin jumped out of bed and greeted Jack with a joyful wiggle.

"It's strange," he continued. "Sherry moved back to her childhood home in the Valley after her parents passed away."

Sherry, Jack's former girlfriend of fifteen years, had always cast a shadow over our relationship. She was the one he was supposed to marry before me. I'd never met her. Jack told me she split her time between the Valley and Paris. Apparently, she fell in love with the City of Light while they were living there together—she, the budding model, he, the talented musician signed to a major record label.

"Actually, I think she's in Paris right now," he added.

"Hearing about Sherry is the last thing I need right now," I grumbled in frustration. Since the day we met, I was haunted by his ex-fiancé. I mean, come on, the rock star and the model. Who can follow that?

"I'm sorry. At least your mom's passing is giving you some time off."

"I miss my mommy," I said, my eyes welling with tears.

Jack attempted to comfort me with a cliché: "At least she's in a much better place."

"Is she?" I mumbled, pulling the covers over my head.

"You know I believe in reincarnation. The soul never dies. Death is just the beginning of another chapter."

"I wish I felt that certain." I turned away to stare out the window at the hibiscus plant, admiring its red flowers. Mom planted it back when I was in grade school.

Jack continued. "Even the Bible says death is not the end." He sat down at the foot of my bed and pulled Baldwin into his lap.

"But I'm worried that heaven doesn't exist," I said, "that when we die, there's nothing."

"Keep living in the question mark. Like they say on *The X-Files*: 'the truth is out there.'"

"I guess so."

"When do you have to go back to work, anyway?"

I turned back to look at Baldwin cuddled up in Jack's arms, looking beyond adorable.

"Thankfully, I have a lot of unused vacation and sick days. I don't have to go back for weeks."

"That's good. It'll give you some time to figure things out."

"What I can't figure out is how to get hold of Angel."

My friend and mentor, Angel, divided her time between Cape Cod and Jamaica. After her much-older celebrity husband of twenty-five years died, Angel found love with a Rastafarian man named Bede while on a trip to Jamaica. Judging from the photos she shared, the two were madly in love. And I didn't blame her one bit. Bede was handsome and fit, looking strikingly similar to Baldwin. I couldn't wait to introduce them to each other.

"I've left messages for her at that bar near the place she stays on Treasure Island. Wish she had a cell phone."

"She'll call you." Jack stood and pulled back the covers. "Come on, sleepy head. Let's take Baldwin on a walk. Fresh air will help you clear your head. And Baldwin needs his exercise."

I sighed and got out of bed. "Fine, let's go."

We made our way down the street, Baldwin stopping to sniff every flower and blade of grass along the way. The quiet neighborhood filled with ranch homes and huge front yards smelled like freshly mowed grass mingled with citrus.

"I wish things could go back to the way they were," I said, breaking the silence.

"I know," Jack said, putting his arm around me. "But we have to keep moving forward."

"I just don't know how to do that without my mom."

"We'll figure it out together," he said, giving me a reassuring squeeze.

"Thanks, Jack. You always know what to say."

"That's what I'm here for."

We continued our walk, Baldwin leading the way, and I felt a small glimmer of hope start to grow in my heart. Maybe things wouldn't be okay right away, but with Baldwin by my side, and Jack's friendship, I knew I could face whatever came my way.

Mom's brother, Uncle Robert, his wife Hanna, and their daughter Liz, my only cousin, flew in from New York for her funeral. Erin and her family had already driven back down, arriving the day before, so the house was overflowing with people.

Despite the crowd, I felt alone in my grief, unable to reach my friend Angel. I held onto the hope that miracles can happen. And when the kitchen phone rang the night before the funeral, I experienced what I believe was a miracle.

"Darling," Angel said, "I just arrived in town."

"Oh, Angel, I've been desperate to talk to you. My mom passed away." I sank into a kitchen chair.

"Oh, Sweetikins, I'm so sorry. Is there anything you need?"

"I need you. The funeral's tomorrow, and I know it's a lot to ask. You're in Laurel Canyon and driving to the Valley..."

"Just give me the address," she interrupted. "What time is the service?"

The next morning, a nasty storm swept in, posing a threat to the final farewell we had planned for Mom. We had no idea that we'd scheduled the service right in the middle of Super Bowl Sunday. With the game and the rain, we anticipated a small turnout.

When I arrived at the church with my family, there was a soaking-wet Angel waiting for me under an awning. I rushed over to her and fell into her arms, sobbing.

"There, there, Sweetikins," she said, stroking my hair.

Closing my eyes, I inhaled her familiar scent of rose, and for a moment, I forgot why we were there. We pulled back and Angel used her handkerchief to wipe away my tears. That's when I noticed her big, baby-blue eyes were welling up too, despite never having met Mom.

"You look so good with your tanned skin." I touched the layers of necklaces she wore. "I missed you terribly."

"I can't believe all you've been through, darling." She took my hands in hers. "You're a strong woman. Remember that."

Arm in arm, we entered the church, pausing in front of the large wooden cross behind the lectern. Angel made the sign of the cross and bowed her head before we proceeded to take our seats—me in the front row, Angel directly behind.

Before the service began, I looked around the sanctuary. I'd never seen it so full. College kids whom Mom had taught in first grade, clerks from Macy's and Albertsons, the mailman, and, of course, her numerous church friends were all there. Mom had an exceptional gift of leaving an impact on everyone she met, and they were all present to commemorate a life well lived.

The congregation fell silent when the minister made his way to the lectern. After taking a moment to survey the crowded room, he began to speak.

"We have gathered here to commemorate the life of Margaret Agnes Hartzler," he began. "As Methodists, we believe that life is a precious gift bestowed upon us by God. Margaret's life was undoubtedly a gift to all who had the pleasure of knowing her."

He paused, casting a glance toward my family in the front row.

"I'd like to start by sharing a wonderful anecdote Erin, Will, and Susan shared with me about the family's unforgettable month-long vacation, during which even Siesta, their beloved Chihuahua, tagged along for the adventure. The plan, I'm told, was to drive from the Valley to New York City where Margaret's brother and his family lived. They were going to camp along the way instead of spending money on hotels. Dick bought a huge tent for the occasion."

The minister smiled at Dad.

"The tent took up most of the space in the trunk, but Dick managed to get everything packed in the family sedan. Of course, being an engineer, he'd mapped out the entire trip ahead of time, carefully selecting each campsite along the way and paying in advance. After spending almost ten hours in the car on the first day, they planned to stop and set up camp at Chicken Creek in Utah."

I nodded, remembering that fateful trip.

"The dirt road that led to Chicken Creek was long, windy, and full of sharp rocks. Dick carefully maneuvered the car, taking it slow. The surrounding landscape was vast, and Will said it looked like something out of a horror movie. The horizon, nothing but uncompromising desert, filled with tumbleweeds and dirt. About halfway down, the car swayed. Dick stopped abruptly. A tire burst. It must have hit one of the rocks just right."

I looked over at Dad, a blank stare on his face.

"After the car came to a halt, everyone stepped out, and Dick began carefully unpacking the trunk to access the spare tire. However, Margaret became uneasy with their surroundings, feeling that Chicken Creek was a treacherous and isolated location. Despite her expressing her concerns to Dick, he remained resolute in his decision to spend the night there."

3. Never Fur-get

"When they reached the campsite, Margaret got spooked. She'd spotted some questionable characters while Dick and the kids were occupied with setting up the massive tent. Eventually, she was able to persuade him to leave. Once again, Dick packed up the car and drove to the nearest hotel, but ... they didn't get far. About halfway down the rocky road, another tire blew."

The entire congregation erupted in laughter.

"And that was the end of the camping plan, much to the delight of Margaret and the kids. For the rest of the trip, they stayed at hotels, never to pull that tent out again."

I turned to look at Angel. She mouthed the words "I love you."

The minister led the congregation in the 23rd Psalm, "The Lord is my shepherd." Then everyone stood to sing Mom's favorite hymn, "I Am the Bread of Life."

My stomach did flip-flops when the minister introduced me. I stood and walked to the lectern, my heart beating, my mouth dry.

Struggling to contain my emotions, I announced, "I would like to share one of my mom's poems. Did you know she was a poet?"

A man in the congregation responded, "Yes, she was a member of our poetry group."

Another member of the church chimed in, "She was incredibly gifted."

I carefully held the piece of paper with her poem and cleared my throat, attempting to steady myself and stop my hands from trembling.

"This one's titled *Sailing*."

Mom in her younger days.

33

The Peace Puppy

Tonight, I feel as if I could sail
Far, far away to the sea.
Along the great Winding Trail,
That leads to my land of dreams.
I'd like to sail, as of yore.
Our ancestors the Norsemen sailed
With never a care or worry,
But a mind free and clear.
And as my mind wanders further,
I see myself standing on a ship
Which is tossed by the wind and the waves
Of a deep, mysterious sea.
Oh! What I wouldn't give tonight
To be able to sail away
Along the great winding trail,
That leads to my land of dreams.

I continued with my eulogy, fighting the grief that placed a heavy weight on my chest.

"My mom was truly one of a kind," I read from my notes. "It's impossible to overlook the interesting parenting style that defined her. She possessed a charm and wit that was uniquely her own—a magical touch that made every day feel like an adventure."

I looked out at my family of friends seated in the pews. I couldn't help but consider the incredible role Mom played in these relationships, guiding me with unwavering support to forge and nurture these invaluable friendships. Heck, she even bought me that little black bundle of joy named Baldwin who waited for me back at the family home.

"One of her most endearing quirks was her uncanny ability to know everyone. And I mean everyone. Whenever Erin, Will or I found ourselves in trouble, her unconventional remedy was to pick up the phone and call one of her many friends—like Bugs Bunny—or even the big man himself, Santa—and tell on us."

I glanced up from my notes and noticed Will nodding his approval.

"Another thing I appreciated was her love of dogs. When the veterinarian told her it was time to put down the family dog Siesta, Mom brought her home to consider his suggestion. After giving the scruffy mutt a donut, she thought, *'I can't put this dog down—she just ate an entire donut!'* Siesta lived for six more years."

I looked out at Erin, her head down in sorrow.

"Mom's sense of humor, whimsy, appreciation of nature and heart of gold made her life unforgettable with laughter, love, and unwavering commitment to make every moment a cherished memory, will be greatly missed here on earth.. Rest in peace, Mom."

My entire body shook as I made my way back to my seat. Once I reached it, I put my head in my hands, overwhelmed by the emotions swirling in my head. When I looked up, my gaze fixated on Will as he stepped up to the lectern, his eyes red and swollen from the same emotions that gripped me.

"My mom was the best mother on earth," he said, his voice breaking. "She made me minute steaks before school and tied my shoes for me every morning through high school."

The congregation responded with a collective "Ahh."

"Once, she encouraged me to do a twenty-four-hour drum solo, never complaining about the noise. I love you, Mom."

When Uncle Robert stepped up to the pulpit, it became evident that his usual unwavering composure had faltered.

"I've … forever … held my sister Margaret in admiration," he began, his cheeks turning ruddy and his eyes downcast. Despite his efforts, words seemed to elude him.

The weight of emotion overcame Uncle Robert, and tears spilled down his cheeks before the congregation. In a poignant display of vulnerability, he took his seat, gently wiping away the tears that bore witness to the depth of his feelings. On that day, his actions conveyed a message more powerful than any words ever could.

The minister stepped up to the pulpit next. "We'd like to hear from any of you who have a story to share about Margaret."

"I loved Margaret," a woman spoke up. "She always said my Amy was the best kid ever."

"Hold on there," another woman interjected. "Margaret told me my kids were the best."

"Actually," another voice chimed in, "Margaret insisted mine were the best of all."

The sanctuary resonated with more and more voices echoing similar narratives, until finally the congregation erupted into shared glee.

I surveyed the room, touched by the profound impact my little cupcake of a mom had on the lives of so many, especially me. After all, she bought me Baldwin.

4

Life Is Ruff

After Mom's memorial service, the rain continued to pour relentlessly for weeks, but I found solace in the gloomy weather. The sky mirrored my depressed mood, and anyway, I welcomed the cool temperatures. Baldwin, with his thick black coat, did too, eagerly nudging me awake every morning, his frisbee clenched in his mouth, begging to get outside and play. How could I resist the adorable pleas of my Muppet-looking dog?

Baldwin had a natural talent when it came to catching the frisbee. He effortlessly leapt in the air and snatched it with grace and agility. However, there was one hurdle we faced in our game: his unwillingness to release the frisbee once he brought it back to me. The concept of letting go of the frisbee didn't register with him, and instead, he insisted on a spirited game of tug-of-war.

One afternoon, during a brief respite from the rain, I decided it was time to teach Baldwin the importance of releasing the frisbee. I threw the disc with precision, and he soared through the air to catch it. When he returned, I urged him to let go, but he stubbornly held on.

"Give, Baldwin!" I demanded.

Despite my pleas, he adamantly held on to that frisbee. Eventually, he released it, but not before I yanked it with all my force, causing my hand to shoot upward. In the chaos of the moment, my thumb collided with my eye, sending a jolt of pain through me.

"Shit, Baldwin!" I scolded him, my eye watering like a fire hydrant. "You need to learn to let go."

"Let go." Those words reverberated in my mind like an echo of pain. I sank to the ground, my hand instinctively covering my wounded eye, which throbbed with intense pain. In my moment of distress, the ever-compassionate puppy, Baldwin, ran to my side. With my vision blurred, I drew the fluff ball of comfort close.

In a whispered tone, I murmured, "No. I'm the one who needs to learn to let go."

As if in response to my newfound understanding, a ray of sunlight broke through the cloudy sky. It served as a reminder of the Serenity Prayer by Reinhold Niebuhr: *God, grant me the serenity to accept the things I cannot change, courage to change the things I can, and wisdom to know the difference.*

Heading back inside, I repeated the prayer over and over again. Once I entered the living room, I caught my reflection in the mirror that hung above the fireplace.

"Damn, my eye looks like it was struck by a bolt of lightning," I told Baldwin. "Ice will help."

I walked to the kitchen, passing Jason on the way, Baldwin trailing at my heels, and opened the freezer.

"Susanna, what happened to your eye?"

"Don't even ask." I grabbed an ice pack and pressed it gently against my throbbing eye. "Looks like you got in fight," Jason said.

"Great," I sighed in frustration. "Just when I have to go back to work."

The following morning, Baldwin woke me up by thrusting his frisbee in my face.

"Ouch!" I winced when the disc accidentally struck my already-tender left eye.

I got up and stumbled toward the mirror, discovering the disheartening sight of my first-ever black eye.

"Thanks, Baldwin," I said, half-jokingly, knowing that he couldn't comprehend what he'd done. Baldwin, still clinging to his beloved frisbee, spun around, then play-bowed. "You're lucky you're so adorable," I mused.

We headed to the backyard for a quick game before I left for my first day back at work. I threw the disc several times, playing tug to get it back and toss it again. Then something I never dreamed possible happened. Baldwin caught the disc in midair, brought it back and dropped the frisbee at my feet for the first time in his short life.

"Good boy!" I exclaimed, rewarding him with pets and kisses. "That's it for now. Always end on a positive note. Anyway, I've got to get ready for work."

Baldwin trailed me to my bedroom, proudly carrying the frisbee, and watched me pull my favorite black pantsuit out of my closet.

"This always makes me feel empowered," I told my canine sidekick. "And today, I need all the help I can get."

The Peace Puppy

This would be the first time I left Baldwin at home for an entire day since we lived in Santa Monica, something neither one of us was happy about. Our feelings were evident in the longing look we exchanged before I stepped out the door.

I braved the morning traffic on the infamous 405 freeway, enduring the slow crawl from the Valley to Santa Monica, which took just under two grueling hours. The thought of returning home to my faithful dog at the end of the day and sharing our evening walk together kept my spirits high.

Once I entered the loft building, home of the public relations firm where I'd worked for the past three years, my optimism crumbled. Not a single person looked up from their computer screens to greet me.

Puzzled, I muttered under my breath, "God grant me the serenity to accept the things I cannot change."

The morning sunlight illuminated the two-story open space. When I reached the top of the stairs, I discovered that a stranger had taken over my desk. Confused, I headed straight to my boss's office.

I knocked on Abby's door. The blonde-haired, preppy beauty, ten years my junior, looked up and gazed at me.

"Whoa, what's the story with your eye?"

"Oh, this little beauty?" I pointed to my black, swollen, bloodshot eye. "Let's just say I engaged in a heated duel with a rogue frisbee."

She raised her eyebrows in surprise. "Hold on, are you telling me that a frisbee managed to give you a shiner like that?"

"Yeah, I know, right? Turns out those innocent flying saucers are actually secret weapons in disguise."

"I'll be sure to stay clear of any coming my way." She stood and walked toward me, holding her hand out to shake mine. "You're back."

"There's a stranger sitting at my desk," I said.

"Oh, right. That's Karen. I didn't think you'd come back."

"Why not? I kept in touch. Even left a message yesterday that I'd be back today."

"Follow me," she said, leading me to the conference room.

The conference room—a space rarely used unless an account executive needed to onboard a new client in person. Abby opened the door, motioning me to take a seat at the modern, oversized glass conference table.

"Karen took over your accounts. We hired her shortly after your sad news. You'll love her."

I felt my face flush.

"Don't worry," Abby said. "We'll get more accounts. I've had several new business meetings. For now, why don't you set yourself up in here?"

I looked around the stuffy, windowless, beige, non-descript room and my stomach churned.

"You know Excel, right?" Abby continued. "We've got lots of contacts that need to be input into our system. I'll have our IT person set up a computer for you here."

I bit my lower lip to hold back the tears. My life, already shattered after losing Mom, and now a demotion. I knew I'd have to consider my options. I also knew I needed a job. And I wasn't in any condition to begin a job search. Anyway, what company would hire such a mess? For the time being, I needed to stay put.

Inputting names into a database is not my forte. The tedious and time-consuming process made my head spin. I did get a kick out of someone named Will Power, but that's about the only thing that made me smile all day. And then, after hours of complete torture manually entering name after name, I had to endure another grueling drive back home in stop-and-go traffic, more stop than go.

When I finally arrived home and walked through the door, Baldwin's greeting gave me that sense of serenity I'd been praying for all day. At the sight of me, his whole body wiggled with excitement. And to top it off, he'd ditched his frisbee for his beloved teddy bear, the two of them almost the same size.

"Hey, boy, I missed you so much."

The teddy bear's arms dangled, swaying to the rhythm of Baldwin's enthusiastic welcome. He followed me, carrying that bear, as I made my way to the den to greet Dad.

"Hi Dad," I said, leaning in to kiss him on the cheek. "I got demoted at work today."

Dad didn't answer, didn't even acknowledge my presence. I wondered if he even knew I'd been gone all day.

I turned my attention back to the black fluff ball. He knew I'd been gone all day, and one word was all it took to make him go even more crazy with excitement.

"Walk?"

At the mere mention of the w-word, Baldwin's stubby tail wagged furiously, his eyes brightening with anticipation, and he ran in circles, all the while carrying that teddy bear. I tried my best to take the bear out of his mouth, but, like his frisbee, Baldwin wouldn't let go.

The Peace Puppy

"You're bringing that along?"

He lowered his head and furiously shook the toy in his mouth, as if to say, "Yes."

"Okay, but don't drop it," I warned with a smile, appreciating his determination to bring his prized possession along for the fun.

Baldwin wagged his stump of a tail so hard when we stepped out the back gate that I thought he'd take flight like a doggie helicopter, with that stuffed bear as his passenger.

Once we reached the end of the driveway, Baldwin bounded ahead of me. Watching him walk, with his bowlegs, shuffling gait, and small, quick steps, made me burst out laughing.

"Has anyone ever told you that you walk like Charlie Chaplin?"

He gazed up at me with those deep brown, soulful eyes as though I'd just revealed the secret to world peace.

The neighborhood was quiet, in stark contrast to the always-bustling streets of Santa Monica. With each house built several feet from the neighboring home, the community had a spacious and tranquil vibe.

"I love how enormous these lots are," I remarked aloud. "That must be why they call this place Sherwood Forest."

We took a right turn at the end of the block and then a left, proceeding up the street where my best friend from childhood, Kat, grew up. We'd been pals since the first grade but lost touch years ago after she got married and relocated to Canada.

I wondered whether her parents still lived in the yellow house with the wood shingle roof. I'd spent a significant portion of my youth there, playing with Kat, her younger sister Dede, and their baby brother Dirk. I stood there, lost in memories.

My mind drifted to memories of us playing in her backyard playhouse. The sturdy structure, built by Kat's father, had a peaked roof and a small porch. The walls were made of polished wood panels, and the windows had flower boxes overflowing with colorful blooms. I can still hear the little brass doorknob turn with a creak when we entered. Once inside, the playhouse was surprisingly spacious, with room enough for all four of us to play together.

Her mom outfitted the interior with a small table and chairs, a toy chest filled with dolls and costumes, and even a tiny kitchenette with a pretend sink and miniature stove. The attention to detail was impressive. From the lace curtains on the windows to the twinkle lights that outlined the structure, it was the perfect place for a group of imaginative children to spend hours lost in make believe.

4. Life Is Ruff

One day, Kat and I convinced the popular boys in our first-grade class, twins Mike and Mark, to spend the afternoon with us. While we stayed inside playing house, the boys climbed onto the roof and jumped off, doing their best Superman impressions. It wasn't what we had in mind, but it was still quite a feat to get the boys to come over.

I was abruptly brought back to the present moment by a voice calling out, "Sue, is that you?"

The voice sounded familiar, but I couldn't quite place it. I turned and saw a figure standing a few feet away. When I focused my gaze, I recognized the person calling me. It was none other than my childhood friend Kat. She headed our way walking a dog roughly the same size as Baldwin.

"Kat!" I called out, approaching her. "Is that really you?"

"Yes, Sue, it's me! What are you doing in the neighborhood?" She opened her arms for a hug. "And who's this little guy?"

"This is Baldwin."

"Hi, Baldwin," Kat said with a smile. "Let me introduce you to Amber Jewel."

Baldwin dropped his teddy bear to greet Amber Jewel the way dogs do—by sniffing her butt.

I stepped back to admire Amber Jewel. "She's adorable. And look at you, all stylish."

Kat sported a trendy hairstyle in the early 2000s, complete with a zig-zag part and chunky blonde highlights that accentuated her stunning emerald-green eyes. She was always a fashion leader; I never forgot the dress she wore in second grade featuring a dachshund wrapped around her waist.

"Your dog is so cute," I said.

"She's a real keener."

"She looks like a mini Golden Retriever to me. Never heard of a keener. Canadian breed?"

"Sorry," she said, "slang from the Great White North. A keener is someone who tries hard to please." Kat tilted her head to one side, staring at my shiner. "What's up with your eye?"

I pointed at Baldwin. "Frisbee gone wrong."

"Looks like it hurts."

"It does. But how can I stay mad at a face like that?" I ruffled the curls on Baldwin's head.

"Impossible," she said. "Are you visiting your parents?"

"No, I live here now."

"Really? I do too—built a little guest house off the back after my divorce from Rod."

"When did that happen?"

"A few years back," she said. "Hey, I thought you were happily living over the hill, your big public relations career and all."

"I was, sort of, until Mom died."

"No!" Kat covered her mouth. "Was she sick?"

"Not that we knew. She died peacefully in her sleep."

"At least she didn't suffer. I lost my dad a couple months ago too."

"Not your dad. What happened?"

"Cancer." Her lips trembled. "He suffered terribly in the end. You're lucky you didn't have to go through that."

"Oh, Kat, I'm so sorry." I squeezed her hand.

"Me too, but let's not talk about that. I've cried so much, I don't have any tears left. Anyway, I want to get caught up on the last ten years."

"Join us on our walk, then. No time like the present."

I shared the details of my work ordeal with Kat, hoping for some guidance.

She listened and then asked a pertinent question that only a lawyer's daughter would consider. "Is demoting someone like that even legal?"

"I have no idea," I said. "If only your dad were here. I could seek his advice. But it doesn't matter." I shrugged. "I've seen it before. My boss waits until an employee's life is in ruins, then goes for the throat. So much for my vice president status. I should've known."

"Remember what my dad always said: 'It's only money.'"

"Easy for him to say. Your dad was a highly respected, and well paid, lawyer. Me, I have no savings at all. I've been supporting an out-of-work musician for the last ten years."

"Oh, Sue, I'm so sorry." She stopped in her tracks to give me a big hug.

"At least I don't have to pay rent right now."

"This is the time to take care of yourself."

"Actually, I have to take care of more than just myself. Dad's got Parkinson's and I volunteered to oversee his care."

"Parkinson's? That's a shame."

"So is getting divorced."

Kat, always one to speak her mind, offered her perspective. "Listen, if there's one thing I've learned, it's that you don't have to tolerate someone else's nonsense. In love, or in a job."

Her words hung in the air, carrying a sense of conviction, and I couldn't help but consider her advice. It was clear that she learned to take a stand against the unacceptable. Maybe I should too.

I drove to work the following day on a mission. Once I stepped into the building, I made a beeline for Abby's office.

I poked my head in her door and asked, "Do you have a moment?"

Abby nodded, gesturing for me to come inside. I closed the door behind me.

"I want to give my official notice," I stated firmly, my eyes fixed on Abby.

As soon as the words left my mouth, my attention quickly shifted to a hawk outside her office window. It perched on a tree, its sharp eyes focused on prey below. With a swift motion, it swooped down, leaving me in awe.

"Are you considering opening your own P.R. firm?"

I shook my head. "No, taking care of my dad demands more of my energy than I'd anticipated."

Abby nodded in understanding. "You're a saint."

"I wouldn't call me a saint, but like that hawk outside your window, it's time for me to find my own path and embrace new opportunities."

"What hawk?"

5

Go, Dog, Go

My friendship with Kat picked up right where it left off, as if no time had passed since we were besties. Having Kat in the old neighborhood brought me a sense of comfort. We walked our dogs together every night and rode our bikes everywhere, just like we did in our younger days.

"I feel like a kid again," I commented as we pedaled to the local ice cream store one sunny afternoon.

"Me too," she replied. "It's like fate brought us back together."

"A godsend, for sure. I always thought you and Rod were perfect together. You, with your gemology degree, and Rod, with his family's jewelry business. It seemed like a match made in heaven."

"More like a match made in hell," she said, steering her bike into the parking lot. "His emotional abuse almost landed me in the hospital."

"No—how could someone possibly abuse you?" We secured our bikes and proceeded inside. "I guess Rod had the nice guy act mastered."

"Sure did. My ex had an uncanny ability to win people over, leaving a trail of admirers in his wake. But, behind closed doors, he was a totally different person."

We placed our orders for ice cream cones and continued our conversation.

"I know how that feels," I sympathized. "I've been there too."

"Really?"

"I wasted three years of my life in my own nightmare relationship with an alcoholic musician only to hook up with another. Not alcoholic, but out of work musician."

"That's terrible," she said. "Isn't it weird that we both ended up in relationships with abusive men?"

Lifting my ice cream cone in a mock toast, I declared, "Never again." Our ice cream met in a playful imitation of clinking champagne glasses.

"All I can say is thank goodness for old friends. And for dogs."

44

"Absolutely," Kat agreed. "And a little bit of chocolate chip doesn't hurt either, does it?"

When the sun set, Dad, Jason, and I adhered to our now-familiar dinner ritual. Nestled in his cherished red leather armchair in the den, Dad held his customary spot, while Jason and I settled onto the couch opposite him. We ate our meal on vintage TV trays, the very ones that my family used back in the day.

That night, Jason reheated one of the casseroles dropped off by one of Dad's friends from church. During times of grief, there's nothing quite as comforting as a casserole, especially if you're a Methodist. The three of us sat there enjoying our homemade meal when, out of the blue, Dad abruptly flung his fork across the room.

"I want to go home," he declared, his face flushed.

Confusion washed over me. "You are home, Dad."

"I said I want to go home," he repeated. "Take me home now!"

I looked at Jason for help, but he seemed as puzzled as I felt.

"Why won't you listen to me?" Dad shouted.

Remaining calm, I reassured him, "Everything's okay, Dad. We're having a nice dinner together."

"No, we're not," he snapped, overturning his plate. "Take me home now!"

Jason rose from his seat and retrieved Dad's wheelchair. "Here, sir," the caretaker said, helping Dad in. "Let's go."

I got up too, headed to the back door to watch the two of them head down the driveway before turning back toward the house.

"Welcome home," I said at the back door they'd just exited a few moments ago. On the way back to his red chair, Dad paused to watch Baldwin tidying up the scattered remnants of his dinner. It was clear that he didn't remember what had just happened.

"Why's there food on the floor? Doesn't your dog eat from a dog bowl?" he asked.

"He's the clean up committee, " I answered. "Just doing his job."

Dad eased back into his red chair while I cleaned up the remaining mess. When I placed a fresh plate of casserole in front of him, Dad thanked me as if we'd just sat down for dinner.

I'd learned in Baldwin's obedience class that without training, a dog's bad behavior just gets worse. It was becoming increasingly clear that I needed to learn how to manage Dad's outbursts before they escalated further.

The following morning, I picked up the phone and made an appointment with Dad's neurologist, Dr. Tapper. This time, the appointment was for me.

Later that week, I was ushered into his office. In his white coat, the hefty Dr. Tapper sat behind a huge desk in front of a wall filled with various medical degrees. He projected an air of professionalism, empathy, and expertise.

"I have some questions about my dad."

"Ask away," he said.

I explained what happened the other night.

"Psychosis, including hallucinations, illusions, or delusions, can affect Parkinson's patients," he told me. "It's called Parkinson's disease dementia and it affects approximately 40 percent of those struggling with the disease. In addition, the medication we use can also cause dementia."

"I see. But what should I do if this happens again?"

"His reality is whatever he perceives it to be. Don't argue with him; it's best to go along with whatever he says."

I took a deep breath, absorbing Dr. Tapper's words.

"How do you know he has Parkinson's?"

"Well, there are currently no blood or laboratory tests to diagnose the condition. And while the symptoms are different in every case, your father displays some of the tell-tale signs: his stiff muscles, his shuffling gate and what we refer to as the Parkinson's mask. You see, Parkinson's causes a lack of dopamine in the brain which can limit his facial expressions."

I nodded before asking my next question. "How did he get Parkinson's in the first place?"

"It's hard to say. Parkinson's is a complex disorder with both genetic and environmental factors. Researchers have identified several genes that are associated with Parkinson's, but having those genes doesn't necessarily mean you'll develop the disease. Other factors, such as exposure to toxins or environmental triggers, are also believed to play a role."

"Could exposure to radiation be the cause? He worked at

Rocketdyne and was there when the Santa Susana Field Laboratory had a nuclear meltdown in 1959."

"Could have..."

"Do I have to worry about getting it?"

"Having a family history of the disease, especially in a first-degree relative like a parent, can slightly increase the risk of developing Parkinson's," he said. "But I wouldn't worry about it."

Armed with this newfound information and understanding, I knew exactly what to do the next time Dad became irate—and it didn't take long for Dad's confusion and anger to resurface.

"I want to go home," he announced one evening the following week.

I called for Jason, relying on his support to fetch Dad's wheelchair and take him outside. And just as before, after a quick walk down the driveway and back, I greeted them with a warm and familiar "Welcome home" as if they'd been away on vacation. This simple act of acknowledging Dad's reality worked like a charm, providing a sense of comfort and stability for everyone involved.

Together, Jason and I became the steadfast anchors in Dad's ever-shifting world, in our effort to provide the support and care he needed as we all navigated the complex landscape of Parkinson's disease. Of course, having Baldwin by my side helped too. There's nothing like the love of a rescue dog to get you through the rough moments of life.

One evening after dinner in front of the TV, the three of us were startled by a loud crash from the kitchen.

"What the hell was that?" I asked.

Dad's eyes twinkled mischievously. "Must be Mom."

Curious, I went to the kitchen to investigate.

"You won't believe this," I shouted over the blaring TV. "The pots and pans from under the stove are scattered all over the floor."

"How could that happen?" Jason asked, joining me into the kitchen.

I scratched my head. "I have no idea."

"I didn't open the cupboard tonight," Jason said.

After stacking the pots and pans back in the cupboard, we returned to the den where Dad's attention had already drifted back to CNN.

"You know what? You're right," I told Dad anyway. "There's really no other explanation. Mom was never a fan of the kitchen."

His answer? "I want to go to bed now."

"It's only 7:30," I objected.

"I don't care. I'm tired."

Jason helped Dad to his bedroom while I cleaned up the dinner dishes. By the time I joined them in Dad's room, he was already in his pajamas.

"I can take it from here," I told Jason.

Baldwin immediately jumped on Dad's bed and covered him in slobbery kisses.

Dad laughed at Baldwin's antics, thank God. Still, I managed to intervene, giving my fluff ball the command to get off. He did, then turned his attention to torture poor Molly the Collie lying peacefully next to her master's bed.

"Knock it off, Baldwin," I said.

"Yeah, knock it off," Dad repeated.

After turning on his bedside light (he liked to sleep with it on) and radio, I tucked Dad in and gave him a kiss on the forehead.

"Sweet dreams," I whispered.

I had turned to leave when Dad suddenly sat up and said, "Your mother was the only person I ever loved."

I was taken aback by his sudden confession, but I turned back and sat down at the foot of his bed to hear more. Baldwin jumped up next to me.

"Ah, Dad, you were so lucky."

He continued, "The first time we made love was after a church gathering. I'd just graduated and moved to New York City where your mom was getting her teaching degree from Columbia. After the party, she came back to my apartment on the Upper East Side. We started kissing, and the next thing I knew, things got out of hand. She was the first and only woman I made love to."

I sat there, stunned by Dad's unexpected revelation. It was as if a hidden chapter of my parents' love story had been unveiled before me. With Baldwin snuggled next to me, I mustered up a response, trying to find the right words to acknowledge Dad's vulnerability and honor the love he shared with Mom. But I couldn't speak. I was stunned silent.

"I ran down to the corner store," he continued as if he were discussing his love life with a friend rather than his youngest daughter, "had to buy condoms. She was my best friend from the moment we met."

I found my voice and said, "Dad, it's beautiful that you and Mom had such a special connection. You created a love story that lasted a lifetime."

He nodded his blank Parkinson's-masked face. "Yes, we did. She was everything to me."

I leaned in and kissed Dad on the forehead again.

"I love you, Dad," I said, hoping that my words would reach his heart. "Now, get some rest. I'll be here across the hall in my room if you need anything."

I left trying to process the mix of emotions I felt—sadness for Dad's fading memories and the impact of Parkinson's on his mind, mingled with my own discomfort and embarrassment hearing the intimate details he'd shared of my parents' sex life.

Later that night, I headed to my room to get some much-needed sleep. Baldwin cuddled up next to me in bed and I tried to drift off, but Dad's words kept playing in my mind. Even Baldwin couldn't work his magic and help calm my tangled thoughts. In the end, I turned to reading as a way to distract myself.

A couple hours into a new book, and I was interrupted by the sudden fluctuation in the volume from Dad's radio. It sounded like someone was repeatedly adjusting the dial. I could have sworn I heard Dad snoring just a few minutes earlier.

"What is he up to now?" I asked Baldwin as the two of us headed to Dad's room to investigate.

I found Dad sound asleep, his radio now blaring. I turned it back down and went back to bed. Yawning, I was getting comfy in bed when I heard Dad's radio go haywire again.

Back in his room, Dad snored like a mad lion, undisturbed by any tampering with his radio. I knew I wasn't the one turning the dial. Jason was in his usual spot, smoking cigarettes in the garage. There was but one plausible explanation—it was another message from Mom. The unexpected shifts in volume, as if the radio adjusted itself, sent a profound message that surpassed verbal communication. The moment I turned down the volume this time, a tingling sensation spread through my body.

I whispered, "Message received, Mom."

Back in bed, Baldwin nudged closer. In that quiet moment, I acknowledged the love that surrounded me.

Thank you, Mom, for buying me this dog," I said out loud "I don't think I'd be able to handle all this without him."

Feeling a renewed sense of peace, I relaxed, knowing that Mom's presence would always be there, guiding and comforting me. And as I drifted off to sleep, I carried her love with me, grateful for the mysterious ways in which it continued to show up in my life.

6

For the Love of Dog

One morning, Baldwin jolted me awake with a frenzy of barks emanating from another room. I followed the noise and found him in the living room trying his best to get Molly the Collie to play. This time, he was determined. I watched Baldwin perform a playful dance to engage her. He hopped from side to side, play-bowed, and ran zoomies around Molly, but the poor girl was not interested.

Molly gave me a glance that seemed to say, "Life was so peaceful before this crazy puppy came along."

I couldn't help but sympathize with her. Kneeling, I gently petted her head, apologizing for Baldwin's behavior.

In that moment, it became clear to me that Baldwin needed an avenue to channel his limitless energy. I remembered his obedience class where he showcased his exceptional skills in conquering obstacles and emerged as the top contender, his first of many blue ribbons. The trainer warned me about his intelligence, saying that he needed both physical and mental stimulation.

"You need a job," I told the fluff ball, who rolled over to get me to scratch his tummy. "Remember how you aced that obstacle course? There's a place in the Valley where you can play on all sorts of agility equipment."

"Woof, woof!" Baldwin voiced his agreement.

Unaware of the world of dog sports at that time, I imagined a dedicated space, akin to a children's playground but designed specifically for dogs and their humans. I did some research and discovered the existence of many nearby agility classes. Who knew the Valley was a hub of dog agility activity?

The following Tuesday, I took Baldwin to a nearby church for his first-ever agility class. We pulled into the parking lot and spotted a cluster of people settled in lawn chairs, all facing a spacious area filled with agility equipment. The air was bursting with anticipation, heightened by

Baldwin, the #1 Puli in agility in 2001 (photograph © 2003 Caryn Levy).

the spirited symphony of barks from dogs eagerly awaiting their chances to participate.

"Look, boy, it's a canine tailgating party."

Baldwin, unable to contain his enthusiasm, shot up in the passenger seat and joined in the chorus. I joined in, too, throwing my head back and howling.

We stepped out of the car and headed toward a gathering of dog owners and their canine companions. In front of the crowd were two obstacle courses. At the first one, we paused to watch a remarkable dog effortlessly leap over jumps and skillfully weave through poles.

"Someday, that could be you," I told Baldwin.

Walking up to the man whose dog had just completed the course, I said, "Wow, that was incredible! I mean, good job! We're new to this. How long did it take your dog to learn all that?"

"Border Collies are natural athletes," he responded, catching his breath. "Especially my Fly." He bent down to leash his pup. "If you're here for the beginner class, Kristen is the instructor you're looking for." He pointed to a woman barking instructions in the adjoining course. She looked to be around my age, fit and athletic, her brown hair in pigtails.

From what I could see, she was actively instructing a group of students, both canine and human, her passionate guidance loudly echoing through the church parking lot and, most likely, the entire neighborhood.

"You suck!" she yelled at a student who'd stumbled on the course. "Keep your eye on your dog. It's always the handler's fault, never the dog's."

I flinched and looked down at Baldwin. "I hope she's not that hard on us."

With a mixture of anticipation and determination, Baldwin and I joined the beginner class, ready to embark on this new adventure together. Little did we know that agility training would not only provide an outlet for Baldwin's energy but also strengthen the bond between us.

Baldwin tugged at the end of his leash, leading me toward another beginner student, a beautiful white Australian Shepherd. It was as if the two dogs recognized each other instantaneously, their connection sparking a playfulness that made it seem as if they were long-lost friends.

"Don't let your dogs socialize at class," Kristen yelled like a drill sergeant.

6. *For the Love of Dog*

"Nice to meet you, too," I mumbled under my breath.

The women with the white Aussie turned to me said, "Don't worry. Kristen's always like that but she's the best trainer around."

We followed Kristen with the other members of the class to a twenty-foot tube made of heavy-duty vinyl.

"This is the tunnel," she said, squishing it up to less than a third of its size. "Running into a dark space is not instinctive for dogs, so it's up to you to help them conquer their fear." She took Baldwin's leash from me. "Go to the other end," she directed. "Stick your head in the opening and call his name."

I followed her instructions, bending down to stick my head inside the opening of the tunnel and calling out Baldwin's name. Without hesitation, he dashed toward me with exhilarating speed.

I lavished him with praise and gave him a handful of Goldfish crackers, something I'd brought as treats, not fully grasping at the time the significance of proper dog rewards. In the beginning, Goldfish crackers seemed suitable to me. They didn't create a mess in my pockets or on my hands; they didn't emit any unpleasant odors. Moreover, in the intervals between Baldwin's turns, we both enjoyed snacking on them.

I've since come to understand the importance of appropriate treats. They come in varying degrees of value—high, medium, and low. It's crucial to have a range of treats during training sessions, reserving the high-value ones for introducing new behaviors, training in distracting environments, or when undertaking behavior modification.

But, for our first class, I'd brought Goldfish crackers. We repeated the exercise several times, and with each repetition Kristen progressively enlarged the size of the tunnel. Baldwin proved to be a quick learner, becoming the first to conquer the entire thing.

"Good boy," I told him, offering more Goldfish as his reward.

Kristen clapped her hands. "Get back in line. We'll tackle jumps next."

She pointed to a set of metal upright bars spaced two feet apart, connected by a PVC pipe.

"Step over the jump yourself if you have to."

To my amazement, Baldwin effortlessly sailed over the jumps as if he'd been running agility courses his entire life. I felt extremely proud of my fluffy canine athlete and he seemed pretty happy with himself too, strutting around in between his turns.

Over time, Baldwin learned how to navigate the dog walk, the teeter, the A-frame, and even the weave poles. Baldwin's newfound agility skills not only provided him with a fulfilling outlet for his energy but also helped boost my self-esteem as we shared the triumphs of his training journey and, eventually, agility trials. In time, I'd buy every piece of agility equipment for my boy and set up his own course in the backyard.

When it came time to leave that first class, Baldwin hopped into the car, curled up in the passenger seat, and fell asleep.

"Good, maybe you'll be too tired to bug Molly tonight."

Soon, I made our weekly class a family affair, bringing Dad and Jason to Baldwin's training sessions. I hoped that the outdoor atmosphere and the lively doggy environment would prove beneficial to Dad's well-being.

I remember the first time they joined us. I carefully positioned Dad's wheelchair right in the front of the course where our class would take place. However, Dad's attention quickly wavered, his gaze drifting aimlessly, seemingly captivated by anything other than Baldwin and me.

Throughout the class, I couldn't help but steal glances at Dad, who appeared increasingly preoccupied with his surroundings. His focus and engagement that I counted on in the past were replaced by a distant look in his eyes, as if his thoughts wandered through some long-forgotten memories. I wondered if bringing him was a good idea.

The class had been intended as a way to spend quality time together and engage him in an outside activity, but his preoccupation raised doubts about whether it was the right choice.

However, my reservations were erased when Dad said, "Your mother would have loved watching you out there."

"So you had a good time?"

"Of course, I did," he answered. "You and Baldwin were the stars of the class."

Though his demeanor had been distant during class, his words inspired me to research other ways to lift his spirits. One idea struck me on the car ride home.

"Dad, do you remember getting physical therapy at Cal State, Northridge?"

"Yeah," he said, staring out the window, "those students got me out of this damn wheelchair."

"Well, good news. I'm enrolling you again."

6. For the Love of Dog

The following week, I accompanied Dad to his first physical therapy session since Mom died. The college gymnasium bustled with activity when we arrived as students tended to seniors like Dad facing a variety of health issues.

A young, athletic-looking woman sporting a Dorothy Hamill '70s haircut and workout attire approached us, addressing Dad by name.

"Hello, Dick," she greeted him, flipping her short hair off her face. Dad nodded in acknowledgment.

"I'm Kiki," she introduced herself, extending a hand toward me. "I'm your dad's physical therapist. I'm sorry to hear about your mom. She was a nice lady."

I shook her hand and expressed my gratitude.

Kiki focused her attention on Dad. "Let's get you walking again."

Over the course of two months, Dad made remarkable progress. While he still experienced stiffness he'd regained a significant degree of mobility—enough to ditch the wheelchair. With the help of a rollator, he could finally walk again.

Witnessing his progress prompted me to do more research on alleviating the symptoms of Parkinson's disease. That's when I stumbled on the potential benefits of massage therapy in mitigating the rigidity and discomfort that comes with the condition.

Personally, I relished the luxury of indulging in a massage, and I didn't forget to pamper Baldwin with the same treat. Whether it was through professional masseurs or my own hands, I made sure my four-legged superstar received the relaxation he deserved. After all, he was undoubtedly a true athlete in his own right.

Consequently, the idea of massage for Dad resonated deeply with me. And, to my surprise, he agreed to give it a try!

I contacted a therapist named Emily, who had experience working with Parkinson's patients, and arranged for her to come to our house and give him his first-ever massage.

It certainly didn't hurt that Emily was youthful and stunning, with her perfect, petite figure. Dad's face lit up with anticipation when she set up her massage table in the living room, strategically positioned by the windows that offered a serene view of the backyard.

After Emily and I helped Dad onto the table, he said, "Not one but two pretty women. Must be my lucky day."

His strange comment made me wonder if he remembered I was his youngest daughter. I stayed in the room, just in case he became irritable. Didn't want to scare off Emily on her first visit.

The Peace Puppy

Baldwin hopped onto the living room couch and nestled beside me. As Emily attended to Dad, I tenderly massaged Baldwin.

She started with gentle strokes on Dad's arms and legs, then moved on to his neck and shoulders, using a combination of massage techniques to release any tension. For the first half hour, Dad seemed to be enjoying the treatment. But then, after Emily asked him to turn over on his back, he sat up and made a crude comment.

"You have nice breasts."

That was bad enough, but when Dad reached out to touch them, Emily looked at me for help. I quickly intervened, apologizing to her on Dad's behalf. This was not the same man who raised me.

After Emily made a hasty exit, Dad went back to the den to watch his beloved CNN as if nothing had happened. Later, I walked through the den to check on him. There he was, sitting in his red chair with a turkey sandwich in hand, half of it in his lap.

"How are you doing?"

"Shh," Dad said, completely oblivious to what just happened. "Can't you see I'm having lunch with Hillary Clinton?"

I glanced at the television and saw the former First Lady being interviewed on CNN. Technically, he was correct, so I apologized and left him to his pleasant hallucination with Mrs. Clinton. It was a relief compared to the uncomfortable massage moment or the unsettling encounters he claimed to have had with squirrels in his bed.

I did manage to find another massage therapist to come, and this time, it was a man. I witnessed a remarkable improvement in both Dad's physical and mental state. Regular massage treatments appeared to alleviate the tense muscles and joints that come along with Parkinson's. Moreover, massage is scientifically known to release happiness-inducing hormones, including endorphins, which played a role in enhancing his overall mood and outlook, ultimately leading to a reduction in his angry outbursts and scary hallucinations.

One night, Baldwin and I woke up to the sound of Dad singing at the top of his lungs.

"Oklahoma, where the wind comes sweepin' down the plain!"

Dad's voice sounded strong and spirited, like the man I knew before Parkinson's. But when Baldwin and I went to check on him, we found Dad snoring.

6. *For the Love of Dog*

"Singing in his sleep?" I asked Baldwin, stretched out in front of me.

This sparked a sudden idea. Perhaps enrolling him in singing classes would be beneficial to his physical and emotional health too. He'd always loved to sing. So, with that thought in mind, I wasted no time. The very next day, I signed Dad up for an adult singing class taking place at my former high school.

I didn't know this at the time, but it turns out that singing has been shown to reduce Parkinson's symptoms by helping to relax muscles and release tension in the back and neck.

Dad seemed enthusiastic about the prospect of joining a singing class, although he had to endure a week-long wait until the class officially began. Patience had never been one of his virtues, even before Parkinson's, and the anticipation seemed to make the wait even more challenging for him.

Every day, without fail, he asked, "Is my singing class tonight?"

"No, Dad. Just a few more days," I'd reply.

Finally, the day arrived, and we set off to my alma mater, Granada Hills High School. Baldwin happily accompanied us to the brightly-lit, spacious classroom with desks pushed back against the walls and chairs arranged in a semi-circle. I noticed some of the other students waiting in silence for the class to start. They were all middle-aged and older, which I took as a good sign for Dad because they could relate to each other, being from the same generation. Once we passed through the doorway, everyone's attention was immediately drawn to Baldwin.

One of the students couldn't help but ask, "What kind of dog is that?"

"He's a Puli," I replied, an ancient breed from Hungary. "And he sings, too."

I threw my head back and let out a howl. Within seconds, Baldwin joined in, harmonizing with me. We howled together, much to the delight of the students.

Then, in walked a substantial, middle-aged man with a beard and mustache, dressed professionally in a suit. He looked a bit surprised to see a dog howling in the middle of the classroom, a sight he'd never anticipated.

"I didn't know we had any dogs signed up for this class," he said, then turned to introduce himself. "I'm your teacher, Mr. Henderson."

The Peace Puppy

I helped Dad into one of the chairs and then approached Mr. Henderson.

"Welcome to the adult vocal workshop," he told me. "Please take a seat."

"I'm actually not here for the class." I pointed to Dad sitting quietly with his shoulders slumped. "My dad is—he has Parkinson's."

Mr. Henderson's eyes lit up with understanding. "That's fantastic! Music and singing can be incredibly powerful for individuals with Parkinson's. It can help with vocal control, breath support, and overall well-being. We've had several participants with Parkinson's in our classes over the years, and they've experienced remarkable benefits."

Encouraged by his response, I continued, "I think my dad will really enjoy it."

"Our classes are designed to be inclusive and supportive. We focus on vocal exercises, group singing, and even some solo performances for those who are comfortable."

That sounds great," I said. "I'm looking forward to seeing how he connects with the music and the group."

I left the conversation with a sense of hope. Enrolling Dad in singing classes felt like another step toward enriching his life and providing him with opportunities to express himself, even in the face of Parkinson's.

While the class was in session, I walked Baldwin around the campus.

"That's the room of my favorite teacher." I pointed at a classroom door. "Of course, Mrs. Garcia taught English, my favorite subject—next to dogs, of course."

I told him about driving Kat to school on my brother's Honda Mini Trail 70. "We drove it right into our first period class," I said, "Boy, the looks we got, two blonde surfer girls on a motorcycle..."

We hit the quad and I told Baldwin about the time Kat and I entered a pie-eating contest.

"I don't know who won, but I can tell you that afterward, I found pie everywhere. There were even pieces inside my ear."

When it was time for the class to end, Baldwin and I made our way back and were greeted by a welcome sight: all eyes were fixed on Dad as he confidently sang his favorite song, "Trees."

"I think that I have never seen a poem as lovely as a tree..."

When he concluded, a wave of applause erupted, and the entire class rose to their feet, giving Dad a resounding standing ovation. Dad humbly bowed his head in gratitude for the heartfelt recognition.

Afterward, Mr. Henderson rushed over to me and asked, "Does your dad have formal vocal training?"

"He was asked to tour with the Roger Wagner Chorale, but he decided to get married and have a family instead."

"Being invited to join such a prestigious vocal ensemble is a significant accomplishment," Mr. Henderson said. He patted Dad on the back. "Thanks for sharing your amazing talent with us."

In my ongoing attempt to keep Dad's mind and body engaged, I signed him up for field trips organized by the local senior citizens center. Jason escorted Dad to a variety of events, his favorite being the horse races.

I remember dropping them off at the senior center and watching Jason help Dad onto the bus for the first time. Talk about role reversals. After waving goodbye, I headed back home.

Kat called me on my way. "Where are you off to this fine morning? I went by your house and no one was home."

"I just dropped Dad and Jason off and watched them board the bus for the horse races."

"Aww, it's so adorable how you've become the parent to your dad. It's amazing how family dynamics change, isn't it?"

"I feel a bit strange," I said. "All my life, he was the one I looked up to—a pillar of strength and dependability. Now the roles have reversed. I'm the caregiver, and he looks to me."

"You're doing a fantastic job, Sue. Your mom would be so pleased of how you stepped up."

"I hope so."

"Your dad is lucky to have you."

"I'm the fortunate one. Caring for Dad gives me the chance to repay him for all the sacrifices he made for me." But not everyone can do what you're doing," she said.

"Maybe not, but I kind of like him more as he is now than as the strict parent he used to be."

At three that afternoon, Baldwin and I returned to pick up Dad and Jason. We arrived just as the bus pulled into the parking lot.

"We won!" Dad exclaimed, sticking his head out the bus window like a child returning from school to find his parent waiting. "Show her the cash!"

Jason fanned out three twenty-dollar bills while Dad puffed out his chest with pride. Much to the delight of all the seniors on the bus, I managed to elicit an exuberant howl of excitement from Baldwin.

The two of us moved to the bus door where I positioned Baldwin in the perfect spot to wave at each senior as they disembarked. Even those who didn't emerge victorious couldn't resist smiling at my adorable, fluffy, canine companion. And I smiled too. Finally, Dad's positive attitude had returned, bringing a sense of relief and hope to all of us.

7

Love Me, Love My Dog

One evening during dinner, Dad abruptly put down his fork and announced, "I need you to schedule an appointment with my attorney. I want to revise my will."

"No, Dad, let's not do that again. Will blew my head off last time you brought that up."

"Your mother and I wanted to leave this house to you," Dad persisted.

"I know," I sighed. "Mom told me when you were in surgery for your aortic aneurysm."

"Your brother and sister have houses. We wanted to make sure you have one too."

"Don't worry about it, Dad. I'll be okay."

"But—"

"Please, let's not talk about it anymore."

"I worry about you," he said.

"Well, don't. What you can help me with is Mom's secret. She said you knew about it but told her not to tell us kids. What was she was hiding?"

"I do recall something," he said, "but I can't remember what it was."

Disappointed, I sighed, acknowledging that I might never uncover what Mom kept hidden from me.

"By the way, my friend Angel is back in town. I have plans to meet her and her new boyfriend for dinner."

"That's nice," Dad replied, his focus once again absorbed by the television screen.

The lights from the Valley twinkled in my rearview mirror on my way to Angel's Laurel Canyon home. I couldn't wait to meet her Jamaican boyfriend, Bede, and introduce the two of them to Baldwin.

The Peace Puppy

The sun began its descent when Baldwin and I took off, making the scenic vistas and expansive views of the canyon even more breathtaking. By the time we arrived at her house, a full moon had risen, illuminating the sky with a soft, silvery light.

Baldwin faithfully trotted beside me as we approached the grand front gate, leading us to a magnificent wooden door that was nothing short of a masterpiece. The door's intricate carvings showcased skillful artistry, casting a cool, ethereal radiance on the porch.

I turned to my loyal canine companion and remarked, "This is how the other half lives."

Just then, Angel opened the door, her blonde flowing hair longer than the last time I saw her. She wore a flowing caftan, and, as usual, had an array of gold and silver bracelets gracing both wrists. Beaded necklaces with precious and semi-precious stones were layered around her neck too. Notably, a gold signet ring featuring a simple cross replaced her turquoise wedding ring, which she now wore on her index finger.

"Sweetikins," she said, greeting me with one of her warm hugs before turning her attention to Baldwin.

"What kind of dog is this?"

"He's a Puli."

"I say he's a Bede." She scooped him up and brought him to the living room where her boyfriend sat on her brown suede couch, transfixed by an action flick.

"Look at this dog, darling," she said, putting Baldwin in Bede's lap.

"Hi, liddle mon," the totally buff Rastafarian said, moving his thick dreadlocks off his face.

"Darling, we've got to take a picture of the two of you." She picked up her camera. "Look here."

"They do look alike," I commented. Despite Baldwin not sporting the typical dreadlocks that the Puli breed is known for, there was an undeniable resemblance between them. They certainly seemed like brothers, especially in spirit.

"Bede, this is my friend Susan," she said, holding my hand in hers. "You know, the one I told you about?"

Angel made the introduction, but Bede seemed completely absorbed in showering affection on Baldwin, seemingly oblivious to my presence. Watching his instant connection with my fluff ball, I couldn't help but feel a sense of appreciation. After all, it was hard to blame him, given Baldwin's irresistible charm.

Just then, from the opposite side of the house, Angel's Scottie dog, Hobson, emerged, his tail wagging in enthusiastic delight.

"It's the happy meter," I remarked.

Angel's rescue Labrador Retriever, Charlie, now a senior, slowly followed.

"Oh, Charlie." I bent down to kiss him on the top of his head. "How old is he now?"

"He's fifteen," Angel said proudly. "Doesn't he look fabulous?"

"If he wasn't black, I'd say Charlie's a silver fox," I chuckled. "I smell your famous chicken wings baking."

"Are you hungry?"

"Starving."

We headed to the kitchen with the trio of dogs faithfully trailing behind us, resembling loyal shadows.

Bede made his way toward the kitchen, too, saying, "Sus. Mi like yuh dawg."

"Me too?" I wasn't sure what he'd said but figured it couldn't hurt to agree.

"Darling." Angel handed me plates, silverware, and napkins. "I wanted to let you know I lit a candle for your mum in our little chapel at the Cape."

"Oh, Angel, that means so much to me," I said. "Reminds me of the time we went to Manhattan and lit candles inside every Catholic church in the city."

"We were on a mission. My first trip after John died."

"Can I help with something?" Bede asked, his voice deep and raspy.

I had a hard time understanding his words, but Angel understood everything he said.

"No, darling, we've got it."

"Just like old times," I smiled.

"Yes, the good old days—they're gone now."

She handed me a fresh green salad to put on the table.

"My life in Jamaica is so different, darling. Every night, Bede builds the biggest bonfire you've ever seen. All the locals join us at the beach. Many of them are criminals. Can you image me hanging out with criminals?"

"Actually, I can. You see the good in people. That's one of the many things I love about you."

We sat around Angel's long teak dining room table, each dog finding their designated spots beneath their person, settling in comfortably.

Angel placed a bowl filled with her famous chicken wings on the table. Bede enthusiastically bit into a drumstick, and sauce dripped down his chin.

"The whole of them family," Bede said.

"Yes, darling, they're all family. Speaking of family, I took Bede to London to meet Mum last month," she said, a sparkle in her icy blue eyes.

"What'd your mom think?" I asked, curious to find out what a friend of the queen of England thought about her daughter in a relationship with a Rastafarian.

"She adores him." Angel touched his buffed bicep. "Called him her 'Little Sunflower.'"

Bede flashed his pearly whites.

"You found your person," I said, feeling goosebumps.

"Yes, Bede's my person. His name means prayer."

"Angel and a prayer—perfect," I said.

"All the Jamaican people are an answer to my prayers. They're so spiritual and loving—so real."

"Which do you prefer: the Hollywood elite or Jamaicans?"

"Jamaicans, of course." She winked at Bede. "Their energy is infectious. I've laughed more over the last year than I have my entire life."

"I found my people too—dog people. You should see Baldwin killin' it on an agility field."

Angel asked, "Is that where dogs run through those poles?"

I nodded. "The weave poles and more. He's a natural."

"I'm so impressed, darling."

"A woman I met is going to help me train him to become a therapy dog. Marilyn says we can visit kids at the hospital with her pack. She's amazing, with her pack of two Australian Shepherds—resembles Elizabeth Taylor."

"Of course, darling," she said. "You're such a good person, always doing for others. Just like you're doing for your dad. You gave up your life to look after him."

"I couldn't do it without the support of Baldwin," I told her. "When things go haywire, he never fails to lift my spirits."

"I can see why," she said. "I mean, look at him."

Right on cue, Baldwin stuck his head out from under the table hoping for a bite of chicken.

"No, Baldwin, this is people food," I said. With that, he settled back down at my feet.

After dinner, Angel and I cleared the table while Bede lit the biggest joint I'd ever seen.

"Ganja?" I understood that word. He handed me the blunt.

"Be careful, darling," Angel said. "It's strong stuff."

"I better not." I handed it to Angel. "I'm driving."

It didn't take long for the two of them to relax; their red, sleepy eyes meant it was time for me to leave. So, I said my good-byes, leashed Baldwin, and headed to my car.

On the ride home to the Valley, I felt a bit high too. Maybe it was the secondhand smoke. Or maybe I just felt intoxicated seeing my friend so blissful. We'd both found our tribes and, for that, my heart felt like it would burst with gratitude.

8

Bark Side of the Moon

After the stormy, gray winter, spring arrived with a chorus of birds singing every morning. A woodpecker drumming on the cypress tree in the backyard reminded me of the circle of life. Each beat represented the countless obstacles of life which I was beginning to embrace as a natural part of my journey—anyone's journey, for that matter. I could grow and overcome anything by facing it head-on.

One evening, Dad's voice beckoned me from the den, calling out, "Suzie, is that you?"

I responded, "Yes, Dad, it's me."

When I entered his TV sanctuary, Dad posed an unexpected question. "Do you think I should ask Kiki out?"

Kiki, his physical therapist, in her mid-twenties.

Without hesitation, I responded, "No."

"I think she likes me," he said, disregarding my answer.

I felt a burning in my throat. I knew what his doctor would say, but honestly, the thought of him having a crush on such a young woman made me want to vomit. I had to get out of there before I upset his fantasy with rationality.

"Let's talk about this later. I've got to meet Kat for our evening walk."

I leashed Baldwin and headed out the front door. The dark evening sky presented an ideal chance for stargazing as we strolled along the tranquil streets of the neighborhood, allowing me to momentarily escape from Dad's inappropriate inquiry.

"Quit pulling, Amber Jewel," I heard Kat reprimand as she and her canine cutie headed our way. Amber pulled Kat down the street toward her buddy Baldwin.

"Sit, Baldwin," I told my boy, and he did, halting in his tracks.

Agility training not only enhanced the fluff ball's physical prowess but also honed his obedience skills. Through his weekly classes Baldwin's attention span increased which, in turn, reinforced his compliance to obedience commands.

8. Bark Side of the Moon

As soon as I released him, Baldwin hurried toward Amber Jewel, and the two dogs frolicked in playful puppy circles around us.

After Kat and I managed to regain control of our furry companions, the four of us set out together. I couldn't wait to get Kat's take on Dad's inappropriate question about Kiki.

"What should I do about that? First, the incident with the masseuse, and now this."

"Your dad is becoming a sexual deviant," Kat chuckled.

"I know, and this is the same man who only had one sexual partner his whole life. Don't ask me how I know that little fact. Maybe it has to do with his Parkinson's?"

"You should call his doctor and ask."

The following morning, I did just that. According to Dr. Tapper, there were a myriad of reasons why a person suffering from Parkinson's disease could focus on sex.

"Certain medications used to treat his condition can have side effects that impact a person's sexual desire," he said. "Or it could be caused by changes in his brain chemistry."

He went on to explain that Parkinson's affects the brain's neurotransmitters and dopamine levels, which are associated with regulating various functions, including sexual desire.

"Fluctuations in these chemicals can result in alterations in sexual interests," Dr. Tapper continued. "Then there are the psychological factors to consider."

"Like what?"

"Like depression, anxiety, or changes in mood. These factors can influence a person's thoughts and behaviors, including their sexual expression. And in the case of your dad, the death of your mother could be playing a role. Any major changes like that impact healthy humans. Imagine trying to grieve while living with Parkinson's."

"Makes sense, but what do I do about it?"

"It's crucial to approach the situation with empathy and understanding. Don't make too big a deal out of it. Just try and change the subject whenever it comes up."

That valuable advice seemed reminiscent of something I'd learned in one of Baldwin's obedience classes. It revolved around the concept of redirecting a dog's attention to curb undesirable behavior and guide them to do the right thing. I retrieved my dog obedience folder from my filing cabinet to review the instructions.

I read: "First, you need to identify the specific behavior you want to discourage, whether it's jumping on people, chewing on furniture, excessive barking, or something else. Providing an alternative activity is crucial. Offer your dog a positive outlet for their energy and redirect their focus away from the undesired behavior."

Looking over at my trusty canine companion lying on the ground with his frisbee in his mouth, I realized I could redirect him from any unwanted behavior with his favorite toy. That's when a thought struck me: "I need to find Dad his frisbee!"

A few months after quitting my job, I received some unexpected calls from former clients.

"We want you back," my contact at JW Marriott Desert Springs informed me one lazy afternoon.

"I appreciate your kind words, Mary. I've missed working with you too."

"No, I'm serious. We're not at all satisfied with the person who took your place. Would you please consider representing us again?"

Her invitation was followed by similar requests from other clients. Each call fueled a growing desire within me to reclaim my place in the industry. It became evident that there was a demand for the quality of service I provided.

And so, with a sense of excitement and renewed purpose, Susan Hartzler Public Relations was born. I embraced the opportunity to make my mark in the world of public relations once again.

With a growing client list, it became evident that I needed assistance to keep up with the workload while overseeing the care of my dad. And there was only one person I had in mind for the job.

"Kat, will you please come work with me?" I asked, hopeful for a positive response.

She hesitated. "I don't know anything about public relations."

"But you do," I assured her. "It's a sales job, except instead of selling jewelry, you'll be pitching stories."

Kat wasn't sure about taking on a new role but I persisted, knowing she had the potential to become a PR star.

"Come on, you're a natural. Just give it a try. Please?"

After careful consideration, Kat agreed. The following morning, she arrived at my house on Dearborn Street, brimming with enthusiasm and ready to dive headfirst into our exciting new endeavor.

8. *Bark Side of the Moon*

Together, we transformed Will's old bedroom into an office, rearranging furniture to create a functional and inspiring environment. Dad's old desk became my workspace, while a table from the living room served as Kat's dedicated workstation. Equipped with our respective laptop computers, we were fully prepared for this new chapter in our friendship.

In a short amount of time, Kat picked up where I left off. Besides being a person I could count on, Kat turned out to be a quick study. Plus, our clients loved her.

With both Kat and Jason there to help, I felt comfortable leaving Dad when I had to lead media FAM trips or take meetings out of town. Good thing, too, because I had another FAM trip on the horizon.

The following week I had eight top journalists from around the country joining me at the luxurious JW Marriott Desert Springs Resort & Spa. With everything going on at home, I hated to leave but I had to go.

I'd rather spend time with Baldwin. Even getting a root canal seemed more appealing, especially since my dentist allowed me to bring Baldwin to my appointments. He'd lie across my lap while the dentist went to work. The comforting presence of Baldwin's warm body helped alleviate the fear I usually experienced at the dentist.

I reluctantly packed for the trip with plans to leave first thing the next morning. And even though I dreaded the trip, the drive to Palm Springs provided a much-needed opportunity to decompress from my responsibilities as Dad's caretaker and shift gears to focus on tending to the needs of the travel media.

Once I pulled into the impressive porte-cochère, I was welcomed by the resort's flock of flamingos. These graceful creatures roamed freely around the meticulously maintained grounds, adding a touch of whimsy. The sight of these pink birds instantly swept away any traces of monotony that the long drive may have brought. With little time to spare, I quickly dropped my luggage off in my room and made my way back to the lobby to meet with my contact at the resort.

Kat and I'd arranged for the travel writers to indulge in a relaxing spa treatment when they arrived. Our intention was to provide a bit of pampering to help them unwind and start the trip in a state of relaxation. By setting a positive vibe from the beginning, we hoped to create an optimistic atmosphere that would influence their entire three-day stay along with the stories they'd write afterward.

The Peace Puppy

The FAM officially kicked off later that afternoon with an immersive tour aboard one of the resort's small boats that took guests around the property on its private man-made lake.

First stop, the resort's championship golf course that boasted lush green fairways with breathtaking views. Next, we passed the spa facilities, where our media guests had already indulged in rejuvenating treatments. We also showed off the resort's ten dining options, with a diverse selection of restaurants, each offering exquisite cuisine. And, of course, the tour highlighted the resort's five shimmering swimming pools, including my favorite complete with underwater music, a sandy beach, and a cascading waterfall.

The boat dropped us off at the resort's Rockwood Grill where we met Chef Ray and dined on delicious American fare made with fresh, local ingredients. I sat back, allowing Chef Ray to entertain the group. My mind was back in Northridge and the burdens that went along with my role as caregiver. And, of course, I missed Baldwin.

The West Coast editor of *Travel Weekly* caught my attention, eager to discuss her spa experience.

"The masseuse applied too much pressure," she complained, rubbing her neck. "I'm in pain."

"I apologize for the inconvenience," I responded, internally pondering why she hadn't communicated her preferences to the masseuse during the treatment. After all, they can't read minds.

Another travel writer chimed in, sharing her suggestion to improve the resort's spa. "The facilities are lovely, but I believe a meditation room would be a fantastic addition. They're all the rage right now."

"Thank you for your input," I replied diplomatically, although secretly I questioned the relevance of her suggestion. With the resort boasting its own lake, a fleet of boats, and flamingos, it seemed to me like there were already ample amenities and unique experiences available.

The remainder of the FAM proceeded as expected, with the media sharing their unsolicited negative opinions and providing feedback on areas they believed could be enhanced—like the height of the bathtubs. Yes, one reporter commented on the bathtubs, as if my client would consider changing them in all 884 rooms based on her counsel.

It was disheartening to witness their lack of gratitude for the experience that Kat and I had worked so hard to create. I couldn't wait to get home to Baldwin who never complained about anything. And the end couldn't have come sooner.

8. Bark Side of the Moon

Overwhelmed by exhaustion, I arrived home feeling drained. Dad and Jason were already fast asleep, but Baldwin greeted me, insisting on a game of frisbee. I was so happy to see him that I acquiesced.

The following morning, Jason woke me up.

"Susanna, your dad! He fell out bed—there's blood!"

With my heart racing, I hurried to Dad's room and discovered him sitting on the edge of his bed, his forehead marred by a deep gash. His hand trembled as blood cascaded through his fingers and landed on his bed sheets, creating a grim scene. A small pool of crimson formed on the floor near his bedside table too.

I barely had a chance to react when Baldwin leaped onto the bed, instinctively drawn to the scent of blood. I gently moved Baldwin back to the floor and motioned for him to stay there. My obedient boy understood completely, watching me with those soulful brown eyes of his.

"I almost caught that damn squirrel this time," Dad said—and he was serious.

I tried my best to adhere to the guidance of Dad's neurologist. *The squirrel is real*, I told myself.

"Shit, Dad, you should've let it go."

Jason rushed in with a towel, placing it on Dad's forehead.

As he applied pressure, I told Dad, "We need to get you to the hospital right away."

Baldwin and Molly the Collie followed us to the back door. In unison, they showed their empathy by lowering their ears and tails, if you could call Baldwin's tiny stump a tail.

"Stay," I told the two of them. Baldwin expressed his concern with a whine, peering at the three of us. Molly tilted her head in confusion.

"It's all right," I reassured them. "We'll be back soon."

Jason assisted me in getting Dad into my car, and we raced to Northridge Hospital as quickly as possible.

When we reached the emergency room at six that morning, it was nearly empty, enabling the triage nurse to promptly evaluate Dad's condition. After checking his vital signs, the nurse turned to me and said, "Looks like he'll need stitches. Let's get him to an examination room immediately."

I followed Jason as he pushed Dad in his rollator to a sterile, white room. A woman in a white lab coat entered, introducing herself as Dr. Aguilar. She wore medical scrubs under a crisp white lab coat and projected a sense of confidence with her hair neatly pulled back.

Removing the bloodied towel from Dad's forehead, she said, "You took quite a fall. Fortunately, it seems to be a superficial wound, so X-rays won't be necessary." Reading Dad's chart, she turned her attention to me. "Given his age and medical history, you'll need to keep a close eye on him."

"Is it serious?"

"No, the cut was shallow enough for me to use liquid stitches. The adhesive usually peels off after about a week, but you should make sure the area stays dry for at least five days."

I nodded my understanding. "Can we arrange to have a hospital bed delivered to prevent this from happening again?"

"Good idea. I'll place the order. Meanwhile, use ice to reduce any further swelling."

As soon as she left the room, Dad said, "I don't need a stupid hospital bed."

"But Dad, I don't want you to fall out of bed again."

"I didn't fall," he argued.

"You did fall, sir," Jason affirmed.

"No, I didn't!" Dad declared, his tone defiant and resolute. "And if you try to make me sleep in one of those contraptions, I'll bust your nuts."

"Okay, Dad," I sighed. "We won't force you to do anything you don't want to do."

Dr. Aguilar returned and proceeded to skillfully seal Dad's head wound with glue. He sat on the edge of the hospital bed with a blank stare, seemingly detached from the situation.

"You're incredibly brave," I praised him. "I bet you never thought you'd be glued back together."

"Yeah, a regular Humpty Dumpty," he said with a grin only, to return moments later to his blank stare.

During the car ride home, I did my best to calm my nerves, but my adrenaline rush could not be contained. Had I done the right thing moving home to look after him?

When we entered the house, we were greeted happily by Baldwin and Molly the Collie. Nothing unusual there. But Baldwin didn't shower me with his customary enthusiasm. Instead, he seemed to focus entirely on Dad. It was as if Baldwin had a singular purpose: to keep a watchful eye on him.

8. Bark Side of the Moon

I observed this intently as Jason helped Dad settle into his familiar red chair. Without hesitation, Baldwin approached with utmost care, gently nudging Dad's leg with his wet nose.

"Well, hello there, little guy," Dad said, patting the fluff ball on the head.

Baldwin positioned himself at Dad's feet, ever watchful for any signs of discomfort or distress.

On that day, Baldwin deviated from his usual routine of trailing me around. It dawned on me that he considered safeguarding Dad as his primary mission. Yes, the little fluff ball had taken on the role of assisting me in looking after Dad.

Kat was already in the office, busy at work, when I entered.

"Where were you this morning?"

I told her about Dad's fall and that a hospital bed would arrive later that week.

"He adamantly said he does not want one. What am I going to do? In his condition, a fall could be catastrophic."

"Just tell him his bed broke," she suggested.

"His bed broke." I contemplated the idea. "I think that could work."

On the day the new bed was scheduled to arrive, I sent Dad and Jason to the local senior center. Once they left, Kat and I sprang into action. We disassembled his old queen-sized bed, the one with the tall wooden posts, and stowed it away in the garage.

"I hope this works," I told Kat.

"It will," she said.

Later that night, when Dad announced he was ready for bed, my nerves began to unravel. What if Kat's plan didn't work?

I picked up Baldwin to ease my angst and called out to Jason, "He's ready for bed."

Holding my breath, I followed Jason as he guided Dad to his bedroom.

Once they reached the door, I announced, "I got you a new bed."

I maneuvered myself in front of Dad and Jason while Baldwin jumped on the bed. He immediately rolled around with pure delight.

"See, Dad? Baldwin approves."

Dad asked, "What happened to the old one?"

73

The Peace Puppy

"It broke. I sent it out to be fixed."

"You're such a wonderful daughter."

How I'd longed to hear those words from him my entire life, but at that moment, I felt terrible. Lying to him had become my new normal. And lying totally sucked.

9

Nectar of the Dogs

It didn't take long for the summer heat to take hold of the San Fernando Valley. And that first summer back, I worried about my loyal, black-coated dog. We stayed inside during the sweltering days, and when we did venture out, I watched him closely, making sure he remained hydrated and cool. It wasn't uncommon for me to stop whenever we passed a local park or school with sprinklers on and let Baldwin play in the water.

Despite the relentless heat, there was a reason to celebrate. It was Dad's birthday, and I wanted to make it special for him. I contemplated what to get him, but my mind went blank. Then I remembered thinking about finding Dad his "frisbee" and it struck me—the television was his frisbee. I knew he loved watching the news, so what could be better than to get him a huge-screen TV?

With his seventy-second birthday on the horizon, I planned a small gathering to celebrate the milestone. Jack, Kat, Jason, Baldwin, and Molly the Collie all gathered at the family home for a summertime barbeque, paying tribute to dad's Kansas City, Missouri, roots. We indulged in some classic dishes from the Show Me State, savoring the taste of his home.

To ensure an authentic experience, I ordered the finest barbeque sauce online, elevating the flavor of the smoked St. Louis–style ribs to perfection. To compliment the mouthwatering main course, I prepared some cheesy corn for the first (and only) time. Rounding out the menu, I prepared Mom's famous potato salad which brought back memories of family gatherings of the past. We dined in the backyard, enjoying the warm summer evening.

Baldwin moved from person to person begging for one of the rib bones.

"No, you don't," I firmly told him, fully aware of potentially life-threatening hazards for dogs concerning bones. When bones are cooked, they become brittle and prone to splintering. These sharp splinters can pierce and tear the delicate tissues of the digestive tract, potentially leading to internal injuries, blockages, or perforations. I certainly didn't want to end Dad's big day with an emergency vet visit.

Fortunately, I'd planned ahead and bought the fluff ball a giant bully stick to gnaw on. It did the trick, and we found it incredibly amusing watching him lug the oversized treat throughout the house.

Jack and I snuck away from the party to set up Dad's new television in the den directly in front of his red leather chair. Once it was up and running, we brought Dad inside for the surprise.

When Dad walked into the den, his eyes widened in amazement at the sight of the enormous screen.

Baldwin, the party boy.

"That's your birthday present from me," I said.

Immediately, he settled into his red chair, ready to experience the magic of his new TV.

When the images flickered to life, he looked at me and said, "You really outdid yourself this time, Suzie. I couldn't have asked for a better birthday."

Our little group of revelers, all gathered in the den, formed a circle around Dad and sang "Happy Birthday." The moment was made even sweeter as we savored the homemade cake I'd prepared for the occasion.

Dad's demeanor took on a touch of sentimentality as he spoke. "Life's true treasures are not found in possessions, but in the precious moments we share with those we hold dear."

Afterward, when I reflected on the day, I felt an overwhelming sense of contentment knowing that I'd succeeded in making his first birthday without Mom truly special—and I knew Mom's spirit oversaw the entire celebration.

Later that summer, I enrolled Baldwin in therapy dog training with Marilyn, the woman I'd met in agility. She worked with us on all the essential basic qualities that a therapy dog needs, which include being well-behaved, calm, and obedient in diverse settings such as hospitals, nursing homes, schools, and other places where people might need a little doggie love.

Marilyn suggested I take Baldwin to a variety of places to prepare him for his important role. We went to Home Depot, Nordstrom's, and parks filled with screaming kids. We stood in front of a nearby Catholic church when mass ended, encouraging people walking by to engage with my fluff ball. Of course, he still accompanied me to our local Starbucks every morning.

I even took him to Hollywood and Vine one sunny afternoon—an iconic and bustling intersection in the heart of Hollywood. This renowned area has a long history intertwined with the glamour of Hollywood, attracting tourists from around the world. And it would be the perfect place to train Baldwin for his work as a therapy dog.

The goal was to see how he fared when encountering the diverse array of people that were drawn there. Besides the visitors exploring the Hollywood Walk of Fame and marveling at landmarks like Grauman's

Baldwin poses at Vasquez Rocks near the town of Agua Dulce, California (photograph by Pamela Marks, https://pawprincestudios.com/).

9. Nectar of the Dogs

Chinese Theatre, the intersection was filled with the homeless along with out-of-work actors dressed in character costumes.

I knew this environment, with all the noise and stimulation, would be an excellent training ground for Baldwin, helping him become more accustomed to a variety of people and situations, ultimately preparing him for interactions with children in hospitals.

We conveniently parked just a short distance away from all the commotion. Under the radiant sun, we made our way through the bustling scene. We passed by people dressed as Batman, Wonder Woman, Captain America, and even Charlie Chaplin. Finally, I decided to engage with Elmo. After all, whoever was under the mask was portraying a friendly character, and I thought they would be kind enough to interact with my fluff ball. With Baldwin by my side, I approached the performer and kindly asked if he (or she) would be willing to pet my dog.

To my surprise, Elmo responded in a strong New York accent, "Five dollars, please."

Perplexed, I questioned, "Five dollars to pet my dog?"

"This is my job, lady," Elmo replied.

Slightly taken aback, I reluctantly agreed and handed over a five-dollar bill. Just as the exchange took place, a guy with a gigantic boa constrictor wrapped around his body passed by. As someone with an intense fear of snakes, I felt panic instantly set in. I swiftly pulled Baldwin's leash and hurriedly made our escape in the opposite direction.

After I put enough distance between me and the snake, my attention was drawn to a family with three young children huddled nearby.

"There we go—some kids."

Baldwin and I approached them, and I asked if they would be interested in seeing some dog tricks.

"No Inglés," the mother responded.

The family reminded me of the time I visited Sweden in my early twenties—blonde and beautiful. Everyone in that country appeared exceptionally attractive. I recalled thinking that the clerk at a liquor store could have easily been a supermodel back in the United States.

The toeheaded kids immediately bent down to pet Baldwin while I tried my best to communicate with their striking parents. But before I could get them to understand, Baldwin started offering behaviors. He gave each child a high five to begin his impromptu performance, followed by a kiss. The little ones were all smiles watching Baldwin twirl in front of them, and they clapped when he rolled over, stopping for a belly rub.

I decided to end my useless attempt to communicate with the parents and simply went for it. Baldwin showcased the rest of his repertoire of tricks, which included weaving through my legs, walking backward, playing dead, catching a treat, waving hello, speaking, and sitting pretty. However, the real showstopper was when the fluff ball sneezed on command, causing the entire family to burst into laughter.

When our performance ended, both Baldwin and I took a bow. It was at this moment that the father attempted to give me five dollars, as if I were one of the costumed actors who'd fallen on hard times.

I politely declined. "No, no, I'm not a performer. I'm just training my boy to become a therapy dog."

The father insisted, placing the money in my hand.

"For dog," he said, pointing at Baldwin.

At least I recouped the money I'd given to Elmo.

Following our adventure on Hollywood Boulevard, Baldwin successfully passed the American Kennel Club's (AKC) Canine Good Citizen (CGC) test. This comprehensive evaluation assessed his behavior and manners, specifically focusing on his ability to work through distractions, interact positively with friendly strangers, and exhibit good manners in public.

The CGC test took place at a local park during an agility trial, and it was a fitting setting considering our triumphs. After securing first place in the novice class on both the standard course and the jumpers with weaves course, we met with a fellow competitor who was certified through the AKC to administer the CGC test. It must have been my boy's lucky day because he aced that test as well. Or perhaps it was the result of all the training I did with him.

The following week, we met with an evaluator from Therapy Dog International (TDI) at a local pet store for the final test. I worried about the setting, with all the yummy smells, but we'd done our due diligence and practiced for months.

I chose this organization because members had the flexibility to choose their own places to visit. Plus, my new agility friend, Marilyn, who'd invited me to accompany her and her pack on visits to the children at Los Angeles County + USC Medical Center, was already a TDI member.

9. Nectar of the Dogs

At the testing venue, four other dogs were present, and their owners shared my hopeful anticipation of passing the test. Our first step was to sign in and complete the required paperwork, all while being observed closely by the evaluator—a stout, middle-aged woman with a sturdy presence, her own Poodle standing by her side.

The evaluation itself involved a thorough temperament test measuring my fluff ball's behavior and sociability as well as his responses in a variety of situations. The evaluator carefully observed how Baldwin behaved with both dogs and people while I was judged on my interactions as well. We were testing to become a therapy dog team, after all. I didn't worry about either one of us. Heck, I'd proven that I could remain calm with demanding travel journalists and had complete confidence that Baldwin's kind and gentle nature would shine through during the evaluation and after.

What I didn't have confidence in was Baldwin's ability to make the right choice when it came to resisting a tasty piece of hot dog. I'd been using hot dogs as high-value treats in agility training ever since ditching those Goldfish crackers. I was concerned about his self-control when faced with the temptation of a juicy morsel right in front of his nose. During practice, he didn't always leave it.

When it was time for that part of the test, I took a deep breath and locked eyes with Baldwin.

"Leave it," I commanded, holding a smelly chunk of hot dog in front of his nose.

Baldwin's nostrils flared at the scent of the tantalizing treat. He leaned forward slightly but then looked up at me and relaxed, shifting his head away from the hot dog.

"Good boy!" I praised, knowing that he expected the treat as his reward. I couldn't give him anything during the evaluation, though.

"You'll get your reward afterward," I told him, and he seemed to comprehend my promise.

Next, the evaluator proceeded to scatter some low-value yet enticing treats on the floor, gesturing for me to guide Baldwin through this tempting obstacle course.

"Leave it," I reiterated, as I walked him forward.

We maintained unwavering eye contact, and before I knew it, he'd successfully navigated his way through without grabbing one.

Baldwin performed admirably during the entire evaluation. He successfully held his sit-stays, down-stays, and greeted another dog with the grace of a seasoned pro. Baldwin had no trouble waiting patiently for me when I left him with the evaluator for a couple minutes, to prove he would remain calm with anyone other than me.

He remained still when the evaluator threw a metal dog bowl down in front of him, demonstrating that he wouldn't bolt if something crashed at the hospital during a visit. Baldwin's calm demeanor truly shone through when a group of noisy kids ran around him, screaming, with their arms in the air in excitement.

He demonstrated impeccable mastery when it came to entering and exiting doors, and his ability to walk on a loose leash filled me with pride. He displayed total confidence and familiarity around wheelchairs and rollators, a skill we had diligently developed with valuable guidance from Dad.

But, as I mentioned, the test didn't focus solely on Baldwin. It was a comprehensive evaluation, assessing both Baldwin's behavior and my ability to effectively partner with him during our therapy dog visits. As the handler, I had to lead him while actively engaging with pretend patients and their families in a friendly and confident manner.

Together, we successfully passed the test, marking the beginning of an extraordinary chapter in both our lives. Equipped with his new status, Baldwin was poised to make a positive impact on the lives of hospitalized children.

After receiving a clean bill of health from his veterinarian and a proper grooming, Baldwin and I set off for his first therapy dog visit. He curled up in a cozy ball in the passenger seat during the car ride to downtown Los Angeles. When we arrived at the parking lot of LA County USC, he sat up as if he sensed that we were about to embark on an unforgettable journey—not just for ourselves but also for the young patients, their families, and the dedicated healthcare professionals we would meet.

In the parking lot, I dressed him in a children's doctor's costume that I'd bought for the occasion and customized to fit his adorable frame. It was a daunting task to navigate through the hospital grounds, as everyone we passed couldn't resist the urge to interact with this four-legged, furry doctor.

After checking in at the front desk, we rode the elevator to the sixth floor. Baldwin surprised me. Despite his usual boundless energy, he was unusually calm, and when those elevator doors opened, he

9. Nectar of the Dogs

herded me out as if he understood the importance of our mission—to bring smiles and comfort to hospitalized children.

We were greeted by Leticia, the head of the hospital's children's ward, who asked, "Who's this little doctor?"

"This is Baldwin." I motioned for my fluff ball to take a bow.

She curtsied back. "Well, hello there."

"We're here to meet Marilyn and her pack," I explained.

"They're already going room to room," Leticia told me. "We have a special little girl waiting to meet you."

Baldwin was an angel here on Earth visiting kids as a therapy dog.

Baldwin was on a mission that day: to share his special kind of love with Maria, a brave seven-year-old cancer patient who'd just undergone chemotherapy earlier that day. Due to her increased susceptibility to germs after the treatment, Maria sat alone in the playroom with her mother by her side.

Maria looked so pale and fragile—until Dr. Baldwin entered the room. Once she spotted my funny, muppet looking boy, she laughed, infusing a touch of color back into her face.

In my limited Spanish, I asked Maria if she would like Baldwin to sit beside her. She motioned for him to join her on the couch, and without hesitation, Baldwin hopped up and gave her a sweet puppy kiss. To my surprise, he nestled on her lap, stretching his entire body across her. I jumped, ready to take him off, afraid he might hurt her, but Maria seemed content and began to stroke Baldwin's fur.

In minutes, Maria was taking deep breaths in sync with Baldwin's soft snores. I watched in awe as the transformative power of their connection unfolded before my eyes. Maria seemed to improve with every inhalation.

I stepped back and took in the beauty of the moment. Baldwin, my high-energy dog, had become an instrument of grace. We spent an hour with Maria and her mother that day, Baldwin sound asleep in her lap. It was remarkable how intuitively he knew exactly what this little girl needed. In that hospital room, the boundaries of language and species dissolved, leaving only the purest form of compassion and healing in their wake. At that moment, I knew we'd uncovered Baldwin's purpose, and mine too.

That evening, Angel called, and I couldn't contain my excitement. I told her all about Baldwin's first day as an official therapy dog.

"Darling, I have to witness this miracle dog for myself!" she exclaimed.

Angel and I made plans for her to join us at the hospital during her next trip to Los Angeles.

Eager to make a contribution to the hospital, Angel asked, "What can I bring for the kids?"

"They always need of art supplies," I replied.

And I didn't have to wait long. The next month when I picked her up at the trendy Chateau Marmont, I found her waiting in the porte-cochère surrounded by piles of shopping bags.

"I mentioned some art supplies, not the entire store."

"I wasn't sure what they might need, so I ended up getting a little bit of everything," she confessed.

When it came to Angel, her definition of "a little bit" clearly exceeded expectations.

We arrived at the hospital, and I dialed Leticia's number from the parking lot seeking assistance unloading Angel's bounty of donations.

"I'll send someone down," she assured me.

While we waited, I dressed Baldwin in a red, white, and blue top hat and star shaped sunglasses. We were celebrating the 4th of July, after all.

Baldwin celebrates Independence Day in style.

"He looks so dapper," Angel giggled. "There's just something inherently funny about dogs wearing sunglasses."

Soon, a young volunteer approached us, pulling a red wagon behind her. We loaded the wagon, and I handed some small flags I'd bought for the occasion to Angel. Holding onto Baldwin's leash, we followed the wagon toward the entrance of the hospital.

On the way, Angel said, "Hobson would never keep a hat on like that, let alone those sunglasses."

"No dog is born with the hat and sunglass gene. I had to train him."

"How'd you do that?"

"With lots of patience," I replied. "I gradually introduced them to him, leaving them on for short periods of time clicking my approval. Of course, treats help."

Baldwin and I led Angel through a labyrinth of corridors on our way to the elevator.

"Darling, you really know your way around."

"You think that's impressive—wait until you see Baldwin in action."

I pressed the button for the sixth floor. When the door opened, Baldwin pulled me into the hallway of the children's ward where Leticia stood waiting.

"Hello, Dr. Baldwin."

She put up her hand out and Baldwin gave her a high five. "We have fourteen patients waiting in their rooms to see you."

I introduced Angel and let Leticia know about her generous donations.

"Thank you very much," Leticia said.

"No," Angel replied, "thank you for all the work you do with children."

The three of us headed down the hallway, stopping at the first room. I watched Angel give a flag to a little blonde girl recovering from severe burns. The pre-teen legs were covered with dark red blisters.

"Here you go, Sweetikins," Angel said, her lower lip trembling.

A member of the hospital staff captured the moment with a photograph. Angel stood by the girl's bed holding three flags, while I held Baldwin in his star-spangled costume.

Baldwin showed off his repertoire of tricks for the burn patient. He waved his paw, rolled over, backed up, and weaved through my legs.

We journeyed from one room to another, spending time with each child and their families. Along the way, we made sure to stop and acknowledge the incredible doctors and nurses with Baldwin giving them high fives.

The time flew by, and before we knew it, Baldwin had entertained all the kids in the children's ward. Back at the car, Angel slid into the passenger seat and pulled Baldwin onto her lap.

"Sweetikins, this little dog is a healer." Exhausted, he closed his eyes. "Look at him. He's already sleeping."

I glanced at my boy snuggled on my friend's lap and my heart melted.

"He gets just as tired visiting the kids as he does when he competes in agility."

"I can relate," she yawned. "I'm tired too." She turned her gaze toward me. "You know, darling, there's something important I've been meaning to discuss with you."

"Oh?"

"I want you to know that I consider you more than just a friend. We are family."

"I just got chills. That's incredibly sweet of you to say."

"I'm not just saying it, I truly mean it. If you ever need anything, darling, anything, please don't hesitate to let me know." She reached over and gently squeezed my arm. "Are you doing okay financially?"

9. *Nectar of the Dogs*

"Yup, business is booming," I reassured her.

"That's wonderful, darling. But if times get tough, remember, I'm here for you."

I was overwhelmed with gratitude as I thought about Baldwin, Kat, Jack, and now Angel—I couldn't have asked for a more perfect family.

After dropping Angel off at her hotel, Baldwin and I made our way back to the Valley. I parked my SUV in the driveway, feeling utterly drained. Baldwin and I trudged inside, heading straight to my bedroom.

On the way, I stuck my head in the office and said, "Kat, we're going to take a nap."

"Sure, boss. I've got everything under control."

I'd just drifted off when a faint voice at my door roused me from my drowsiness.

"Sleeping Beauty," the voice whispered.

"Did someone just call me Sleeping Beauty?" I sat up and saw Jason standing in the doorway, gazing at me with a smile.

"It's me," he said, flashing a grin. "I'm leaving for vacation tomorrow."

"You're leaving?" I asked, hoping it was just a bad dream.

"Don't worry, my friend is covering for the next two weeks."

It hadn't even been a full year since I took on the responsibility of overseeing Dad's care, and I was already well aware of the burnout that came with caretaking. Jason definitely deserved some time off.

"Well, I appreciate you finding someone to step in," I said, standing up to stretch.

"Yes, Terrance will do a good job."

I didn't feel entirely comfortable with a caretaker I'd never met, but I couldn't care for Dad on my own.

"Next time, could you give me a heads-up? I would have liked to interview your substitute."

"Sure," Jason replied, making his way back down the hall, his hands clasped together as if in prayer.

Deep down, I knew my request was futile. Jason had a habit of agreeing with me about everything, but he didn't always follow my requests. He did things his own way. I referred to it as Jason's way. Nonetheless, Dad liked him, and we needed his help.

The following morning, the dogs barked to alert me of a stranger in the house. I headed toward the kitchen and found Jason standing with a short, skinny, baldheaded man.

"Susanna, this is Terrance."

The Peace Puppy

The stranger bowed as if he were meeting a holy person. At least he looked the part in his comfortable yet practical light green scrubs suitable for caregiving responsibilities.

"He doesn't speak English," Jason added.

Terrance placed his overnight bag on the kitchen floor, then turned his attention to Jason. The two of them spoke in their native language. I enjoyed the soft, melodic, sing-song quality but had no clue as to what they were saying. Their conversation ended and Jason made his way to the den, leaving me and Terrance alone in the kitchen without a translator.

Jason saluted Dad on his way out. "Bye, sir."

I motioned for Terrance to follow me into the den. "This is Jason's substitute, Terrance."

Dad nodded at the stranger as if he were a long-lost friend.

"Suzie, why don't you offer a drink to our visitor?"

I stood there for a moment trying to figure out how to answer Dad's request.

"You brought all these guests with you?" Dad gestured at the empty room.

This new hallucination was a first. Terrance looked at me for guidance.

I was saved by the sound of commotion from Molly the Collie and Baldwin in the kitchen. They were so noisy that I had to investigate. Terrance followed me back to the kitchen. As we turned the corner, we were greeted by the sight of the two dogs doing their best to get into Terrance's bag.

I ran over and picked it up to keep them from ripping it open. "Do you have food in here?"

Terrance looked at me and said, "No English."

The dogs were still frantically scratching at the bag, so I lifted it above my head then placed it in the center of the table well out of reach.

"There must be something inside."

"Suzie, I told you to look after our guests," Dad yelled from the den.

"I'll be right there."

Baldwin couldn't contain himself and jumped onto the table. He'd never done that before.

"No, Baldwin. Get off, now!"

Reluctantly, he jumped off, but his full attention was still on that darn overnight bag.

I motioned for Terrance to open the bag and there it was—a whole dried fish just sitting there on top of his clothes. Both dogs lunged forward to grab it.

Terrance picked up the fish, causing the dogs to go ballistic.

"Don't let them have any." I held Baldwin and Molly back. "Fish bones can be fatal to dogs."

Terrance just stood there with that fish in his hand as I pulled Baldwin and Molly outside.

I closed the door and headed back to Terrance. "Here, give it to me."

Terrance handed me the fish. I took it by the tail in an attempt to minimize direct contact. With caution, I placed it in a baggie and promptly stored it in the refrigerator.

"Tragedy avoided." After I washed my hands and let the dogs back inside, Terrance followed me back to the den where we found Dad holding court with his invisible friends.

"Here she is," he said. "And look what she's got."

That was my cue to mimic holding a tray filled with imaginary hors d'oeuvres and beverages.

I circled the room. "Would you like something to drink? How about a pig in a blanket?"

"Suzie, why don't you take them upstairs? We have a beautiful view of the lake from up there."

There was no upstairs in our single-story ranch-style home. And we didn't live anywhere near a lake.

"Sure," I told him, motioning for the invisible group to follow. "You got here just in time to see the sun rise."

The sun had risen hours ago.

After Terrance's problematic start, I couldn't wait for Jason to return. With Jason around, everything operated smoothly. The three of us had settled into a comfortable routine.

But for the time being, I'd do my best with the help of Terrance. One morning, I completed the grocery shopping before work, and when I returned, Terrance volunteered to put everything away.

"All right, thank you," I acknowledged, making my way to my office to get some work done.

Later in the day, Dad called out, "Suzie, could you bring me a glass of milk?"

"I'll be right there."

The Peace Puppy

I made my way to the kitchen, intending to retrieve the carton of milk that I'd bought earlier that day from the refrigerator. However, it was nowhere in sight. I searched the freezer, only to discover that the beautiful beefsteak tomatoes I'd brought home were there, frozen solid. It wasn't until I checked the pantry that I finally found the milk. I had to go back over my entire grocery list and make sure everything was in its place.

The next morning, I proceeded to the garage to do my laundry. Terrance had taken care of it for me, folding my clothes neatly and placing them on top of the dryer.

"Thanks, Terrance," I said gratefully, passing him as I made my way to my room, my arms full of clean clothes.

I began putting my things away only to make a disappointing discovery. My favorite black cashmere sweater had shrunk to a size fit for a Barbie doll, clearly subjected to hot water.

Terrance was not the only obstacle I had to confront while Jason was gone. The constant need to deceive Dad was taking a toll on me, and his frequent bursts of anger only intensified the strain I felt.

The following day, after I returned home from an exceptionally demanding meeting with a client, Dad confronted me.

"Why'd you do it?" he asked, his hands trembling, his face red. "Your mother and I raised you better than that."

"Do what?"

"Rob that bank!" he exclaimed.

I later learned about a bank robbery, the top story on CNN that day. Despite the absurdity of his allegation, it still stung.

Thankfully, Jason's return brought some relief, but it did little to alleviate the difficulties in my life. Dad's accusations and demanding behavior were weighing heavy on me, causing immense emotional turmoil. And when I reached out for help, instead of receiving the support I needed, I was met with suggestions of additional tasks and responsibilities I could take on.

"Start a book club," the minister of Dad's church suggested, "or a movie night."

When I reached out to Will, he suggested I "just think positive."

"Don't you get it? He has a neurodegenerative condition. My thinking positive won't do anything for him."

"But it might help you."

He did have a point there.

Erin suggested I look for a Parkinson's support group for Dad.

In my desperation, I turned to an online caregiver support group.

9. *Nectar of the Dogs*

When I entered the chat room, I waited patiently, hoping someone would join, but the realization slowly sank in that I was alone both online and in real life. It felt like a never-ending cycle of expectations and obligations, leaving me feeling overwhelmed and unheard.

The next day, Erin called with what she believed was the ultimate solution.

"I've been thinking," she started, "Dad should move up here."

"What?"

"I looked at a few nursing homes nearby and there's one close to me that would be a good fit."

"But he doesn't want to move. And anyway, what about his doctors? They're all here."

"It sounds like you're in over your head."

"Just because I ask for help you think I'm in over my head?"

"It would be good for him to live near me. He'd be closer to his grandkids."

My body tensed. "Let's discuss the possibility during our next phone meeting."

We hadn't had a phone meeting for months and my effort to keep everyone in the loop with emails only seemed to make matters more difficult for me.

I turned to Baldwin, my canine caregiver. I buried my face in his soft curls, finding solace in his unwavering affection. "At least this dog loves me."

Reflecting on the situation now, I see how I misinterpreted Erin's suggestions that Dad move near her as a lack of appreciation for my efforts. At the time, I didn't fully consider the range of options available to us for Dad's care. It wasn't a matter of choosing between one extreme or another. We could have explored the possibility of Dad staying in a facility near Erin for a few months at a time. This approach would have allowed me to take a much needed break while honoring my older sister's desires. If only I could turn back the clock…

10

What Would Baldwin Do?

That weekend, Kat and I drove to a picturesque hiking spot she'd recently stumbled upon. Accompanied by Baldwin and Amber Jewel, we headed toward the rolling hills that encircle the San Fernando Valley.

Following Kat's directions, we arrived at a secluded trail enveloped by majestic sycamore trees, their lofty branches reaching toward the sky. The moment I stepped out of my SUV, I took a deep breath, inhaling the fresh, clean, slightly sweet smell of the trees.

"That smell—reminds me of Girl Scout camp."

I knew Kat would relate since we were in the same troop.

"I remember those trips! And your mom, always the chaperone."

"Did you know she actually hated camping?"

"She did? I don't believe that."

The crisp autumn leaves crunched beneath our feet, composing a soothing and melodic backdrop to our expedition.

"Some years back, I asked her why we never went camping as a family. That's when she confessed her profound dislike for every moment spent at Girl Scout camp."

"Then why'd she go?"

"She told me she only went to make sure I didn't get into trouble."

Baldwin and Amber Jewel bounded ahead, stopping to wait for us on a bridge that overlooked a meandering creek.

"That was her, always looking out for me," I said. "There are moments when the mere thought of never seeing Mom again sends me into a panic attack."

"I know," Kat said. "I miss my dad every single day. While I try my best to go with the flow, sometimes grief takes over."

"Exactly. Sometimes I just feel lost without her."

"What do you do with those feelings?"

"That's a great question," I pondered, pausing for a moment to gather my thoughts. "One thing I do is cry every night when I'm taking a bath."

"That's a good start. We each grieve at our own pace. The goal, I'm told, is to find a way to live with the pain."

"Have you been able to do that?"

"Not yet," Kat admitted, her gaze distant. "You remember my dad's obsession with trains?"

"How could I forget? He had all those vintage trains sets set up every Christmas."

"Well, after he died, I cried whenever I saw a train go by. I'd just sit there in my car bawling my eyes out. But now, I see trains as a message from him—a sort of gentle kiss from heaven."

"I like that."

"This is going to be our first holiday without them," Kat reminded me. "I'm still going to set up his trains."

"That's a lovely way to honor his memory."

"I think he'd get a kick out of me keeping his tradition going, don't you?"

"I'm sure he would. I'm considering starting a new tradition of my own. Angel invited me to spend Thanksgiving with her in Jamaica."

"That's a wonderful idea."

"I suppose so. But what about Dad? This will be his first Thanksgiving without her, too."

Kat paused. "It's important to consider your dad's feelings," she said, "but if he wasn't sick, I'm sure he'd want you to live your life to the fullest. Maybe you can find some sort of balance that allows you to be there for him while also taking care of yourself."

Her words resonated with me, reminding me of the importance of self-care.

"Balance. I keep forgetting about that."

"You could celebrate Thanksgiving before or after your trip."

"That's true."

"He won't know the difference anyway. Maybe he can celebrate the actual day with Will or Erin."

"Maybe."

"It's okay to have your own life, too, you know."

"Okay, then, Jamaica it is. Thanks for listening."

"Of course. That's what friends are for, right?"

The Peace Puppy

I planned to tell Dad about my Thanksgiving plans that night, but before I got a word out, he said, "Your Mother and I almost made it to our fiftieth wedding anniversary."

"Loving someone for forty-seven years," I said. "You guys were lucky."

"I guess so," he replied. "I miss her so much. Life is lonely without her."

"What do you think was the key to your success in marriage?"

"We were best friends, and we both put God above all else. Proverbs 3:6 says, 'In everything you do, put God first, and He will direct you and crown your efforts with success.'"

"That's beautiful, Dad. I always knew that faith played a significant role in your marriage."

Dad nodded. "We faced our fair share of trials, but we always supported each other—and committed to our marriage. We were a team."

"And you both loved to laugh. Remember the time you two walked through the living room with lamp shades on your heads when Kat and I were studying?"

"I remember the peanut M&Ms and Doritos. I guess they helped you study?" He turned away from his beloved CNN for a moment and looked at me. "Love will come your way when the time is right."

"Thank you, Dad," I whispered. "You and Mom were great role models."

With that, we sat together, embracing the silence. Perhaps he was right. Love would come my way some day. For the time being, though, we'd find solace in supporting each other process our grief. And I did have an incredible dog. If only they lived as long as humans.

I cherished my morning routine, despite not being a morning person. I remember a doctor once told me that I was "allergic" to mornings, an observation I found rather astute. Or maybe it had to do with how Mom woke me in my formative years. She'd enter my room banging a tambourine while singing a gospel song at the top of her lungs. And Mom couldn't sing.

Her raspy voice was replaced by an enthusiastic wakeup call from Baldwin. With his frisbee in his mouth, he'd jump on my bed and stare at me until my eyes opened. I'd roll out of bed, and together we'd venture into the backyard for a lively round of frisbee. Then it was off to our neighborhood Starbucks, and on the way home, we'd take a walk in the charming community park adjacent to the coffee shop.

10. What Would Baldwin Do?

In my mind, Baldwin had become the unofficial mayor of the Northridge Starbucks store. Patiently sitting unleashed by the door in front of the store's floor-to-ceiling window, he watched me, never moving from his spot.

One morning, a woman standing in line ahead of me commented on Baldwin's obedience. "It's so cute how he stays there, staring at you," she remarked.

"It is cute," I replied. "The crazy part is that I stare at him."

When I got to the front of the line, my favorite barista handed me my latte. The tall twenty-something then gestured toward his visibly bruised and swollen right eye.

"This is all your fault," he declared.

Confused, I responded, "My fault?"

"After you left yesterday, things got crazy around here. I found myself caught in the middle of a fight between Homeless Manny and Todd Bridges—you know, the former child star who's a regular here?"

"Yeah, I've seen him holding court on the patio. But how does their fight have anything to do with me?"

"It all started after you left. Todd complained about your dog being off leash."

"Well, there is a leash law."

"Manny stood up for you saying, 'Leave her alone—Baldwin is a therapy dog.' Todd didn't agree."

"But how'd you get the black eye?"

"I went out to stop the yelling."

"There was yelling?"

"Oh, yes. And hitting."

"What?"

"Todd went to hit Manny but missed and ended up punching me instead. Thankfully, the police arrived, and an ambulance took me to the hospital."

"You had to go to the hospital?"

"That Todd, he knocked me out cold. Luckily, I didn't have a concussion or anything. Just this damn black eye." He pointed to his injured eye again.

"Oh my God! All that drama over me and my dog? Well, from now on, I'll follow the leash laws," I said, embarrassed.

Baldwin obediently followed me back to the car and hopped inside.

"We caused quite a ruckus yesterday," I mused, stroking his curls.

The Peace Puppy

"If only people could be more like dogs, the world would be a better place."

After a quick walk around the park, I rushed home, eager to dive into a towering pile of work that awaited me. But before I could get to my office, Dad intercepted me. It was evident that he wanted to have a conversation, and despite my workload, I knew it was important to listen to him.

"Your mom," he began, his voice trembling, and his eyes welling up with tears. "It feels like I've lost a part of myself."

"She was truly one of a kind," I responded, acknowledging the depth of his grief.

"I don't think I'll ever come across someone who can appreciate me the way she did," he confessed.

"I understand that you're going through a tough time," I reassured him. "Perhaps you'd find it helpful to discuss your feelings with others who are going through a similar loss."

To my surprise, Dad agreed to the idea. Later that day, I delved into some online research and stumbled upon a weekly grief support group facilitated by a local psychologist. It occurred to me that the group might help me process my own grief as well.

While it was undeniable that Baldwin provided me with an immeasurable amount of comfort, it wasn't fair to place the sole burden of filling the void in my heart on a little dog's shoulders. So I took the initiative and picked up the phone to arrange for both of us to attend the upcoming meeting.

Later that week on a cool fall evening, Jason helped me get Dad into the car, and we drove the few blocks to the campus of California State University, Northridge, where the meeting took place.

When we stepped foot on campus, I remarked, "Dad, we're college students now."

"Your mother would be so proud," he said with a wry smile.

When we entered the classroom, a handful of people were already there, immersed in conversation. The room was arranged with chairs around multiple desks that had been pushed together, creating a sizable square formation.

After helping Dad to his seat, I whispered to Jason, "I'll come get you when the meeting is over."

10. What Would Baldwin Do?

The room slowly filled, everyone exchanging warm greetings as they settled into their usual seats. It became evident that, apart from me, everyone in the room was well over seventy.

A hush fell over the group as a man with horn-rimmed glasses entered. He was dressed in jeans paired with a plain white button-down shirt, giving off a distinctly psychologist-like vibe.

I leaned over and whispered to Dad, "I suppose he must be our facilitator."

The man took a seat in one of the two remaining chairs, leaving the last empty chair right next to me. I couldn't help but feel a sense of relief, as I welcomed the idea of having a bit of personal space.

"Hello, everyone," he greeted the group. "For those of you who may be unfamiliar, my name is Dr. Wyne."

He glanced around the room.

"I see we have some new members tonight, so let's begin with introductions. Please share your name and what brings you here tonight." Dr. Wyne gestured toward me. "Let's start with you."

With a slight lump in my throat, I mustered the strength to speak. "I'm Susan, and I'm here because I've been struggling with the loss of my mom. She passed away earlier this year."

Hoping to swiftly move on, I gently touched Dad's arm.

He began, "My name's Dick, and I lost the most important person in my life, my wife Margaret. She passed away suddenly in her sleep back in January, and I've been feeling empty ever since."

The entire group nodded in understanding, a shared sense of grief uniting us all. As the others shared their stories, I found it increasingly difficult to concentrate. My mind wandered. I didn't snap back to reality until the introductions were nearly finished.

It was then that a woman around my age hurriedly entered and took the empty seat beside me. She turned her attention towards Dr. Wyne, and in that moment, I had an unobstructed view of her beautiful, thick, long brunette hair gracefully cascading down her shoulders.

"Sherry, welcome back," Dr. Wyne said.

Wait, is her name Sherry? Could this be Jack's ex?

"We've missed you these past couple of months. How was Paris?"

Didn't he just tell me she was in Paris?

When Sherry turned toward me, I noticed her flawless features—high cheekbones, youthful skin, big eyes—a perfectly symmetrical face.

The Peace Puppy

"We're doing introductions," Dr. Wyne said. "Why don't you share what brought you here?"

"I've been a member of this group since my parents passed away ten years ago," Sherry began.

This is Jack's Sherry. I'm positive.

"When I first lost them, I felt completely alone and isolated, disconnected from my friends and the world. Joining this group provided me with a safe space to express my feelings. I receive the support and understanding I need, and I've also learned so much by listening to all of your stories."

Jack's Sherry. Sitting right next to me.

"Grief has been a tumultuous journey for me." Sherry said. "I've faced significant health issues of my own, including ongoing symptoms of fibromyalgia. Even after all these years, there are moments when I still feel like my life is spiraling out of control from grief. But being here gives me a fresh perspective and helps me regain some semblance of control."

"Thank you, Sherry," Dr. Wyne acknowledged her contribution. "Your words lead us perfectly into tonight's topic: control."

At that moment, my mind became a whirlwind of conflicting thoughts. It was impossible to focus on anything else but my inner dialogue. The little voice inside my head engaged in an intense debate.

Should I tell her? No. Yes. No. But then again, we could discuss Jack and his fear of commitment. Why would I want to dwell on negativity? Perhaps negativity contributed to her health struggles.

The heart-wrenching story of a gray-haired woman sitting across from me snapped me back to reality again. Her trembling hands and anguished voice painted a devastating picture of her struggle.

"He had a severe drug problem," she confessed. "I tried everything to help him, but nothing worked. I resorted to tough love, and it ended up backfiring. Within days, Michael took his own life. My son's death is entirely my fault."

Oh. my God. At least Mom didn't have to face the loss of a child.

Sitting next to her, a skinny seventy-something-year-old man placed a box of tissues on the table in front of her. "You can't blame yourself, Helen."

"But it is my fault," she sobbed, her face now red and tear-streaked. "I should have..."

Dr. Wyne intervened, his voice gentle yet firm. "Helen, remember what we discussed last week about self-condemnation? Beneath your self-blame lies the recognition that we are not in control. None of us are."

10. *What Would Baldwin Do?*

He paused for a moment, his gaze sweeping across the room. "Let's continue."

I checked out while the other members spoke. I couldn't get over the fact that I was sitting next to Sherry, the woman who caused me such angst when I first started dating Jack.

"Thank you all for bravely sharing your stories tonight. Let's conclude by showing ourselves compassion through a guided meditation."

Dr. Wyne dimmed the lights, and the room became still, bathed in the soft glow of the full moon shining through the windows.

"Close your eyes, place your hand over your heart, and focus on the natural rhythm of your breath. As you exhale, count backward starting from fifty-nine."

A serene silence enveloped the room, interrupted only by the gentle sound of my own breath. In my mind I struggled to quiet the voices arguing in my head, and with each exhale, they gradually faded away.

"On your next inhale, imagine yourself breathing in mercy for the part of you that feels out of control," Dr. Wyne's soothing voice continued. "If you wish, silently express your intention to be released from your suffering."

By following his guidance, I gained a sense of peace—a fleeting respite, but a welcome one.

"Remind yourself that you are not alone," he said, his voice barely above a whisper. "Pray that those suffering in this room, and in the world, also find release."

I couldn't tell you how long we sat there, connected through our grief in this meditation. But when we finished, a wave of relief washed over me. I hoped Dad felt that wave too.

My newfound peace didn't last long. The internal debate over Sherry reignited within me. With a deep sigh, I headed outside to inform Jason that the meeting had concluded.

Once outside, I contemplated calling Jack. Grabbing my phone out of my purse, I began dialing his number, but just before hitting send, an awareness struck me. Sherry's presence was a message to me from a higher power. I could choose to meet her for coffee and trash Jack, or I could work on forgiveness as a way to prevent myself from becoming a bitter person.

What would Baldwin do? He would see this peculiar coincidence as a lesson—a reminder that love transcends the ups and downs of life. I needed to follow the example of my little fluff ball and embrace the same outlook.

11

The Dog-ter

Later that month, Mom came to me in my dream. There she was, my little cupcake with her frosted hair wearing one of her muumuus. This one was pure white, giving her an angelic appearance.

"Stop worrying. I'm watching over you, taking care of everything. I'm proud of you, looking after your dad. But don't stop living your own life..."

She faded away when I was abruptly awakened.

"Susanna, Susanna!" Jason shouted urgently from outside my bedroom door.

I sat up, adjusting my eyes to the early morning light. It was then that I heard the anguished cries of Dad reverberating down the hallway.

"Ow!" he howled. "Suzie, help!"

Without hesitation, I leaped out of bed and hurried to his room, nearly stumbling over Molly the Collie peacefully asleep on the floor by his bed. Dad writhed and contorted his entire body in pain.

"My back ... something went wrong when I tried to get out of bed. Ow..."

"Try to relax," I reassured him, gently caressing his shoulder, while simultaneously reaching for the landline to contact his doctor.

The nurse who answered advised me to call 911. "That way, he'll be promptly admitted to a room."

"Do something, Suzie!" Dad swatted my hand and clutched his lower back. "The pain is unbearable!"

"Hold on," I said, dialing 911, "help is on the way."

Jason came back with a cold, damp washcloth.

"Here, sir," he offered, placing it on Dad's forehead.

Dad angrily yanked the washcloth off and hurled it against the wall. In a frenzy, Baldwin dashed over and snatched it, vigorously shaking it as if possessed. He grew more animated every moment, tossing his head about, spewing droplets of water all over the room.

"Give me that," I said.

Baldwin ran from me, refusing to release his grip. The emergency operator picked up the call.

"There's something wrong with my dad," I said. "He's in severe pain."

"Did he fall?"

"No. I'm not sure what happened."

"Quit jabbering and help me already!" Dad shouted.

I placed my hand over the receiver to muffle the conversation. "I am."

"He woke up in pain," I explained. "He's had multiple surgeries, but he's never complained like this before."

"We'll dispatch help immediately," the operator assured me. "Stay on the line until they get there."

I kept the phone to my ear while simultaneously trying to calm Dad down. "Take a deep breath."

"I can't breathe," Dad yelled. "I'm in too much pain."

The 911 operated asked, "Can he stand?"

"I don't know," I answered.

"Well, I know," Dad yelled. "I know I can't take this pain any longer. Do something!"

"Are you inside the home?"

"Yes," I answered the operator.

"Yes, what?" Dad yelled.

"What room?"

"We're in his bedroom."

"Is the door locked?"

"I'm sure it is but I can send someone to open it." I turned to Jason and mouthed the words "Unlock the front door."

"OK, I'll let them know to enter through the front door."

The sound of an ambulance siren pierced the air. Baldwin finally let go of the damn washcloth only to throw his head back and howl.

"Help has arrived," I told the operator and hung up.

That's when two paramedics entered Dad's bedroom—one young and the other short and robust. They got right down to business.

"His vital signs seem stable," the robust paramedic informed me, a stethoscope in his ears.

"Please, give me something for the pain!" Dad pleaded.

"Hang in there, sir," the young paramedic said, patting Dad on the shoulder.

Mr. Robust inquired, "When did the pain start?"

"This morning," I answered. "Any idea what it could be?"

"I'm not sure," he replied while he and his partner secured Dad to a backboard.

The younger EMT asked, "Does he have any pre-existing medical conditions?"

"He suffers from Parkinson's and has undergone two heart surgeries. He also has peripheral neuropathy in his feet and severe sleep apnea. Oh, and before his last surgery to repair an abdominal aortic aneurysm, his surgeon mentioned he has more than twenty-eight health issues."

"Please, give me something for this pain!" Dad cried out.

The robust EMT asked, "Does he have diabetes?"

"No, that's one health issue he doesn't have."

"Hang in there, sir," the young paramedic reassured him. "Whatever's causing him so much pain, it doesn't seem to be related to his heart. We'll get him to the hospital to find out what's going on."

Dad moaned as they wheeled him on the gurney, carefully maneuvering past Molly the Collie, who'd slept through the commotion.

"You can meet us at the emergency room," the young paramedic directed me before closing the ambulance door.

I hurried back inside to change out of my pajamas.

"He was fine yesterday," Jason remarked. "What could be wrong?"

"I have no idea, but we need to get going."

Baldwin followed me back to my room with that damp washcloth in his mouth again. He sat in front of me while I changed my clothes, then placed the now-filthy thing on the floor by my feet.

"Not now, boy," I patted his head. "We'll play when I get back."

The fluff ball looked at me as though I'd just sentenced him to the pound.

"Come on, Jason, let's go." I grabbed my keys and rushed to the car, heading to Northridge Hospital.

When we arrived, I ran directly to the information desk.

"Yes, your dad is already here," the nice person behind the desk said.

"Can I see him?"

"Not yet. He's getting X-rayed. Please go to the waiting room. Someone will meet you there."

With no available seats, Jason and I leaned against a wall.

11. The Dog-ter

"I've never seen the hospital this packed before," I said.

"I will step outside, all right?" Jason headed toward the door for his morning cigarette.

Inside the waiting room, the sound of a crying baby filled the air. An elderly man sat hunched over moaning in pain, and several people coughed uncontrollably. A teenager grimaced while clutching his arm, which was wrapped in a blood-stained towel.

It didn't take long for the emergency doctor to find me. He was ridiculously handsome, with his broad chest, and dark wavy hair peeking out of his surgical cap. I could imagine him like Asclepius, the Greek god of healing, wearing a crown of laurel leaves instead of his green scrub cap.

"I didn't want to leave you here worrying," he said, pulling off his medical gloves. "It appears that your father is experiencing fecal impaction."

"Oh, that's a relief," I said with a sigh. "I was afraid it was something much worse."

"Fecal impaction can be a serious condition," he explained. "It's nothing to fool around with. If left untreated, it can cause ulcers, colitis or obstruction of the colon. And that can be fatal."

"I had no idea."

"The elderly are at greater risk due to decreased mobility along with possible neurological disorders. Some medications can also be the culprit."

"Makes sense. He isn't too mobile, as you can see, and he does have Parkinson. That's a neurological disorder, right?"

"Yes, Parkinson's causes changes in nerve cells in both the brain and the nervous system. These changes affect movement and the body's functions, resulting in the symptoms of Parkinson's."

"Well, he has been consuming a lot of comfort food since my mom passed away. You know, the salty, starchy stuff."

"That can definitely cause constipation."

"Is he going to be all right?"

"You brought him here in time, so I believe he'll be fine. It's important he gets lots of fiber in his diet. I recommend giving him daily doses of Metamucil. Ensure he drinks plenty of water, too."

"All right," I said, feeling the tension in my chest subside.

"We provided him with something for the pain, but we need to be cautious about administering too much, as it can worsen constipation. Regular aspirin should suffice, and he'll find relief after you give him an enema at home."

The Peace Puppy

"Give my dad an enema?" A wave of disgust washed over me. "Can't you do that?"

"Unfortunately, no. The emergency room is currently overwhelmed."

"Okay," I reluctantly agreed, even though I felt a strong urge to vomit.

On the way home, I stopped at the pharmacy to pick up the dreaded Fleet enema and a box of latex gloves.

When we arrived home, I decided that the only way I could do what needed to be done was by transforming myself into Nurse Ratched. You know, the villain from *One Flew Over the Cuckoo's Nest* who ruled a psychiatric ward with an iron fist?

Dad was comfortable again, high from the pain reliver he'd received that the hospital. He sat in his red chair watching television, oblivious to what was about to take place. I quickly got into character, donning a pair of latex gloves while reading the instructions on the Fleet box.

"It says here that you need to empty your bladder first," I informed my patient. "Jason, can you take him to the bathroom?"

Jason helped Dad to his feet, and the two of them disappeared behind the bathroom door. Summoning the spirit of one of the most notorious literary villains, I closed my eyes and imagined myself metamorphosing into the overbearing and heartless tyrant, complete with a 1960s nursing uniform, nurse's hat and rolled hairstyle.

When I heard the toilet flush, Ratched's cold energy surged through my veins. I entered the bathroom, ready to take control.

"It's time for your enema," I said, surprising even myself with the assertive tone of my voice. Snapping the gloves and placing a towel on the bathroom floor, I declared, "Call me Nurse Ratched!" I steadied myself. "Jason, please help the patient kneel on this towel," I commanded.

Jason's eyes widened. "Here, sir." He assisted Dad into position.

"Dad, lower your head so the left side of your face rests on the towel." I removed the orange protective covering from the plastic bottle and said, "this will hurt me more than it hurts you. Now, bear down."

With gentle precision, I inserted the tip of the bottle into his rectum, closed my eyes, and squeezed until almost all the liquid was gone.

"Don't move! Stay still for at least one minute. Jason, you stay here too and assist him to the toilet when I say he's ready."

"I'm ready now," Dad said, lifting his head.

"No, Dad, you have to keep it in there for at least one minute."

Dad complied quietly, resembling a little boy obeying his mother. I exited the bathroom.

A minute later I announced, "It's time."

I heard the toilet flush. Dad emerged moments later fully dressed and made his way back to his red leather chair.

"Thank you, Suzie," he expressed. "I feel much better now."

"Good. Now, I'm going to take a shower and banish Nurse Ratched from my psyche."

And just in time. Kat showed up for work to find my sopping wet self.

"How are you this fine morning?"

My reply? "Don't ask."

The next evening, Dad asked me to teach him how to email.

"That's easy," I assured him, assuming he would grasp the concept quickly. "I'd be happy to show you."

I grabbed my laptop and placed it on the TV tray still in front of his red chair. Dad stared at me instead of looking at the computer.

"You need to look at the screen," I said.

He struggled to even locate the computer that sat directly in front of his eyes. To make matters worse, typing proved to be an impossible task with his constant tremors.

I patiently sat with him, repeating directions. Whenever he accidentally pressed a key, I praised him, saying. "You did it!"

Reward-based training worked for Baldwin; I figured it would work for Dad too. But it didn't. Dad had neither the mental capacity nor the dexterity to use a computer. It didn't take long for me to come to the conclusion that this wasn't going to work.

"That's enough for today. We'll do more tomorrow."

My hope was that he'd forget all about it, but the next day, Dad approached me, eager for another lesson.

"Oh, Dad, sorry. I've got piles of work waiting for me."

It was heart-breaking to watch him struggle. I did my best, but my attempts were futile. Then I remembered the times he tried to tutor me in math. He'd lose his patience within the first few minutes. Karma, I thought. It can be a bitch.

12

Bone Voyage

I had a hectic week ahead of me with work deadlines breathing down my neck, including finalizing preparations for another media FAM. This time, I'd invited six significant journalists and needed to do my best to make sure they enjoyed each and every minute of the trip. Our destination—Las Vegas to promote the JW Marriott Las Vegas Resort & Spa, an upscale Mediterranean-style property located off the strip in nearby Summerlin.

Kat stayed behind and took care of the business. She was also there to watch Baldwin and fill in for me with Dad. Erin and her family would be spending a night with Dad too. They arranged the stop on their way to Disneyland.

Before leaving, I made sure the refrigerator and cupboards were stocked with food for Erin's family. I wanted them to feel welcome and let Erin know how much I appreciated her help filling in for me.

On the morning of my trip, I awoke when my big fluff ball licked my face. Quite an alarm clock! The instant I opened my eyes, he hopped off the bed and grabbed his frisbee, ready for playtime.

"Not today, boy," I told him.

With the frisbee still in his mouth, Baldwin made his way to my already-packed suitcase and proceeded to sit on it, his chin trembling.

"I'll only be gone for a couple of days this time. You have to stay here and take care of things for me."

Reluctantly, Baldwin hopped off my suitcase and approached me, his body wiggling in an effort to make me change my mind. When that didn't work, he picked up his frisbee again and headed to the back door, hoping I would join him.

"I'm sorry," I said, "you'll have to wait until Kat gets here." Baldwin tilted his head, his expressive eyes pleading. "You're breaking my heart with that face. I need to hurry and get to the airport on time so I can make money and buy you treats."

12. Bone Voyage

At the sound of the "t-word," Baldwin dropped his frisbee and hurried to the kitchen. I followed and gave him a bully stick to keep him occupied while I left.

Since we had only one car, Dad and Jason planned to drop me off that morning.

"Hey, guys," I shouted from the kitchen, "we need to leave."

Dad shouted back, "Where are we going?"

I rolled my suitcase to the den. "I'm headed to Las Vegas," I replied, reminding him of my business trip, which I'd mentioned several times over the past week.

"I'm not going with you?"

"No, Dad, you're staying here."

"But I want to go to Vegas. I haven't been there since you were a kid. Remember when we stayed at Circus Circus?"

Letting out a sigh, I acknowledged, "Yes, I remember." The previous night, Dad and I had meticulously recounted every aspect of that family vacation. "We'll take a trip together soon, I promise."

"No," he insisted, behaving like a stubborn child. "I want to go with you now."

"But Erin and her family are coming here to spend time with you. Don't you want to welcome them?"

"I said I want to go with you," he retorted, his faced reddening.

"Okay, okay, don't get upset. This is a work trip, remember? I need you to take care of the dog and the house. But you're going for a drive to drop me off at the airport and pick me up, okay?"

Jason helped Dad out the back door.

Once my suitcase was in the car and Dad sat comfortably in the passenger seat, I handed my car keys to Jason. "Here you go."

I boarded the plane and settled into my seat for the short, hopefully uneventful flight. But little did I know that my journey to the JW Marriott Las Vegas Resort & Spa would be filled with, well, let's say *interesting* conversation, much to my dismay. While the flight to Vegas was barely an hour, I needed to shift my focus and prepare for the demanding travel journalists that expected the VIP treatment. But that was not to be.

To my left, a slick-haired guy sat determined to charm me with his smooth talk. To my right, an elderly woman took the window seat, eager to strike up a conversation.

The Peace Puppy

As the plane taxied down the runway, the slick-haired Casanova wasted no time in unleashing his rather unique pick-up lines.

"You're so beautiful," he whispered in my ear. "Are you part of the mile high club yet?"

I tried to ignore him, but he continued.

"The things I could do to you. I'd like to rip your clothes off right here in front of all these people and…"

"Sorry, sir, but my heart belongs to press trips and hotel reviews," I quipped. "Oh, and my dog."

Just as I thought I'd escaped the clutches of the smooth operator, the woman to my right peered at me over her bifocals to ask, "Excuse me, dear, do you know if they serve peanuts on this flight?"

The entire hour was spent having my ear talked off by the woman to my right, who seemed determined to share her life story, and the man to my left, who wanted to ravish me. The woman delved into her travels, her grandchildren's accomplishments, and her extensive knowledge of airplane snacks. The man described, in detail—well, you know. I should've asked to be relocated, but the flight was filled to capacity, and besides, this nightmare flight would be over soon. So I smiled and nodded, doing my best to be polite while secretly yearning for a moment of peace and quiet.

After landing, I got out of there as quickly as possible. Once in the baggage claim area, I spotted a tuxedo-clad driver holding a sign with my name on it. I made my way toward him, feeling a hint of celebrity status. Together, we maneuvered through the airport and headed outside where a sleek limousine waited.

During the half-hour limo ride to Summerlin, I gazed out the window, captivated by the scenic beauty. Vibrant hues emanated in the distance from the red rock mountains, painting a picturesque backdrop for the luxury property. The resort stood as a testament to opulence, offering an escape from the neon lights and bustling crowds of the Strip. Who knew you could find a haven to unwind and relax amidst nature in Vegas?

I had just enough time to check into my room before I had to meet my media guests. I'd sent them each a welcome amenity in the form of a bottle of wine and a charcuterie board loaded with Mediterranean flavors, plus a personal letter from the resort's general manager—written by yours truly, of course—along with a copy of the itinerary. That would start things off on a positive note, right?

I headed to the lobby and was happy to see a white-gloved waiter already there holding a silver tray with signature Red Rock martinis, a little something I'd arranged to keep the journalists happy.

12. Bone Voyage

Ginger, a freelance writer for prestigious food and wine publications, was the first to arrive. She'd traveled with me before.

I extended my hand as she approached. "I hope you're ready for a truly decadent dining experience."

Ginger shook my hand. "Of course, but let's not forget I still need to interview the chef for my story. That's top priority."

"Yes, I've arranged for that," I said, handing her an itinerary—this one with her exclusive interview included.

Ginger took a sip of her Red Rock martini just as four other journalists arrived.

"I wanted to thank you for the toothbrush you left in my room," one of them said.

Toothbrush? I didn't leave a toothbrush. Must be part of the property's amenities.

Another writer chimed in, "I didn't get a toothbrush."

"Neither did I," an older, gray-haired man from a local parenting publication announced, "and I am the most important person here!"

That got a laugh from the group. Thank God. For a minute, I thought he was serious.

"Oh, I'm so sorry," I said, "I'll make sure you all get one."

Really? The welcome amenity wasn't enough?

We waited another twenty minutes for the last journalists to show up to our pre-dinner cocktail soirée. Mandy, who wrote for a spa publication, was a no-show. Her tardiness was no surprise, given her track record on my past FAM trips. I excused myself from the group and pulled out my cell phone to call her.

"Hello?" she answered, mid-yawn.

"We're waiting for you in the lobby," I said, making sure to keep my tone even.

"Oh, I didn't know we were meeting tonight."

"It's on the itinerary." I gritted my teeth.

"I forgot mine," she said. "Anyway, my flight was delayed."

"Don't worry, I have an extra itinerary for you. Why don't you get yourself together and meet us at the restaurant in an hour."

Before returning to the group, I headed to the concierge to have those toothbrushes sent to each travel writer.

"Just add it to the box of spa goodies they're receiving tonight," I told the girl at the desk. I always sent the journalists attending my FAMs nightly gifts. Ah, the bribes I provided...

We made our way to the resort's Spa Tower for dinner at the

The Peace Puppy

Hawthorn Grill, a sophisticated restaurant renowned for its mouthwatering American cuisine. Before we took our seats, I paused to gather the group's attention, pointing out the mesmerizing desert sunset.

"Look," I said and gestured toward the window. "Have you ever seen a sunset so beautiful?"

My comment was met with an enthusiastic chorus of oohs and ahhs from the group.

There was still no sign of Mandy, but I couldn't hold up everyone any longer. The meal must go on!

I began with a toast. "To our important guests, may this dinner be the start of an incredible trip. I can't wait to read about your experiences. Cheers!"

All the journalists raised their glasses.

"I'll drink to that," the old guy from the parenting publication said before clinking his glass with the others.

Before the final course, Ginger, the red-headed food writer who worried about her interview with the chef, accidentally knocked over her large purse, causing its contents to spill out onto the marble floor. Among the scattered items, I noticed full-sized bottles of shampoo, conditioner, and lotion, all branded with the spa's logo. The sight was peculiar, leaving me to wonder if Ginger had gone on an impromptu shopping spree or if she had a tendency for unintentional pilfering.

I was contemplating making a comment when Mandy finally arrived, just in time for dessert.

"You made it," I said, then turned my attention to the waiter. "Please put a plate together for our new guest."

"Yes, I'm starving," Mandy said, taking her seat.

She wore grungy sweatpants with a matching gray sweatshirt, her hair in a messy bun on top of her head. The waiter quickly rushed to deliver the delectable meal that the chef had prepared to Mandy, while the rest of us indulged in an irresistible slice of lemon ricotta cheesecake. Once the rest of the group finished every last bite of this light, elegant dessert, all five of them excused themselves from the table, headed back to their rooms. I had to stay, sitting there watching Mandy eat.

"That was delicious, but I ate too much," Ginger said on the way out. "Can you have some ginger ale sent to my room?"

What, she doesn't know how to dial room service herself?

"Of course," I said. "I hope you'll feel well enough to join us tomorrow for Cirque du Soleil."

"I wouldn't miss it."

110

12. Bone Voyage

Sipping my chamomile tea, I couldn't wait for Mandy to finish so that I could escape to the solace of my room and prepare for the next day. However, she seemed to eat at a snail's pace, and with each passing moment, I struggled to keep my heavy eyelids from closing.

I finally mustered the courage to speak up. "I apologize, Mandy. I know it's unprofessional, but I'm absolutely drained. I need to head back to my room."

Mandy paused mid-bite. "No need to apologize," she replied. "I'm exhausted too. I lost my mother last month and all I really want to do is sleep."

"Really? I recently lost my mom too."

Mandy dropped her fork, reached out and covered my hand in hers. "Then you understand the profound emotional devastation that follows losing your mom."

"I do."

"I find myself cycling through the five stages of grief. One moment I'm bargaining with God to bring her back to me, the next, I feel so depressed that I can't get out of bed. Then I go through denial hoping she's really not gone, and when I realize she is, I get so angry. When will I ever get to the acceptance stage?"

"I can totally relate. My mom passed away in January and my mind's still in a fog."

"I know what you mean. Just when I think I've hit bottom, I hurt more."

"And to add to that, I moved back home to take care of my dad who is battling Parkinson's."

"That's a lot of emotional upheaval."

"It is indeed," I nodded in agreement. "Hey, I have an idea. Why don't you take the rest of your meal to your room? That way, we can both get a good night's sleep."

She agreed, and I asked the waiter to have her meal delivered to her room promptly.

As we rode in the elevator together, Mandy said, "I feel as if I was meant to be late tonight so we could have some time to talk with each other."

"Me too. Our mothers must have been behind our kismet meeting."

I bid her goodnight and expressed my gratitude to her for sharing her loss with me.

In the safety of my room, I took a deep breath and relaxed in the knowledge that it's perfectly all right to not be okay at this moment.

The Peace Puppy

The following day flew by in a whirlwind of activities and overindulgence. Amidst the extravagance, I missed my Baldwin and worried about Dad. Still, I needed to do my best. I had to remind myself over and over again of the significance of being completely engaged in the present moment, something Baldwin taught me.

One of the perks of working in public relations was the ability to incorporate activities into a FAM that *I* genuinely wanted to experience. Typically, attractions offered complimentary tickets to the media in exchange for coverage. So, for this trip, I managed to secure comped tickets to the breathtaking extravaganza "O" by Cirque du Soleil at the Bellagio. After all, it was only fair to grant the writers one night to explore the Strip, right?

Ginger was the first to arrive for the limo ride to the Strip. "I can't wait to see all those synchronized swimmers."

"Me too," I said. "I've only been to one other Cirque du Soleil show. I loved it so much I didn't want to leave."

"This will be my first," she said. "I guess you can call me a Cirque virgin."

She had a hard time stepping into the stretch limo; her slinky black dress was way too tight. I noted she'd ditched the huge purse for a gold lamé evening bag. Mandy arrived next, and we greeted each other with a warm hug, embracing like old friends. The rest of the group showed up, along with the resort's general manager *and his wife.* He'd overheard me discussing our plans and expressed interest in joining. I'd managed to get him a last-minute ticket, but it hadn't crossed my mind to inquire whether he would be bringing someone along. Consequently, there was no ticket available for his wife unless I forfeited mine. Guess which choice I made?

Stay cool, Susan. Life goes on.

When we arrived at the will-call window, I handed everyone their tickets and said, "I'll meet you for our final dinner tonight after the show."

"Aren't you joining us?" Mandy asked.

"No, n-no," I stumbled on my words, "I've got some work to do."

With that, I turned and pulled out my cell phone to call the office.

"Susan Hartzler Public Relations," Kat answered.

"It's me," I said. "How's it going there?"

"I swear, Baldwin knew it was you calling. He ran in here the minute the phone rang and jumped in my lap. Here, say hi to him."

"Hi Baldwin! Mommy will be back tomorrow!"

"I wish you could see how cute he is, tilting his head at the sound of your voice."

"I wish I could too. This group is exhausting."

"But you get to go to Cirque du Soleil tonight, don't you?"

"No, I don't. Our GM wanted a ticket at the last minute then showed up with his wife. I only managed to get him a ticket, so I gave her mine."

"That sucks."

"Not half as much as some of the journalists. I don't know what's wrong with me. I used to love traveling with the media, but lately, everyone's driving me nuts."

"Be kind to yourself," Kat said. "Losing your mom so suddenly like you did is an emotional tidal wave."

"But losing a parent is an inevitable fact of life, isn't it?"

"That doesn't make it easy. It does give you a new perspective, though."

"I certainly don't have the patience I used to have."

"I'm not surprised," Kat said. "You've got the added stress of looking after your dad. In a way, when your mom passed, you lost them both."

"I guess you're right."

I looked around me. The Strip was crowded, filled with groups of people having fun together. Me? I stood there—alone.

"Is Dad okay?"

"He's been mumbling something about pennies. Do you know what that's about?"

"Oh," I said, forgetting about the press trip for a moment. "He used to walk around the block and throw pennies so kids would find them on their way to school."

"Really? I'm sure I found some of those pennies back in the day."

"Tell Jason to take him out front with a handful of change. He can walk down the street and throw some pennies."

"Good idea. Here, let me put him on the phone."

"Ahem, ahem." Dad cleared his throat.

"Are you okay, Dad?"

He proceeded to cough. "I woke up with this darn cough."

"Did you use your CPAP machine last night?"

"No," he answered, "I hate that contraption. I can't sleep with a stupid mask, makes me feel like I'm swallowing air all night."

I was well aware of the severity of Dad's sleep apnea. Not long after I moved back home, I asked his doctor about Dad's recurring headaches and morning coughs. The doctor prescribed a sleep study. That resulted with the diagnosis of sleep apnea, a condition that leads to the relaxation of the upper airway muscles during sleep, which can result in airway constriction. In severe cases like Dad's, a person's breathing can pause for ten seconds or more.

The doctor ordered Dad a CPAP breathing machine, emphasizing that without using it, Dad was depriving his body of oxygen, which could lead to fatigue, mood swings, and various health issues, including heart disease and high blood pressure. There was one problem, though: getting him to use it. Dad was as stubborn as they come.

After doing my best every night, I finally managed to get him used to the darn thing. But my guess was that, since I was gone, Jason let it slide. Hence, Dad's cough.

I turned the corner and the intense sun momentarily blinded me, forcing me to halt. Fortunately, I found myself right in front of the magnificent fountains of the Bellagio. The golden sunlight enveloped the scene as the water danced gracefully into the sky, almost like a ballet performance, framed by the picturesque backdrop of fluffy desert clouds.

At least I got to see a water show.

I walked past the Mirage, and for a brief moment, the thought of visiting Siegfried & Roy's white tiger habitat crossed my mind. However, the voice of the animal advocate within me vehemently objected to the idea. My moral principles held strong; I couldn't endorse live animal shows.

I strolled along the famous Las Vegas Strip, savoring the sights and sounds. Despite the throngs of people around me, I relished the tranquility of being alone. And before I knew it, I needed to make my way back for the elaborate dinner I'd planned for our final night.

I arrived at the Bellagio's Prime Steakhouse in time to make a quick adjustment. We needed to add a place setting to accommodate the general manager's wife.

"We don't have a larger table available," the tuxedo-clad maître d' informed me.

Undeterred, I decided to take matters into my own hands.

"Can't we squeeze one more chair here?"

A figure clad in chef's whites entered the scene. It was none other than the renowned Bellagio chef Jorge, with his crisp white apron over a white double-breasted jacket and black-and-white houndstooth pants.

He took my hand in his and asked, "More guests?"

"Yes," I confirmed. "Just one more, but if it poses an issue, I don't have to eat."

"No, no. Here, let me help."

The two of us shifted a couple of plates and rearranged the silverware to create the necessary space.

"I think it'll work," I said. And right in time. The media arrived, in high spirits.

"How was the show?" I asked.

"Breathtaking," Ginger said. "We were so close that I felt like I was part of the performance."

Mandy chimed in next. "It's incredible how the stage turns into water."

"I'm so glad you had a good time. Please, take a seat."

As the first course arrived, Mandy caught my attention from across the table and mouthed the words "Change my seat?"

"Of course," I responded without hesitation, jumping to my feet. "Let's switch."

Moments later, Mandy caught my eye again, signaling another request.

"Can I move again?" she pleaded. "I'm left-handed."

I obliged, of course, getting up for the second time. I guided Mandy to the head of the table, where she could enjoy her meal without anyone seated on either side. So much for our connection on the first night.

I looked around. Everyone seemed to be savoring their meals. Me? I was a bundle of nerves, feeling so stressed that I couldn't even take a single bite. I'd learned long ago that by pushing my food around the plate, it would look like I'd eaten.

The final dinner was a huge success, and once we returned to the resort, my work was finally done. The only thing left was to make follow-up calls and request copies of their stories.

On the plane the following morning, all my worries dissipated. For that brief moment, I had no responsibilities or obligations to attend to, and before long, I would be reunited with Baldwin.

Dad and Jason waited for me at the Burbank airport's baggage claim area. I ran over to hug them both.

"Welcome home, Suzie," Dad greeted me.

The Peace Puppy

Jason chimed in, "We have surprise for you in car."

My luggage arrived quickly, and we hurried to my car. And there was Baldwin, his stump of a tail wagging in a symphony of elation.

"What an excellent surprise!" I exclaimed, opening the door and slipping into the back seat with him. "I missed you too."

Jason tried to hand me my car keys. "Why don't you drive us home?"

"I can drive," Dad insisted.

What? Not this conversation again. He can't even see the computer screen when it's right in front of him.

"I'm sorry, Dad, we sold your car after Mom died," I said, forgetting to play along.

"Then I'll drive yours."

Jason came to my rescue. "It's okay, sir. Let me chauffeur."

With that, Jason helped Dad into the passenger seat while Baldwin nuzzled his wet nose against my face, his tail still wiggling.

"How do you like driving my car?" I asked Jason.

"I like it," he replied, his hands steady on the steering wheel in the classic ten-and-two position. "Drives smooth."

"Glad to hear it. I've been thinking, Jason ... perhaps you could take over Dad's transportation—you know, accompany him to his doctor's appointments and his physical therapy, when I'm out of town or busy."

Jason's face lit up. "That sounds great, Susanna!" He turned to face Dad. "Sir, I'll be your partner in adventure."

"At least you won't have to wait for hours to get a ride from that free service through Medicare."

"Last time, it took so long, we missed his doctor's appointment."

"That's settled, then. I'll add you to my car insurance on Monday."

13

Pee Mail

The whirlwind media FAM, although exhausting, proved to be highly successful, resulting in a valuable collection of "free" editorial worth thousands of dollars. Reflecting on the trip, I thought that perhaps Kat was right when she suggested that losing Mom had shifted my perspective. True, I no longer handled media demands as effortlessly as I had in the past. It was high time for me to get my act together before clients started considering their options.

The trip made it evident that I needed to work through the five stages of grief that Mandy had brought to my attention. While I'd somehow skipped denial and bargaining, I found myself stuck between a deep state of depression and raging anger, far from attaining any form of acceptance.

Amidst my struggles, there was a consistent source of comfort that never failed to lift my spirits: Baldwin, the precious gift Mom gave me. That adorable fluffball had a remarkable knack for coaxing me out of bed each morning, serving as a gentle reminder to embrace the day. Whenever sorrow engulfed me, he curled up in my lap, instantly changing my mood for the better. And the reception he gave me every time I crossed the threshold of home, well, it truly took away any lingering anger. Who could be upset when a Muppet-looking dog loved you so much?

The morning following my return, Kat arrived at work earlier than usual.

"Have I got a story for you," she began. "You'll never guess who your dad worked out with yesterday."

"Who?"

"The president."

"What?"

"You heard me correctly. I went to check on him at lunchtime, and to my surprise, he was doing chair exercises, laughing with his new buddy George."

The image of Dad, engrossed in conversation with George W. Bush, seemed comical.

"I remember him telling me about his lunch with Hillary Clinton," I said using air quotes. "But Bush? Dad's not even a Republican."

"Well," Kat said, "you know how he always has the TV on, right? Bush held a press conference yesterday, and I guess in your dad's mind, he'd become his esteemed lunch companion."

"It's surreal. He sounds like the man who raised me, but his thoughts are so delusional."

Dad's hallucinations served as a painful reminder that the person I once knew and loved was slipping away. His mind played tricks on him, and despite my best efforts, I couldn't bring him back to reality every time. Each day felt like a fresh loss.

Fortunately, Erin and her family planned to make another stop the next day on their way back from Disneyland. Dad's spirits were up at the prospect of seeing his granddaughters again.

Erin and company showed up just as I was leaving for my morning Starbucks fix.

"Do you want anything from Starbucks?"

"No, thank you," Erin said.

"Okay. I'll be right back. Dad's waiting for you. We can make breakfast together."

When Baldwin and I returned from Starbucks we were greeted by the sound of a heated argument emanating from the den. Baldwin dashed ahead of me toward the commotion.

"I want to go home!" Dad shouted.

"You are home, Dick!" my brother-in-law, Alan, shouted back.

"If you don't get me out of here, I'm gonna call the police!"

I entered the den to see Alan standing over Dad, his face red with anger.

"It's okay, Dad," I interrupted. "Jason will take you home."

At the sound of his name, Jason magically appeared with Dad's rollator.

"Here, sir," he said, helping Dad to his feet and leading him outside.

"I was just trying to help," Alan told me.

"I know," I answered, "but reasoning with him doesn't work. His doctor explained to me that Dad can have a completely different reality that he genuinely believes."

13. Pee Mail

"Oh, I had no idea," Alan said.

"Some Parkinson's patients have what's called Parkinson's disease dementia."

"Dementia?"

"Yes. Their reality is just as real to them as our reality is to us. So it's not helpful to confront him."

Erin entered the room. "What's all the noise about?"

"We were just discussing Dad's challenges," I explained.

"Can you turn down the TV, then?"

I grabbed the remote and muted Dad's TV.

"About that TV," Erin said. "You shouldn't let him watch it so much. It's not good for him. Besides, what's he doing with a gigantic set like that? You've got to be more responsible. He's not made of money, you know."

"I bought it for him for his birthday."

Erin raised her eyebrows skeptically, as if she doubted what I was saying. When we were kids, she always had a hard time believing anything that came out of my mouth. Admittedly, I did have quite the imagination back then. But to her, I was still that mischievous little brat.

I'd hoped that by moving back home to oversee the care of our dad, she'd finally realize I'd grown up.

I welcomed Dad and Jason back inside after their quick walk around the backyard.

"You're home," I exclaimed. By my side, Baldwin wiggled his greeting.

Once back in his red chair, Dad relaxed.

"Want to watch some news?" I turned the sound back on and motioned for Erin to follow me into the kitchen. Baldwin followed as if we were heading on an exciting journey.

"I thought I'd mentioned before that many Parkinson's patients experience dementia," I explained.

"You did tell me," she acknowledged.

"The medication he takes can exacerbate things, so I keep a close eye on him. He can become agitated in an instant. He's not the same Dad he used to be."

"Even more reason it's time to move him to a place that can take better care of him. Remember, I checked out several senior living homes near me. I found one that is less than one mile from my home. It looks like a Marriott and everyone I saw looked content and happy—both the residents and workers. The people who live there are part of the community

119

and participate in many activities together.. Even local school kids visit. Anyway, don't you want him to live closer to his grandchildren?"

"Erin, I asked him about moving last time you brought it up and he is adamant that he wants to stay here. Anyway, changes in routine and environment can be troublesome for someone in his condition. His doctor says change can increase his confusion and agitation, which, I must say, are already impacting his quality of life. Don't take my word for it. Go ahead and call his neurologist yourself. He'll explain."

Erin let out a forceful breath, but I chose to ignore it.

"I wanted to talk to you about something else," I told her. "I'm having a hard time with this grief stuff."

"What does your therapist say?"

"I'm not in therapy right now."

"You're not? Don't you think talking this out with a professional would do you some good?"

"I was hoping I could talk to you," I said under my breath. "I really need a break."

"You just had a break."

"A business trip is not a break."

My nieces interrupted us when they entered the room.

"Hi Aunt Sue," they chimed in unison.

Baldwin spotted them and sprinted over to greet them. They bent down to pet the fluff ball.

"What are you two up to?" I asked, making my way past Baldwin to embrace them.

"Not much," Frankie replied.

"Are you enjoying your time visiting Grandpa?"

"Yes," Frankie said.

"I wish we were back in Disneyland," Charlie added.

Frankie shot a disapproving look at her younger sister, prompting her to quickly change her answer. "Well, I mean, I do love visiting Grandpa."

"And he loves spending time with you. I do too."

Watching Dad with his grandchildren took away the stings of the day, replacing them with a belief that everything would be all right.

Life resumed its usual rhythm after Erin and her family left. However, her lack of knowledge about Dad's health condition made me recognize the importance of keeping Erin and Will better informed. So I decided to send them regular email updates. The first one went like this:

Dear Erin and Will:

It occurred to me after Erin's recent visit that the two of you are in the dark when it comes to day-to-day life with our dad. So I've decided to remedy that situation by sending you email updates. This is the first of what I hope will be an ongoing diary of sorts, keeping you both in the loop.

First, I want to express how much it meant to Dad (and to me as well) to have Erin and her family visit. I am truly grateful for your presence, especially while I was away on a business trip. I hope you'll come again soon.

Dad had his physical therapy session today and was in good spirits. He meets with his church friends at Cracker Barrel tomorrow. I do have some concerns about his persistent cough, so I'm scheduling another appointment with his doctor. We'll be going later this week, and I'll be sure to update you as soon as we have more information.

Love, Sue

A few days later, I received a response from Erin. It read:

Dear Aunt Sue:

Thank you for sending an update about Dad and for everything you are doing to take care of him. It's hard to find out what's really going on when I live so far away. So often during phone calls people only share the good things that have been happening. I've found a wonderful retirement place that is less than one mile from my home. It looks like a Marriott hotel and everyone I saw looks contented and happy (both the residents and the workers). If it becomes too much for you to continue, Sue, I hope you would consider this option and allow me to take my turn caring for him. I know you are trying to help Dad meet his request to live at home but is that still the best place for him? If he did move up here, he could spend more time with his grandkids, which, as you mentioned, brings him great happiness.

Best wishes, Erin

Looking back, I wish I'd taken her wishes into consideration. Instead, I allowed my life to get so entangled with Dad's that I couldn't accept any alternative. In the grand scheme of things, looking after our ailing parent should've involved all three of us. Life is nothing without family. I know that now.

14

Yappy Hour

We still had a way to go before winter arrived, but the transformation of the golden-brown hillsides into a lush green expanse, coupled with the leaves on the trees turning to shades of orange, red, and yellow, painted a picturesque scene. The crispness in the air brought joy not only to me but also to my faithful companion, Baldwin.

Despite the beauty that surrounded me, my mind was preoccupied with the demands of my professional life. Metaphorical fires raged in my thoughts, overshadowing my appreciation for nature's unfolding wonders.

Back at the office, Baldwin took his spot beneath my desk. I kicked off my shoes and rubbed my feet against his soft fur. Another media FAM was coming up and I needed to prepare. That morning, while client issues seemed to multiply, Baldwin's steady breaths reminded me to breathe.

A phone call interrupted my positive thoughts. The general manager from the Las Vegas resort called to complain about an error in the *USA Today* article I'd secured.

"You need to get this fixed," he said.

"I'm on it," I promised.

But before I could reach out to the journalist responsible for the mistake, another urgent call came in.

"The reporter from the *LA Times* has arrived," the marketing director from the Renaissance Hollywood informed me. "She says that you had a lunch appointment scheduled today."

"Oh shit, I mean, darn." I grabbed my appointment book. "I had our meeting down for tomorrow. Can you introduce her to the chef and let them know I'm on my way?"

I hung up and quickly slipped my shoes back on, bracing myself for the inevitable traffic.

"What's happening?" Kat asked.

"That *LA Times* reporter showed up for lunch a day early. I have to get to Hollywood, fast."

"Drive carefully," Kat cautioned.

"Oh, and Kat, can you call the *USA Today* reporter and get him to fix his story? The details are on my desk."

"Sure, boss."

"Oh, shit," I added. "I'm going to miss Dad's doctor's appointment. Can you take him? I need my car."

"Of course," Kat responded, extending my purse toward me. "You might need this."

I pulled out of the driveway, feeling a sense of urgency. Before I got very far, I called Kat.

"It's me," I said. "I forgot to tell you about Dad's appointment." I proceeded to share my concerns about Dad's persistent cough, adding, "And make sure the doctor checks for pneumonia."

"Didn't he receive a vaccination for that?"

"Yes, but I read online that there are various types of pneumonia, some not covered by the vaccine."

The traffic on the 101 was light for once in my life, so I got to Hollywood in less than thirty minutes. From the road, I left a message for the *LA Times* reporter letting her know that I'd be there shortly.

Next, I called Jack, the car guru. "I need to get a car."

"What about your SUV?" Jack asked. "The lease can't be up yet."

"I'm keeping my car," I explained. "I need to get a used car, not too expensive." For Jason.

"What's the budget?"

"No more than four thousand."

"I'll find one for you, Dudan," Jack assured me.

"Appreciate it more than you know."

As soon as I hung up, I pulled into the hotel entrance and handed my keys to the valet. In a rush, I sprinted through the lobby and ascended the stairs with a determined stride, taking two steps at a time. When I finally arrived at the restaurant, I felt a sense of relief. The handsome chef Thomas, with his dark hair and ice-blue eyes, had my back. There he was, sitting with the food writer, engrossed in conversation.

"Sorry I'm late," I gasped, attempting to catch my breath. "I mistakenly thought our lunch was scheduled for tomorrow."

"No worries," Thomas said.

The *LA Times* reporter announced, "We're just about to have dessert."

The Peace Puppy

The fair-skinned journalist looked far too thin to be a food writer. But there she was, enjoying a meal with my favorite rock star chef. She wiped the corners of her mouth with her napkin, her nails polished a deep red.

Dessert was the last thing on my mind. I hadn't eaten a thing all day. But one look at the flourless chocolate cake and my tastebuds disagreed. The first bite of the dense and velvety delight melted in my mouth.

The reporter's eyes widened. "A perfect balance of sweetness and bitterness."

"Do you need anything from me for your story? Like images or recipes?"

She held up her reporter's notebook. "I interviewed Thomas before you got here. And I have the menus." She shoved her notebook into her briefcase. "Someone from the art department will be calling to arrange a photo shoot. Other than that, I think I've got everything I need."

At that, she said her goodbyes, promising to publish the story the following week.

The moment she left, I sighed, turning my attention to Thomas. "I apologize for being late. I truly owe you."

"No, no," he replied, placing his hand on my shoulder. "I'm the one who owes you. Being featured in the *LA Times* is a remarkable opportunity."

"I wish all my clients were as appreciative as you."

I hopped in my car, buckled my seatbelt, and answered my ringing phone. It was Jack, his voice brimmed with excitement.

"I found your car," he said. "It's a Honda, priced at just under three thousand dollars, and it has remarkably low mileage. I've even organized its delivery for you."

"Fantastic!"

After hanging up I felt relieved. I didn't have to worry about Dad's transportation anymore.

Next, I dialed the office to get an update on Dad's doctor's appointment.

"He's doing fine," Kat informed me. "It's just a common cold."

"That's good news."

"The doctor advised him to drink plenty of fluids and get plenty of rest. He also recommended a humidifier and a saline nasal rinse."

"What about antibiotics?"

"Antibiotics don't help with viruses," Kat explained. "But the doctor suggested over-the-counter medication for his congestion. Thankfully, he's not running a fever."

On my way home, I made a brief detour to the pharmacy and purchased the items that the doctor recommended. Back home I tended to Dad's needs, hoping to clear up his congestion in time for the weekend. I had something planned and I didn't want any of us to miss it, especially Baldwin.

That Saturday, Baldwin, Dad, Jason and I headed to the Earl Warren Showgrounds in Santa Barbara for the fluff ball's first agility trial. On the way, I glanced at Dad in the passenger seat and noticed how small and frail he looked.

"Did you take your cold medicine this morning?" I asked.

"Yes," Jason replied from the back seat. "But the cough not getting better."

"I feel fine," Dad insisted.

I reminded Jason to make sure Dad stayed hydrated throughout the day with the water I'd packed in the cooler.

When I parked the car, my stomach did somersaults. I tried to ignore them, but my jitters persisted. A competition of any kind stirred up those familiar feelings of test anxiety that I'd grappled with back in school. Baldwin, ever perceptive, sensed my anxiety and did his best to lift my spirits by offering me his repertoire of tricks. When he finished, I got Dad and Jason situated near the agility courses.

The trial took place at the showgrounds' spacious outdoor area. The first thing I noticed was two agility courses. Quite a few people were milling around while others sat in folding lawn chairs, their dogs in crates or what I later learned were x-pens—portable metal enclosures, a sort of doggie play pen. I'd never seen one before.

"Look, Baldwin," I said to my canine sidekick. "I'll have to get you one of those for next time."

A burst of energy inside one of the rings caught my attention. I stopped to watch an Australian Shepherd, with a red coat as breathtaking as a summer sunrise, maneuver through the weave poles in a blur of precision. I marveled at the sheer athleticism displayed by this four-legged athlete.

The Peace Puppy

When the time came for the novice dogs, my anxiety had intensified. I didn't need to worry, though, since only one other dog was competing against us.

Without the proper preparation of an x-pen or even a dog crate, I handed Baldwin's leash to Jason, asking him to watch Baldwin while I walked the course. Walking the course at a dog agility trial refers to the process of getting familiar with the layout and obstacles before the actual competition begins. The handler walks through the course. Without their dog, handlers study the sequence and positioning of the obstacles, such as jumps, tunnels, weave poles, and contact equipment. This allows the handler to plan their strategy, determine the best handling techniques, and visualize their dog's path to success. The goal was to get a "Q" or qualifying run.

My hands trembled when I returned to take Baldwin's leash from Jason.

"Good luck, Sleeping Beauty," Jason said.

Dad patted my hand as I passed. "Break a leg," he said. "We'll be watching."

When Baldwin and I stepped onto the agility course, my nerves sent me back to my younger self. I remembered the time I sang a solo of "Rudolph, the Red Nosed Reindeer" at the school Christmas pageant. My heart pounded, my palms sweated, and my voice quivered as I belted out the lyrics. It was just me, a third grader, standing alone in the spotlight. I scanned the audience for Dad and found him, beaming with pride. His supportive gaze gave me the confidence to finish the song.

That day at the agility trial I yearned for the same confidence boost I'd received from Dad all those years ago. But the most I could I hope for was that Dad would be able to focus on us without being distracted by any real or imagined squirrels.

I took a deep breath and stepped onto the course, ready to give it my all. It was time to create a new memory. We made our way to the start line, and I gave Baldwin an encouraging pat on the head before putting him in a sit-stay behind the first jump.

I looked at him and said, "Let's have some fun," before releasing him. The two of us started running and I could feel our connection grow stronger with every step. Each obstacle he cleared caused adrenaline to course through my veins, driving us forward.

Baldwin weaved through the poles, soared over jumps, and maneuvered through tunnels with precision. The obstacles blurred together as we raced toward the finish line, my arms in the air in victory.

126

I knew our run was clean, so I picked Baldwin up and praised him. "Good boy! We did it!"

Baldwin also aced the jumpers course, speeding along so fast that I had a hard time keeping up with him. I swear, that boy could read my mind. He flew ahead of me as if sensing where I wanted him to go next.

Later, I learned he took first place in both the standard and jumpers

Me and Pepper.

courses. First place at his very first agility trial! In that moment, I felt as though the two of us could conquer the world together. Not bad for the girl who was never very athletically inclined. By the end of our first year trialing, Baldwin would be recognized as the number one Puli in the entire United States.

Back in the car, the exhilaration from our victory faded, replaced by Dad's hacking cough.

"I don't like the sound of that," I said. "I'm going to make another appointment with your doctor, and this time, I'm coming with you."

"I told you," Dad said, "I'm fine."

"Well, you don't sound fine." Glancing at him beside me in the passenger seat, I saw that he held Baldwin's blue ribbon tightly in his grasp.

"I can't believe you finished in first place," Dad said. "Siesta flunked obedience."

Siesta, the family dog, only listened to me. The little Chihuahua mix was a terror when Dad took her to the park to learn some manners. Before her, we had Pepper, a beautiful Dalmatian pup. Dad didn't even try to train that wild boy. After only a few months, Pepper was sent away to live out the rest of his life on a farm. At least that's the story Dad told us.

On Monday morning, I wasted no time scheduling another appointment with Dad's doctor.

"We have a cancellation this afternoon," the nurse told me. "Want to take that?"

"Yes, the sooner the better."

The afternoon arrived and Dad and I headed for his appointment, Dad hacking the entire way there. While we sat in the waiting room together, the faint scent of disinfectant triggered a rush of emotions, reminding me of his numerous hospital visits since I've moved back home. I pushed the memory away. Surely his cough wouldn't put him in the hospital.

Dad's body trembled as he coughed. I felt a pang of helplessness, wishing I could take away his discomfort with a magic wand.

"Hang in there, Dad."

Time seemed to crawl as we waited. Finally, his name was called, and we made our way to the examination room.

Dr. Lee, a middle-aged Asian man, carried an air of confidence and professionalism. As he was Dad's primary doctor, we'd met several times. He greeted me like an old friend.

After a thorough examination, Dr. Lee said, "Your father has developed a secondary infection in his respiratory system. I'm going to prescribe a course of antibiotics and recommend plenty of rest and fluids."

"So no hospital?" Dad asked before coughing again. "No surgery?"

"Nope," Dr. Lee said. "You'll be back to your old self in no time."

After the doctor left, I turned to Dad and said, "I promise you'll never have to go through another surgery again."

A small smile tugged at the corners of Dad's lips. "Thank you, Suzie. I'm lucky to have a daughter like you."

The following week, the new used car was delivered as planned. I gave the keys to Jason.

"What's this?" he asked.

"These are for you. I bought a Honda so that you can take Dad to his appointments when I'm not around."

The car wasn't the only thing delivered that day. I also got something special in the mail—an envelope from Angel with my plane ticket to Jamaica. Thanksgiving was just around the corner, and I couldn't help but smile at the thought of reuniting with her and hearing all about her adventures with her Rasta boyfriend.

With Will's reassurance that he'd check on Dad daily, I knew he'd be in good hands while I was away. The prospect of temporarily escaping the responsibilities that consumed me since Mom died brought a sense of liberation. And even though I'd miss Baldwin, the time had come for a much-needed respite.

15

Dirty Paws

Even with the prescribed antibiotics, Dad's cough persisted, worsening with each passing day. The situation reached a distressing climax when he woke me up in the middle of the night struggling for breath. Thankfully, Baldwin heard Dad's muffled cries and roused me awake by nuzzling his cold nose against my face.

When I rushed into his room, I saw Dad sitting at the edge of his bed, his breathing obviously labored. Drawing closer, I noticed Dad's face was pallid, and his skin felt cold and clammy to the touch.

Without hesitation, I grabbed the phone and dialed 911, my voice trembling. Once again, the wailing sound of the approaching ambulance pierced the quiet neighborhood.

"A-ooo, a-ooo, a-ooo," Baldwin unleashed a series of howls, joining the sirens.

I followed the ambulance to the hospital, my tires screeching when I pulled into a parking space.

Dad will come through this. He has to.

At the triage desk, I caught my breath and said, "Dick Hartzler, I'm here with Dick Hartzler, 'H-A-R-T-Z-L-E-R.'"

After the young nurse typed his name, her eyes meet mine. "He's being admitted. You'll find him in the intensive care unit."

"ICU again?"

Quickly, I hastened my steps toward the elevator. My hand trembled when I pushed the button for the fourth floor. When the door opened with a gentle chime, I exited, feeling my heart race in my chest.

I navigated the bustling corridors of the fourth floor and quickly found the nursing station. Even in the middle of the night, it was a hub of activity.

A busy nurse looked up from her paperwork.

"Excuse me, could you please point me to Dick Hartzler's room? He was just admitted."

15. Dirty Paws

She looked at her computer screen, then pointed me to the end of the hall. Wringing my hands, I made my way down the corridor.

"Dad, I'm here," I said upon entering. Then I noticed—he was already hooked up to a breathing machine.

A nurse gently took hold of my hand.

"I'm sorry, but your father is currently sedated. His breathing has become compromised, and the doctor made the decision to put him on a ventilator." I nodded, trying to absorb the information.

With a gentle touch on my arm, the nurse assured me, "We're doing everything we can to support him. He's in good hands."

"Is he going to die?"

"Not on my watch. The ventilator will provide life-sustaining oxygen to support his breathing. We'll do everything we can to give him the best possible care."

Her words offered a glimmer of hope. She directed me to the waiting room and told me the doctor would meet me there.

With no windows, the waiting room felt suffocating. A row of chairs faced a television that was turned on, but the sound was muted. I noticed it was tuned to Dad's favorite channel, CNN.

Maybe that's a good sign?

I took a seat, feeling the weight of the situation settle on me. The empty waiting room mirrored the emptiness I felt inside.

A middle-aged couple entered, breaking the stillness, their expressions etched with sorrow and despair. In a hushed voice, the man muttered something while the woman anxiously tugged at her hair. A teenager with a hoodie pulled over his head entered and joined the couple.

Time seemed to stretch endlessly as I waited for news about Dad. Seconds turned into minutes, minutes into hours until the door to the waiting room swung open and Dr. Lee stepped inside.

"He has pneumonia," he stated.

"But you said last week he'd be fine," I said, my voice trembling. "And I've been diligently giving him the antibiotics you prescribed."

"His heart issues and weakened immune system make his condition tricky," Dr. Lee said, motioning for me to take a seat. "We've put him on a ventilator so he can rest and recover."

"So you're saying he'll recover?"

"It's hard to say. Pneumonia in elderly adults can progress quickly," he said taking the seat next to me.

"I should've brought him to the hospital earlier," I cried. "This is my fault."

"You did nothing wrong," he countered, "and he's here now. We'll have to take it day by day."

"You mean there's a chance he might not recover?"

"Well, there's always that chance but your dad's a fighter," he said. You can go see him, but he's sedated."

I entered Dad's room and was immediately struck by the sound of the ventilator breathing for him. Dad looked peaceful, his eyes closed, his chest moving in rhythm to the whooshing noise. He was still, hooked up to a variety of machines with an IV bag hanging on a hook next to him dripping life-saving medication into his veins.

"Oh Daddy," I said softly, pulling the only chair in his room over to his bedside. I sat down, put his hand in mine, and sobbed. "You're such a good man. You don't deserve any of this. Don't leave me, please. I need you." I leaned in close and added, "I'm not giving you one of those end-of-life talks," my words carrying a resolute tone. "Did you hear me? You're going to pull through this."

On the way home, I called Will.

"What? He's in the hospital? I thought you said he was feeling better."

"He was," I replied. "I'm just as surprised about this as you are."

"I'll head over there this afternoon."

"Call me when you go, and I'll meet you."

I called Dad's minister to ask for prayers. "I'll let our church family know. Is he going to make it?"

"His doctor sounded hopeful."

Next, I called Erin but got her answering machine.

"Erin? Dad's in the hospital," I said, my chest tightening. "Call me."

Back home, I collapsed onto the couch and Baldwin instinctively curled up beside me. I buried my face in his soft fur, clinging to him as tears streamed down my face. I poured my heart out to my loyal pet, and he sat there quietly, his presence reminding me that I was not alone.

Over the next week, the question of whether Dad was going to make it became my nemesis. The constant stream of calls from well-meaning church friends only intensified my internal struggle.

"When will he be able to come home?"

15. Dirty Paws

"Is he going to make it?"

"How dire is the situation?"

Part of me wanted to respond with a sarcastic remark or suggest that they seek divine intervention for the answer. But I knew deep down that their inquiries came from a place of genuine concern.

When I met Will at the ICU, his eyes were wide with concern.

We exchanged greetings, and without wasting any time, Will asked the burning question. "What happened?"

I explained how Dad woke up in the middle of the night and could barely breathe.

"Is he going to make it?" he asked.

"The doctor says he's strong, and we both know how stubborn he can be. So yes, I firmly believe he's going to pull through. Definitely, yes."

When we entered the room together, Dad looked so small and frail lying motionless in his hospital bed. I extended my hands, gently moving them in a fluid motion above his body—a practice I'd learned called Reiki, a Japanese form of energy healing.

Will asked, "Is that some sort of voodoo?"

"Voodoo? That's funny," I said. "It's called Reiki. My palms are transferring healing energy."

My hands continued their gentle movements above Dad's body, radiating what I hoped was a sense of calm and positive intention. Though I never had any formal training, I believed in Reiki's potential to heal.

"Here, let me try," Will said, stepping closer to Dad's bed.

I wasn't sure how much healing would come from his jerky movements, but after a few moments, Will exclaimed, "You're healed!"

Will and I met at Dad's bedside every afternoon and performed our own special Reiki treatments, and they seemed to work. By the end of the week, the doctor planned to take Dad off the ventilator.

"He'll be okay then?" I asked.

"We think so, but you have to be prepared. Some elderly patients can't breathe on their own after being taken off a vent."

"But he's not going to die, is he?"

"A considerable number of patients admitted to the intensive care unit die following withdrawal of mechanical ventilation."

I informed Dad's friends about the doctor's plan, and word quickly spread among the members of the church choir. Many expressed a desire to be present when the ventilator was removed, wanting to offer their support and prayers during this crucial moment.

"Sure," I said. "Why not?"

I certainly didn't expect eight members of the choir to show up, but his singing companions, along with Pastor Mark, were determined to be there. They formed a circle around Dad's bed, clasping each other's hands, creating a united front of prayer.

I stood at the door of Dad's room and watched.

"Let's start with 'Healer of Our Every Ill,'" Pastor Mark suggested.

> Healer of our every ill,
> Light of each tomorrow,
> Give us peace beyond our fear,
> And hope beyond our sorrow.

Their voices filled the air with a sense of hope, transcending the sterile hospital environment. Before I knew it, doctors and nurses from the ICU gathered around Dad's room to watch. As soon as the song ended, a couple of nurses gently squeezed past me, signaling for the choir to make way. It was time to initiate the delicate process of removing Dad's life support.

The choir moved back but continued to sing, belting out one of my all-time favorites, "I Will Raise Them Up on the Last Day."

> I am the living bread that came down from heaven.
> Whoever eats of this bread will live forever;
> and the bread that I will give for the life of the world is my flesh.

Dr. Lee entered the room, mimicking a conductor, swaying his hand in sync with the music. His spontaneous gesture momentarily lifted the weight of the tense situation.

Taking his place alongside the nurses, the doctor assumed his professional role, ensuring that Dad's transition to breathing independently went smoothly after the removal of the breathing tube.

Once the tube was out, a hush fell over the room. Dr. Lee then carefully listened for Dad's breath and nodded his head, acknowledging a positive sign. Addressing the choir, he shared some encouraging news.

"Your voices have worked," Dr. Lee proclaimed. "It appears that he has made it through the critical phase. He should regain consciousness within the hour."

Choir members broke out in applause as relief washed over me. Crisis averted.

Dad came home the following week. Baldwin and Molly the Collie greeted him as if he'd just returned from war. And in a sense, he had. A war with death. And he had won.

"You know what the best part of coming home is?" Dad asked.

"No, what?"

"Being greeted by the dogs."

I laughed and gave him a hug. "I can relate to that. As Mom always said, we are dog people."

16

Doggie Paddling

November arrived, ushering in the Santa Ana winds, which swept through the valley with relentless force. The National Weather Service issued a red-flag warning, alerting us to the heightened fire danger. From my home office, I gazed out the window, observing the mighty olive tree in our front yard as it danced and swayed in the powerful gusts.

The winds carried a sense of urgency. As I watched the olive tree bend and twist, I couldn't help but marvel at its strength. It stood tall and proud, weathering everything the storm sent its way.

I needed to tap into that resilience and cancel my plans with Angel. After Dad's close call with death. First step, I needed to stay home. Yes, he was out of the woods, but I wanted to make sure he stayed that way.

Because she didn't have a cell phone, I tried to reach Angel at the Treasure Beach bar where she received messages. I knew it might take some time for her to get my message, but to my surprise, within minutes she called me back.

With a mix of disappointment and sadness in my voice I told her I wouldn't be making it for Thanksgiving after all.

"Oh Sweetikins," she said, "I'm so sorry to hear about your father. Of course, I understand. Just keep the ticket and we'll plan another trip together." Ahh, my Angel, so understanding, so loving. "I'll light candles for him," she promised, "and pray."

Later that day, Kat invited me and Dad, health willing, to her house for Thanksgiving. At that moment, I felt a profound sense of gratitude, appreciating the unwavering support of people like Kat and Angel, reminding me of the power of love and friendship.

By the time Thanksgiving arrived, Dad's cough was completely gone. However, any remnants of the gratitude I'd cultivated dissipated when I awoke on Thanksgiving morning, engulfed by an overpowering feeling of foreboding. It was as if vultures were ominously circling above, casting a dark shadow on the day.

16. Doggie Paddling

"What's wrong with me?"

Baldwin responded with a yawn and a stretch.

"I'm supposed to be grateful today, not freaked out."

I rolled over and squeezed my eyes shut, hoping to open them to a new reality, but my plan didn't work.

"I know what's wrong," I told my canine sidekick, now cuddled in my arms. "It doesn't smell like Thanksgiving. You never got to experience one of Mom's New England Thanksgiving feasts. They were delicious. Even before the first bite, the aroma made your mouth water. She'd put the turkey in the oven early in the morning, and by the time I got my butt out of bed, the smell permeated the entire house. The turkey in the oven, a homemade apple pie made the night before, the boiled onions and her fluffy stuffing complete with sautéed onions, celery, and butter—lots of butter—gone, all gone."

Mom unleashed her culinary skills on holidays, especially Thanksgiving. During my childhood, I didn't appreciate her efforts, but on the first Thanksgiving without her, I missed her more than I thought possible. And I missed those boiled onions too.

Baldwin bounded out of bed, and I trailed behind, preparing myself for the day ahead. He darted outside with his frisbee clutched in his mouth, eager to get the day started. I followed his wiggly butt to the back door, making a quick stop in the den to greet Dad.

"Happy Thanksgiving," I said.

"It's Thanksgiving?"

"Yeah, Dad. Remember? We're going to Kat's house later to celebrate."

"Oh, that's right," he replied. "I guess I forgot."

"That's okay, Dad. We all forget things sometimes, don't we?"

Baldwin tugged at my pajamas and pulled me toward the backyard. We passed through the living room where Molly the Collie was sleeping peacefully, her presence a comforting sight. But before I got out the door, a pungent odor stopped me in my tracks.

"You doing okay, girl?"

She looked up at me with eyes that said "no."

"What is it?" I asked, wishing dogs could talk.

She rolled over, begging me to rub her belly. That's when I saw a puddle of pee.

"Oh, poor Molly," I murmured softly.

I got a warm, damp cloth and carefully cleaned her up. Next, I took care of the puddle she left on the living room floor. After I was done, Molly looked up at me, her once brown eyes now cloudy with age.

"Come on, girl, let's go outside."

The fresh November air helped change my mood. The wind had finally died down, leaving the air crisp and cool, and the sun was shining. I had plenty to be grateful for—my dog, my dad, my friends, my growing business.

"I need to get it together," I said, watching Baldwin catch his prized possession. "This grief thing is a real bitch." He bounded back and, as usual, played tug of war. "It strikes you when you least expect it."

"Susanna," Jason called from the doorway, "I'm leaving now."

"Oh, okay," I responded. I had given Jason the afternoon off so he could spend the day with his sister who ran a care home for the elderly nearby. "Have a great time."

A couple hours later, fully dressed in a deep blue sweater and jeans, I gently woke Dad from his nap. "It's time to go."

"W-Wh…. Wh-What?" Dad stammered, still groggy from falling asleep in his red chair. "Go where?"

"We're going to Kat's," I reassured him, trying to jog his memory. "It's Thanksgiving, remember?"

Cupping his hand over his right ear, he asked, "We're going where?"

"To Kat's house," I repeated patiently.

After positioning his rollator, I clasped Dad's hands firmly in mine. "On three. One, two, three." I used all my strength to lift him from the chair.

Wrapping my arms around his waist, I helped him to his rollator. Together, we made our way toward the back door, where Baldwin waited.

"Not today, buddy," I told the fluff ball. "You'll stay here and keep an eye on Molly the Collie. Don't worry, we'll be back soon. And I promise to bring you some turkey."

Baldwin turned and slowly walked away. At least he had Molly the Collie for company, even though the old girl was asleep on the couch. I walked over to give her a kiss.

A strong stench made me step back.

"Did you pee again? This is the second time today."

"What? Molly peed on the couch?" Dad pushed his rollator toward her. "She's never peed in the house—easiest puppy ever to potty train."

I grabbed a sponge to clean up the mess. "Luckily, it's only a little. But I think I need to take her outside before we leave."

Dad turned to me and asked, "Where are we going?"

16. Doggie Paddling

"Kat and her family invited us to join them for Thanksgiving dinner," I replied, trying to infuse enthusiasm into my voice. "It'll be fun."

Repeating the same information to Dad over and over became a heartbreaking reminder of his disease. As a respected engineer, besides being meticulous when it came to details, he prided himself on his excellent memory. Not anymore.

"We don't want to forget this," I said, grabbing the bottle of wine off the kitchen counter. I'd bought a special pinot noir for the occasion.

I drove us around the block to Kat's house. The smells I'd missed of turkey, stuffing, mashed potatoes, and freshly baked pies greeted me when we entered.

The dining room table was draped with a white linen tablecloth. I could see that Kat's mom, Joan, pulled out her fine china for the occasion, complimented by her special silverware that sparkled from sunlight shining through the French doors that led to the backyard.

I helped Dad into a chair next to Kat's younger sister, Dede, and her husband, Jim.

"Happy Thanksgiving, Mr. Hartzler," Dede said.

"I don't know about you, but I am very grateful to be here," he said, a smile on his face.

He'd known Dede since she was a child, but I wondered if he even recognized her now. It didn't matter—sweet Dede engaged him in conversation while I joined Kat and her mom in the kitchen.

"Look at you two," I said pointing to mother and daughter in their matching orange aprons with the words "Eat, Drink and Be Grateful" printed above a dancing turkey. "Need some help?"

"Sure, Suzie-Q." Joan pointed to the serving dishes on the kitchen counter, steam coming off the traditional Thanksgiving favorites. "Start by taking those out to the table. We'll bring the turkey."

With heaping bowls of mashed potatoes and stuffing in hand, I returned to find Dad fully engaged in conversation with Dede, a glass of pinot in his hand. Dede's cheeks were flushed, her eyes wide open.

"I said I have to pee," Dad's volume increased. "Can't anyone in this place take me to the damned bathroom?"

"I'm here, Dad," I said, setting the side dishes in the middle of the table. "I'll help you."

Dede jumped to her feet to retrieve Dad's rollator while I helped him to his feet.

Once in the bathroom, Dad became self-conscious.

"I can do this myself," he demanded.

The Peace Puppy

"Are you sure?"

"Yes, I'm sure. I've been going to the bathroom all by myself since I was potty trained. Now get out of here and close the door."

"Okay, I'll be right outside if you need me."

Within seconds, I heard a crash. I opened the door and there was Dad on the floor, his pants pulled down to his knees, his rollator across the room.

"Are you all right?"

Dad covered his private parts with his hands and rocked to his side.

"You didn't break anything, did you?"

"No, just get me up. The darn rollator got away from me."

Dede, Jim, Kat, and Joan appeared at the bathroom door.

"What happened?" Joan asked.

"Did he hit his head?" Kat asked, a tea towel over her arm.

"I think he's okay. At least I don't see any blood."

Dad yelled, "Get them out of here!"

The three ladies waited outside while Jim and I helped Dad to his feet and pulled up his pants.

Jim placed Dad's hands on his rollator, and together we made our way to the dining room. The room was silent while I helped Dad to his seat.

Joan broke the awkwardness of the moment by declaring, "We're ready to eat."

Dad appeared unruffled, raising his wine glass for a toast. "Happy Thanksgiving, everyone," he said. "I'd like to express my gratitude to Joan for inviting us and preparing this magnificent feast."

In unison, everyone clinked their glasses.

"We are delighted to have you here," Joan said. "Would you like to say a prayer before we begin?"

"I'd be honored," Dad said, sounding like the cordial man who raised me, not the angry Parkinson's patient from moments ago. I found it difficult to keep up with his mood swings.

"Everyone, join hands," he said, then bowed his head.

"Our heavenly Father, we thank you for this meal and the people around this table, especially for the generosity of our hosts. We thank you for our loved ones who are no longer here with us. As it says in Psalms 100: 'for the LORD is good; his mercy is everlasting; and his truth endureth to all generations.' Amen."

When he pulled his hand away from mine, Dad accidentally hit his wine glass, toppling it over. Deep red streaks of pinot ran across Joan's beautiful white tablecloth.

"Whoops," he said.

I grabbed some napkins and did my best to keep the red liquid from spreading.

"And that's why they call it the nectar of the Gods," I said, trying to lighten the mood. It worked. Everyone laughed. "If only Mom was here. She could get stains out of anything. I called her the stain goddess."

"Don't worry, Sue," Kat said. "My mom's a stain goddess too."

Joan sopped up the rest of the spill with more napkins and said, "No big deal," adding an exuberant "Let's eat!"

After Dad's fall and the wine debacle, the rest of the evening seemed uneventful, thank God. But I couldn't wait for Jason to come back from his sister's house. One thing I knew for sure that Thanksgiving, I was grateful for his help.

In the first week of December, the heavens unfolded once again, and it rained like cats and dogs. With our ongoing drought in California, this much-needed rainfall was a welcome sight. However, the excessive water caused flooding in the streets of the Valley, making it difficult to venture outside.

The wet conditions didn't deter Baldwin. His enthusiasm for walks remained resolute. After the last downpour, I prepared him with an adorable yellow rainproof jacket. Seeing him in it, with the hood over his head, made me laugh out loud.

"You're funny," I said. We ventured outside, both of us outfitted in our best rain gear. "My last dog, Blondie, hated the rain. She didn't like getting her dainty little feet wet. But you—you don't let bad weather ruin your day."

In no time, the hood of his rain slicker came off. When he looked up at me, his now wet curls covered his eyes. I bent down to push the hair off his face.

"There you go," I said, "now you can see."

And right then, Baldwin spotted a puddle, jumped in, and splashed me, then did his happy dance, twirling in the water.

That night, Dad, Jason, and I braved the rain and headed to church for the annual silent auction. We'd donated several items, including the telescope I'd bought Mom and Dad for Christmas the year before. When I moved back home, I set it up in the backyard, but Dad's Parkinson's symptoms made it impossible for him to use it. Trying only made him frustrated. Best to give it a new home.

The sanctuary was filled with auction items generously donated by members. Among the contributors was Duane, a man I remembered from my time teaching Sunday School during my teenage years. Duane, who considered himself an artist, was auctioning an original portrait, painted by him, for a lucky member of the congregation. All they had to do was be the highest bidder. He showcased one of his recent art pieces—a portrait of Pastor Mark.

Early in the evening, Duane stood proudly in front of the painting, exuding a sense of pride. However, as the night progressed, things were not going so well for him. Despite his optimism, no one had placed a single bid.

The lack of interest in Duane's artwork was disheartening. I could see the disappointment in his eyes. In a spur of the moment decision, I decided to place a bid and get the ball rolling. If I won, I figured I could have him paint a masterpiece of Baldwin. And by the end of the night, I won the auction.

When Duane found out I was the winning bidder, he walked up to me with a smile that couldn't be contained. I hoped he'd still be pleased even after he discovered the subject I wanted him to paint.

But before I could get any words out, Duane gently touched my shoulder and said, "I am so honored to paint your father." He was so sincere; I didn't have the heart to tell him I really wanted him to paint a portrait of Baldwin.

The following week, Duane came over with a blank canvas and a bucket of paint supplies. The rain had subsided by then, so we sat outside under a Maxfield Parrish–like sky with the sun's gentle rays filtering through the trees, casting a soft glow on Dad's face.

I was pleasantly surprised by Dad's willingness to participate. Then again, I understood that Parkinson's Disease could amplify one's desire for attention. Dad eagerly following Duane's instructions to remain still throughout the process.

As the portrait slowly took shape, it appeared to me that Duane was, in fact, painting a lovely portrait of someone—just not Dad. I watched as the artist worked until, with a final flourish, Duane stepped back, clapping his hands together.

"Voilà!" he said, his eyes sparkling with satisfaction.

I knew Duane meant to immortalize Dad on canvas and didn't have the heart to tell him otherwise.

"Wow, Duane, nice job," I said. "Thank you so much."

"My pleasure," he said.

I noticed him wiping a tear from his eye when he gathered his things preparing to leave.

After Duane left, I asked Dad what he thought.

"Looks more like George Burns, if you ask me."

Having passed the first Thanksgiving since Mom's passing, I shifted my focus to Christmas, then Mom's birthday on January 23, and the solemn first anniversary of her death the following day. My emotions were nothing short of tumultuous. However, I had my own private superpower in the form of a Muppet-looking fluff ball. Whenever I felt overwhelmed, I'd turn to Baldwin for help. He seemed to grasp the message, promptly grabbing his frisbee and darting off to the grass. I appreciated the reminder to stay in the present moment.

17

Dog Eat Dog

My favorite month of the year has always been December, mainly due to the holidays—especially the gifts. During my childhood, Christmas morning was magical. Mom orchestrated the whole thing, filling the living room with toys for each of us kids. But as we grew older, the gifts became less predictable. One year, I received a simple red electric pencil sharpener, and the next, an extravagant zoom lens for my cherished Nikon camera.

But it wasn't receiving the gifts that made the holiday special. It was giving gifts to the people I loved that gave me joy. Over time, I developed a personal strategy for finding the perfect gifts. Throughout the year, I'd keep an eye out for meaningful presents. Whenever I stumbled upon something that reminded me of someone, regardless of the time of year, I bought it, without hesitation. I still do.

There was one person who proved to be difficult to shop for: Mom. At Christmas or her birthday, I found myself scrambling to find her the ideal present.

One particular year stands out vividly in my memory. Determined to find something exceptional, I dedicated an entire day exploring the shops at the Beverly Center mall. I searched tirelessly for a set of towels that would truly resonate with Mom.

After what felt like an eternity, I found a set of exquisite towels from France. They were incredibly soft, with delicate flowers and butterflies set against a light blue background, the color of her bathroom. Admittedly, they carried a hefty price tag, but the anticipation of seeing a genuine smile on Mom's face outweighed any monetary concerns.

When the time came to exchange gifts, I watched Mom unwrap the package. Her eyes lit up like I'd hoped. At that moment, I knew that my efforts had been worthwhile. It was not merely about the towels themselves, but the love and care that went into finding something she'd like.

Since I was now living at home and no longer responsible for

supporting my ex-partner Jack, I had the finances to purchase meaningful gifts for my family that year. And by September, I'd completed the
task. That meant I had no practical reason to visit the mall during the
Christmas rush, except for one cherished tradition: getting a picture of
Baldwin with Santa.

I dressed Baldwin in his adorable Santa hat and a festive doggie
tie for his close up with the big man. That little black fluff ball looked
beyond adorable.

While we stood in line patiently waiting to meet Santa, the sound
of children crying filled the air. Without hesitation, I guided Baldwin
over to them so he could cheer them up with a high five. And it worked.
Baldwin possessed an extraordinary knack for connecting with kids,
instantly lifting their moods.

When our turn finally came, Santa welcomed Baldwin into his
arms and placed him on his lap. It was a sight to behold, witnessing the
jolliest Santa Claus I'd ever seen holding the cutest dog in the world.

Santa exclaimed, "I want this dog for Christmas!"

I quickly interjected. "Oh no, Santa. Sorry, but he's mine."

Erin and family made their way down on Christmas Eve. The cloudy
sky hung low, giving the day a muted ambiance, as they pulled into the
driveway in the afternoon. Baldwin, ever the gracious host, bounded
toward them with his new teddy bear clutched in his mouth, wagging
his tail in excitement.

Together, we entered the dining room, where Jason and I'd arranged
a feast to welcome them. A honey-baked ham took center stage, accompanied by a crudité platter which included Erin's favorite ranch dip. I'd made
a sweet and tangy pear salad with citrus dressing and baked some rolls too.

We sat down to eat and out of the corner of my eye I noticed Baldwin eying the delicious-smelling ham. Unable to resist the enticing aroma, he had surreptitiously made his way toward the table and
attempted to swipe a slice for himself. With a gentle reprimand, I swiftly
moved the ham to the center of the table, out of his reach.

After our early dinner, we all gathered around the twinkling
Christmas tree to exchange gifts. Dad sat there, a huge smile on his face
replaced his usual Parkinson's mask.

"Being with my granddaughters is the best present I could ask for,"
he said.

The Peace Puppy

As for me, I couldn't contain the excitement of presenting my family members with the special presents I'd bought. I reached for a beautifully wrapped box and handed it to Erin.

"This one's for you," I said.

She carefully opened the package. "Oh wow," she said. "A Coach bag."

"I know how much you like that brand."

I handed two smaller boxes to my nieces, Frankie and Charlie.

Frankie opened the gold necklace I gave her and clasped it around her neck. The pendant displayed her Zodiac sign, Virgo.

"I love it," she exclaimed. "It's like a perfect reflection of who I am."

Charlie proudly displayed her new bracelet adorned with cultured pearls.

"You know, Aunt Sue, pearls are my birth stone," she told me.

"I know and the meaning fits your personality," I said. "You are direct in your communication style, preferring to get straight to the point."

"That's true," she said. "What else do you know about pearl people?"

Erin cast a disapproving gaze in my direction. "You always find the perfect gifts, but this time, you spent too much money."

Silence hung in the air for a moment as Erin placed her new Coach bag back in the box. She handed me a sweater from Lands' End, wrapped in its shipping package.

"It's from me and the girls."

I wrapped my arms around Frankie and Charlie in a grateful hug. "Thank you, girls."

Their response? "Can we go watch TV now?"

I'd hoped for a heartwarming exchange that night. However, in reality it was only a momentary interaction, swiftly transitioning to the allure of television. But sitting with my nieces in the den I realized that true holiday magic is not in elaborate gifts but in the simple act of being in the company of loved ones. And, after all, Baldwin was with me.

The rain returned Christmas morning, doing little to deter Erin and her family from packing up to head back to Disneyland after breakfast.

I asked, "You're going in the rain?"

"Yes," she answered. "It's the happiest place on earth, no matter what weather. Besides, it's usually not as crowded when it rains."

I walked her to the door. "Maybe Dad can come visit you some weekend?"

"Maybe," she shrugged.

"He'd like that."

Dad, Jason, Baldwin, Molly the Collie and I stood in the driveway waving goodbye. Dad laughed when Frankie and Charlie squished their faces against the rear window.

"That was a nice visit," I said.

We watched the car disappear around the corner. "I wish they'd stayed longer," Dad said.

Jack arrived later to enjoy Christmas dinner with us. Secretly, I think he wanted to spend time with Baldwin, but he'd have to celebrate with all of us. The minute Jack stepped through the back door, Baldwin made a mad dash toward him, his legs a blur of motion, propelling him at full tilt. He couldn't help but scrunch up his entire body, as if to gather all his love and happiness into a single, tightly wound package. Jack bent down to meet the fluff ball at eye level and welcome the affection that Baldwin showered on him.

Once Baldwin settled down a little, Jack followed me to the den with the fluff ball herding us. "Merry Christmas, Mr. Hartzler," he said.

Dad smiled and asked, "Are you ready for our annual Christmas football game?"

Jack tilted his head in a question but said, "Sure am!"

Once we were out of Dad's earshot, I leaned in close and confided. "He says that every year, but we've never actually played football together on Christmas or on any other day, for that matter. I'm surprised he's never asked you before."

"Well, that's a relief. I just got these new shoes, and I really don't want to get them dirty."

I glanced down at his feet and noticed his bright red Vans. Must be a fashion thing, I thought.

Jack set the table while I cooked the leftover vegetables from last night's crudité plate. We'd have those with the honey-baked ham and some fresh muffins that I'd baked earlier. Will and his wife Charlotte showed up with an apple pie.

"It's not as good as Mom's," he said, "but I thought you'd like it."

"I want a piece à la mode," Dad said, which didn't surprise me. He loved his ice cream.

After dinner, we settled down with Dad to watch some television.

Dad even allowed us to change the channel from CNN, and we opted to watch the classic film *It's a Wonderful Life.*

I looked at Baldwin nestled comfortably in Jack's lap.

"They should make a movie about him," I whispered.

"Yeah," Jack agreed, "called *It's a Wonderful Dog.*"

Shortly after Christmas, it became evident to me that Molly the Collie needed to see the vet again. Her accidents were increasing in frequency. Jason and I loaded Dad and Molly the Collie into the car. As soon as they were situated, Jason got in the back seat with Molly, her head resting in his lap.

When we arrived at the vet's office, fate seemed to conspire against me. When Jason and I helped Molly out of the car, she stumbled and fell face-first in the parking lot, landing in a large puddle.

"Poor girl," I sighed, helping her back to her feet. "Dad," I called out, concerned that he might also lose his balance on the wet asphalt. "Stay in the car."

Turning to Jason, I instructed him to go inside and inform the staff that we needed help.

Dad watched me steady his dog back on her feet.

"Here, let me help," he insisted, attempting to step out of the car.

"Please, Dad, stay where you are," I pleaded. "Right now, I can only assist one of you, and it's Molly's turn."

Dad hesitated, torn between his desire to support Molly and his understanding that his presence could hinder rather than help. Molly made another feeble attempt to move forward before succumbing to yet another fall.

"Molly," I murmured softly.

The reality of Molly's advanced years had become increasingly apparent, manifested not only in her physical struggles but also in her moments of vulnerability. I'd catch her in the kitchen staring at the wall. Or, from time to time, she'd get stuck in a corner. Her accidents were another reminder of the inevitable passage of time.

I stood there with her in the parking lot, gently coaxing Molly to stay down. At least she wasn't in a puddle any longer.

"It's okay, girl." I stroked her back, waiting for help to arrive.

In what felt like hours, Jason returned with a member of the veterinary staff following him with a large dog-sized stretcher. The young man, in his white veterinary coat, had a look of concern on his dewy face.

"What happened?" the young man in the white coat asked.

"I'm not sure. She can't stand on her own. This has never happened before."

With great care, he lifted Molly onto the stretcher, his touch tender and comforting. I watched as he assessed her condition right there in the parking lot.

"You're an old girl, aren't you?" He addressed Molly directly. Next, he motioned for Jason to assist him at the other end of the stretcher.

"We made an appointment because she's been having lots of accidents. It seems like she's losing control of her bladder."

"Let's get you inside and figure out what's going on," the young man told Molly.

While they prepared to move her, Dad opened the car door and tried to step out.

"Wait, Dad, have a little patience," I urged, my voice tinged with frustration. "I'll be right there. Let Jason help the doctor."

"I'm a vet tech, not the doctor," the young man clarified. "We'll meet you inside. There's a room waiting."

With that, the two men cautiously transported Molly while I turned my attention to Dad. I took his rollator out of the car, locked it in front of him and helped him to his feet.

"Finally," he said. "I was beginning to feel like a second-class citizen."

Together, we entered the examination room just in time to witness Molly being transferred from the gurney to the floor.

"You'll be more comfortable here," the young man told her, "instead of on that cold examination table."

I noticed a small puddle on the gurney. She had another accident. Determined to help, I promptly reached for some paper towels.

"I'll take care of that," the vet tech told me.

As if on cue, the veterinarian entered. He looked even younger than the vet tech, his dark hair slicked back, a stethoscope around his neck. He was wearing jeans and a red Polo shirt on his tall and lanky frame.

"Hello there." He held out his hand to shake mine. "I'm Dr. Stevens." He knelt next to Molly and carefully stroked her white muzzle. "Tell me, how long have you noticed the accidents?"

"It's been happening more frequently over the past few weeks. This is the first time I've noticed her having difficultly standing on her own."

Dr. Stevens nodded, his expression thoughtful. "I see. Has she experienced any other changes in behavior or appetite?"

"Well, she has had occasional moments of confusion," I explained. "She's been sleeping more and sometimes she seems to get stuck standing in a room just staring at a wall. But her appetite's been okay."

Dr. Stevens listened attentively, his focus solely on Molly the Collie. Crouched down next to her, he began a thorough physical, checking her vital signs, examining her abdomen, and assessing her mobility and neurological responses.

"Do you think she's in any pain?" I asked. "We want to make sure Molly's comfortable and receives the best care possible."

"Rest assured, we'll do everything we can to help Molly."

"She's my dog," Dad interjected.

Dr. Stevens nodded; his focus reminded on his four-legged patient. But as soon as Dad spoke, Molly tried to stand.

"It's okay, Molly," I told her.

"How old is she?" Dr. Stephens asked.

"Well, we got her as a puppy," Dad reminisced. "Suzie brought her home from the pound. You should have seen how cute she was. My wife gave her fresh turkey every day," he went on. "It had to be fresh."

"She's about twelve," I interjected.

Dr. Stephens paused for a moment. "Given her age and the symptoms you've described, we'll need a full blood panel to understand what's going on. Meantime, I'll prescribe a medication to help manage her incontinence. It should provide some relief while we wait for the results of the blood panel."

"She's been such a good dog," Dad said.

"Then let's get her feeling better," Dr. Stephens said. "I'll call you tomorrow with the results."

Little did I know that this visit to the veterinarian would mark the beginning of a new chapter in our journey with Molly the Collie.

18

Pack Loyalty

At the end of December, my loyal and energetic canine companion helped me navigate New Year's Eve without incident. The evening threatened to overwhelm me, but Baldwin's presence was a calming force that kept me grounded.

We sat with Dad in the den watching the ball drop in New York. Throughout the evening, Baldwin was by my side, his expressive eyes showing an understanding of my emotions that was hard to fathom. As the clock struck midnight and the world seemed to erupt in cheers, I hugged Baldwin. That hug gave me the comfort and reassurance I needed that everything would be okay.

I needed him that January more than ever. We were approaching what would have been Mom's eighty-first birthday coupled with the somber first anniversary of her passing the following day.

I asked Dad one evening, "How about we do something special to remember Mom? The one-year anniversary of her death is only a week away."

"Has it been that long already?"

"Yes," I said. "I've been thinking we could plant a special rose bush in the garden in her honor."

"She did have a green thumb," he said.

"Then again, we already have so many rose bushes. We should do something truly special, something that captures her spirit."

"Okay," he said, his hands shaking.

We sat there together in the den, our hearts heavy with grief.

"We could throw her a birthday party and eat lots of cake," I said.

"She did have a sweet tooth."

But I soon concluded that a party wasn't quite right either.

"We could make a donation in her name. Can you think of a charity she liked?"

"She loved the church," he said. "We could donate to the new memorial garden."

"Yeah, but you guys have been tithing forever."

I glanced around the room, my eyes scanning the familiar surroundings decorated by Mom. On the sofa end table, her beloved faux Tiffany lamp cast a soft glow. Across from me, the wooden clock she found on sale faithfully ticked and tocked, its familiar sound a testament to the passing of time. The wall across from me featured a framed poster of Saint Johnsbury, Vermont, a visual connection to the town where she'd grown up.

I took in the things she'd carefully chosen, each one holding a piece of her story and a reflection of her eclectic personality.

Suddenly an idea formed, seemingly perfect in its simplicity and profound in its meaning.

"I've got it," I exclaimed. "On Mom's birthday, we'll buy something special for her, and the very next day, on the anniversary of her death, we'll return it."

"She did love to shop," Dad acknowledged.

"And to return. Yes, this is perfect. Buying only to return—a symbol of temporary ownership. Anyway, no physical object could hold the true essence of Mom. This will be a way to honor her spirit and then let it go."

And so, with the idea firmly in place, Dad, Jason and I headed to Macy's on her birthday. Mom's favorite department store seemed like a fitting place to embark on this journey to honor the woman who gave birth to me.

I had no idea what to get her. But when we passed the jewelry department on our way to the elevator, the dazzling displays stopped me in my tracks.

"She did have a thing for jewelry," I said, browsing the display cases. Dad looked bored. He leaned his back against the counter, holding his rollator tight.

He turned to me and asked, "Ready to go?"

"Just give me a minute," I said.

And then I found it—a stunning pendant, with a delicate rose etched in rose gold.

"That's it," I said.

I asked the sales clerk to see it. Once I held the pendant in my hands, a sense of peace washed over me.

"And even better. It's on sale."

Dad asked, "How much does it cost?"

I leaned in close and whispered, "We're retuning it tomorrow, remember?"

Dad nodded. "Can we go now?"

I took a moment to close my eyes, knowing this would serve as a beautiful tribute to Mom's memory—the rose, the gold ... all of it encapsulated her love.

Dad yawned. "Are we done yet?"

Then I remembered that Mom never shopped with Dad. In fact, Jack was the only man I knew who loved shopping (and returning) almost as much as Mom.

"Yes, you can head to the car," I said, motioning for Jason. "I'll catch up in a minute."

After paying, I carefully placed the pendant and the receipt in my purse.

On the way back to the car, I grasped the powerful meaning behind this silly little gesture. It represented a willingness to embrace impermanence. But I didn't share my thinking with Dad. Instead, I took him for some ice cream, something he loved as much as Mom loved a good sale.

The following day, I made my way back to Macy's. This time, only Baldwin came along, leaving dad to his beloved CNN. It wasn't easy to get through the mall with a Muppet-looking dog by my side—especially one that sported giant green peace signs. Everyone we passed stopped; some even took pictures of my boy.

Once we got to the jewelry department, I handed the receipt and the pendant to the clerk. And in the act of returning, I found the acceptance I'd been looking for, the final stage of grief.

Baldwin and I left the store and the weight of my grief eased just a little. To this day, I still honor Mom's memory at Macy's every year, with gratitude, compassion, and a touch of Mom's shopping prowess.

When we got back from returning Mom's gift, Baldwin grabbed his big stuffed teddy bear. With it in his mouth, the fluff ball danced around me, which I knew meant he wanted to go for a walk.

"OK," I told him and leashed him up.

Once outside, I led Baldwin to a little park adjacent to my

grammar school. There was always something going on there, kids playing on the swings, an intense game on the basketball court, an ice cream truck.

The park was small, but the paths winding around mature oak trees made me feel like I was in the mountains, not in the middle of the Valley. When I thought it safe, I took the leash off Baldwin to let him stretch a little but immediately regretted that decision.

"Noooooo!" I yelled.

Too late. Baldwin was already running full speed after a ground squirrel. Luckily, the squirrel ran up one of the stately oaks, leaving Baldwin barking like a mad dog below.

I ran to him as fast as possible, afraid he'd find more squirrels to torment.

"Come here," I panted, recovering my breath. "Leave that squirrel alone."

I took hold of his collar and was on the verge of fastening his leash when a young girl ran over and enveloped him in a tight embrace.

"Baldwin!" I shifted my gaze to the girl, perhaps eight years old, her hair woven into braids with colorful beads. But how did she know my fluff ball? Perhaps we'd met at the park. Or maybe from one of Baldwin's many classroom visits as a therapy dog. The notion of meeting her at LA County USC never crossed my mind. The hospital was more than thirty miles away.

In no time, she was planting affectionate kisses on Baldwin's velvety curls.

"I'm Bella," she smiled up at me. "Do you remember me?"

I delved deep into my recollections in an attempt to pinpoint where she'd met Baldwin, but my mind drew a complete blank.

"Um, well..."

"You visited at the hospital," she recalled, reclining on the grass while Baldwin showered her with slobbery adoration.

"Of course, we'd never forget you," I replied before steering my gaze away to shield the tears that were welling up in my eyes. "I'm so glad to see you're all better."

"Me too," she agreed. "I hated that place. The only good thing was Baldwin. I still have the picture, you know."

Bella rose onto her knees right in front of Baldwin's Muppet face and bestowed him with butterfly kisses—you know, when someone kisses another with their eyelashes by fluttering them against the person's skin, or, in this case, against a cute black dog's curls.

18. Pack Loyalty

That's when the memory of Bella resurfaced. She'd been a patient the previous Easter. I remembered Baldwin in his Easter Bunny ensemble—floppy ears and a cotton ball tail I'd bobby pinned above his stub. He'd been keenly aware of his cuteness that day, parading down the hospital corridors as if he owned the place.

We were never privy to any personal details about the children we visited or the challenges they faced. However, in Bella's case, I recall her appearing pallid, her deep brown eyes bloodshot and swollen.

When she saw Baldwin, Bella's response was immediate. She sat up in her hospital bed and clapped her hands in delight. With rapt attention, she watched as Baldwin showcased his repertoire of tricks—waving a paw in greeting, executing a rollover, deftly maneuvering through my legs. He even playfully wiggled his hindquarters, proudly displaying his cotton tail. When his performance ended, Bella gestured for the fluff ball to join her on the bed.

Understanding the protocol, I looked for a nurse to put a clean sheet down on Bella's bed before allowing Baldwin to jump up and cuddle with her. Swiftly, a fresh sheet was added, providing Baldwin the invitation to leap onto the bed and shower Bella with a cascade of affectionate puppy kisses.

As Baldwin nestled beside her, finding a snug spot, Bella leaned over to give him some butterfly kisses, just like she did at the park. That's when I comprehended that Baldwin was more than just a dog; he was a source of solace and healing. Mom would have been profoundly proud.

I took a picture of her and Baldwin with my Polaroid camera that day and handed the instant photograph to Bella, along with a bag of goodies I'd brought for each child we met. I had no idea she'd keep the photo as a treasure all this time.

There was no denying what Baldwin gave her and all the other kids we visited at the hospital. He brought each and every one of them a little bit of happiness during a difficult time.

Back at the park, Bella turned and yelled, "Mom!" motioning to a young woman heading our way.

Bella's mom joined us under the oak tree. She looked exactly like Bella, only older, with her matching beaded braids and beautiful dark skin.

Bella stood and said, "This is Baldwin, remember? The dog that visited me in the hospital?"

"Oh, yes," Bella's mom exclaimed, shifting her focus toward me. "You can't imagine how often she talks about your dog. She loves him."

I glanced down at Baldwin, now kissing the little girl with abandon. "I believe the feeling is mutual."

On the way home, my heart swelled, as if it could burst at any moment.

"I'm certain Mom is watching over us from heaven," I whispered to Baldwin. Gazing upward, I added, "Thank you, Mom, for buying me this bundle of fluff. He's continuing your legacy."

19

Bow Wow

I found it hard to believe that a year had passed since I bid farewell to my cozy Santa Monica apartment, just a block from the beach. Business lunches were replaced by therapy dog visits, networking now took place at agility trials, and my daily walks with Baldwin in the sun-kissed neighborhood where I grew up became a cherished routine.

However, I couldn't help but miss some of the more exciting aspects of my former life, like attending glamorous Hollywood parties. Besides the occasional business trips and media FAMs, my life had become simple, revolving around taking care of Dad and spending time with Baldwin, while my public relations business hummed quietly in the background.

By this point, my agility dog trainer, Kristen, had relocated our weekly classes from behind a church to her own backyard, a mere ten minutes away. Her vast yard, roughly half the size of a football field, was brimming with agility equipment. She even had sheep on her property, and that spring, I witnessed the birth of baby lambs. Watching them hop around and frolic was an absolute delight.

In addition to our agility training, Baldwin and I enrolled in one of Kristen's weekly sheepherding classes. Mastering the skill of sheepherding was a gradual process for me, and in the beginning, Baldwin struggled to contain his enthusiasm, dashing about after the sheep in a haphazard manner. While his instincts were sharp, Baldwin needed to learn to contain his energy.

In time, I managed to control his instinctive actions, but he always retained his distinctive approach. Stationed at the pen's edge, Baldwin locked his eyes on the sheep. With his right foot pointed toward them as if he was a bird dog, Baldwin waited like a statue for the moment one moved. His natural urge was to pick one off and chase it down, while my task was to get him to keep the sheep united, guiding them toward me.

With the utterance of the magic words, either "come bye" to

instruct him to move clockwise or "away" for the opposite direction, he would take off, leaving a cloud of dust in his wake. The key was to guide him to run in a wide semi-circle around the sheep, keeping them together while gradually herding them toward me. This mesmerizing canine/sheep dance became my ultimate escape.

Still, amidst the responsibilities of my current life, there were glimmers of my past. And an exciting opportunity was just on the horizon. A media friend of mine had extended an invitation to be her guest at a big Hollywood party. The fundraiser for PETA would be my chance to momentarily immerse myself in the world I'd once known. This event had an illustrious lineup, with none other than Ellen DeGeneres as the host and Sir Paul McCartney headlining the evening's entertainment.

The thought of attending such a high-profile gathering filled me with a touch of nostalgia. The prospect of dressing up to experience the magic of a star-studded affair became a sliver of light in my otherwise demanding routine—a chance to momentarily step into a world far removed from my current reality.

The day finally arrived. I carefully selected my outfit, ready to immerse myself in the enchantment of the Hollywood scene. But before getting all decked out for the occasion, I needed to take Baldwin for a walk. He proudly carried his new teddy bear in his mouth as we made our way toward my old junior high school, the perfect spot to unleash him and let him run free.

Reaching the school's entrance, I unclipped his leash. After an intense case of the zoomies, running in circles around me, he darted under a nearby bush and lingered there a bit longer than I was comfortable with.

"Get out of there," I urged, worried that he might stumble upon something repulsive to eat, like an old slice of pizza or, heaven forbid, cat poop.

When I bent down to grab him, he shot out at me like a bullet, his soft black curls now a deep brown color. All it took was a whiff of him to know what he'd gotten into.

"Shit!" I exclaimed. "You rolled in poop again, Baldwin?"

He gazed up at me, seemingly delighted with his aromatic adventure, as if to say, "Isn't it fantastic?"

My adorable little fluff ball, was now entirely covered in foul-smelling excrement, from his head all the way down to his tiny tail stub.

I choked on the rancid smell. "Really?"

The last time he rolled in poop, I consulted my agility trainer,

Kristen, for some insight into this unpleasant behavior. She explained that dogs have an instinctual inclination to roll in feces as a way to camouflage their own scent. To a dog, smelling bad made hunting for prey easier.

I recalled Kristen's wise words the last time. "It can be quite difficult to teach them not to roll in poop or other nasty-smelling things. You have to be vigilant and consistent. When you're outside with your dog, closely monitor them and watch for signs like excessive sniffing, pawing, or digging. They might perk up their ears or make snorting noises in a particular spot. Even seemingly playful behavior like pouncing or circling could indicate your dog is thinking about rolling in something nasty. As soon as you notice those signs, intervene immediately."

"I guess I missed those signs today," I told the stinky fluff ball.

I didn't have time to take him to a groomer, and I definitely didn't want to wash him in my bathtub. The solution? Hose him off outside.

We headed directly home and I wasted no time washing to stink off him. Baldwin followed me out to the grass where I hosed him off then poured heaps of lavender-smelling dog shampoo all over him. The fluff ball leaned into my hands as if he were receiving a luxurious massage.

I heard the sound of the backyard gate close and in moments Will walked up and watched us. He laughed at Baldwin who struggled to get away from me to greet Will.

"He rolled in poop," I told my big brother.

Will held his nose and said, "Don't come near me."

"He's clean now," I said. "But I've got to shower and get ready for an event."

Baldwin shook, spraying water all over us.

"I guess you just took your shower," Will laughed.

We headed back inside and joined Dad in the den.

"I told Suzie to make an appointment with my attorney," Dad announced.

I gritted my teeth. *Oh no, not this again.*

"Your mother and I wanted to leave the house to Suzie."

Taking a deep breath to steady myself, I responded. "We've gone over this already, Dad. We're not changing your will."

With a voice filled with anger, Will said, "That's right, you're not. This is the family house. It goes to all three of us."

Months before her passing, Mom had expressed her wish that the family house be left to me. Even Uncle Robert called after Mom died to remind me of his sister's wishes.

The overwhelming grief that engulfed me when she first died left me in a daze, and without thinking, I asked Will about our parents' will. To my disappointment, they had never revised it to reflect Mom's desire.

This revelation brought a significant shift in the dynamics of my relationship with my siblings. Feelings of hurt and confusion made our grieving process all the more complex for all of us.

The house, once a place of cherished memories, became a symbol of unresolved tension and unmet expectations. I found solace in the memories of Mom's love and the bond we shared, and in the end I accepted that her wishes would not be met. I wanted a relationship with Will and Erin more than a house.

Dad brought the topic up frequently, and every time, I shut him down. This wasn't the first time he did it right in front of Will. But I hoped it would be his last.

"Mom loved all three of us," Will said sharply. "You're not getting the house. Don't even think about it. And you've got to stop spending Dad's money. He's not rich, you know."

I picked up a sopping-wet Baldwin for courage. "I understand," I told Will, fearing the conversation would escalate further like it did the last time we broached this subject.

Throughout the heated exchange with Will, Dad chose to stay silent. The absence of his support left Will and Erin with the impression that I'd fabricated the story and that Mom had never mentioned anything about leaving me the house. They both acted as if I'd lied to them, something that bothers me to this day.

But I've done some research on the topic and learned that I am not alone. It can be difficult for siblings grappling with the grief of losing their parents to cope with their emotions while also navigating the practical aspects of handling finances and assets. Misunderstandings and a lack of open communication can further complicate matters. The sentimental value of family possessions adds to the complexity, as each family member may have emotional attachments to certain items, leading to difficulties in reaching a consensus when it comes to the division of assets.

I didn't know about the intricacies of dealing with Will and Erin back then. But when I looked up at the wall clock, I understood I'd missed my opportunity to shower before the big soiree that night.

"Shit," I muttered. "I need to get ready to leave."

19. Bow Wow

With a renewed determination and a silent prayer, I changed into my black pantsuit and headed out to my car. I did my best to steady myself after the uncomfortable conversation I'd had with Will, but once I was inside the car, tears streamed down my face. My heart felt heavy, burdened by the weight of the situation at home which I feared would only get worse once Dad died.

My stomach churned with anxiety, twisting and turning as I drove to Paramount Pictures Studio for the party on the backlot. I stole a glance of myself in the rearview mirror and noticed tracks of mascara staining my cheeks. With a sigh, I reached into my purse and retrieved a pack of Kleenex. Carefully, I wiped away the remnants of mascara, hoping to restore a semblance of composure.

Despite my efforts, my eyes still looked red and puffy, so I reached in the glove box for my blue-tinted prescription glasses. I hoped their cool hue would conceal the vulnerability etched on my face.

"Let it go, Susan. Let it go."

By the time I arrived at the iconic art deco studio lot, the weight of my worries began to fade, as if the entrance gates, emblazoned with the studio's name, stood as a gateway to another world.

I parked and headed toward a crowd gathered near some towering palm trees. Though my heart still ached, and the worries of home lingered, I allowed myself to embrace the magic of the moment.

I found my journalist friend, also named Susan, in front of the grand fountain. Susan, with her striking long, blonde hair, looked elegant in her blue silk dress—the color a perfect match for her eyes. We linked arms and made our way toward the backlot, our steps synchronized in excitement.

20

Paw-ty Animal

After we checked in at the VIP desk, we were instructed to walk the red carpet with the celebrities—this royal treatment was something new for a lowly PR flack like me.

"I could get used to this," I remarked to Susan.

When I first got into the world of public relations, I was enchanted by the red carpet, drawn in by its irresistible allure of opulence and splendor. However, my profession compelled me to remain in the shadows, choreographing the intricate interplay between the media and celebrities. Finding myself on the opposite side of this world was novel. Even if it lasted a short time, the sensation was electrifying, and I savored every single second of it.

As we made our way down the red carpet, I found myself waving to the audience that lined the barricades, their faces showing their excitement, their cheers and squeals filling the air. To my surprise, some of them appeared genuinely thrilled to catch a glimpse of me.

This unexpected attention took me by surprise. The sight of people waving and beaming at me felt surreal. A group of enthusiastic young girls who excitedly jumped up and down at the sight of me felt particularly peculiar. I turned to my friend Susan in search of an explanation.

"Does this happen every time you walk the red carpet?"

Susan's eyes sparkled with amusement. "Never," she replied. "I think it's you."

I ransacked my thoughts to discern the cause of this newfound fascination with me. Then, a timid little girl approached, her eyes brimming with wonder.

"Hello, I know who you are," she said, her voice barely audible.

I halted, lowering myself to her eye level, and asked, "Who do you think I am?"

Blushing, the little girl hurried back to her mother in the crowd, leaving my question unanswered.

Turning to Susan, I asked. "What is going on? Who do these people think I am?"

"It seems you've become an enigma, my dear," she remarked. "Embrace it!"

Her words prompted a shift in my perspective. Instead of seeking answers to the mystery, I decided to take it all in. Yes, I went along with it, whatever it was, waving and smiling at my newly discovered fan club.

With champagne flowing, we dined on a delicious vegetarian meal designed to be healthy and nutritious. The looks continued off the red carpet as Susan and I made our way to our seats.

As the show began, the pieces of my popularity puzzle started falling into place. It became clear that the source of the attention fixed on me stemmed from my remarkable similarity to the event's hostess, Ellen DeGeneres. We had the same haircut, for starters. Both dressed in black pantsuits and, to top it off, she sported a pair of blue-tinted glasses identical to mine. Susan and I had a good laugh.

After dinner, we strolled around the venue, taking in the atmosphere. We passed Woody Harrelson unapologetically smoking a joint near the scantily-clad Pamela Anderson smooching with her new beau. Susan pointed out actor Alec Baldwin, standing just a few steps away from us.

"You need to tell him you named your dog after him," she urged.

Indeed, the name Baldwin was inspired by the 1995 movie *Clueless* in which the protagonist used Baldwin—as in the handsome Baldwin brothers—to describe attractive guys.

"No, he won't care that I named my dog after him."

"Come on," she said, "you'll never have a chance like this again."

She did have a point. Seizing the opportunity, I mustered up the courage to approach him, my heart pounding.

Taking a deep breath, I said, "Hi, Mr. Baldwin, it's such an honor to meet you. I wanted to let you know I named my sweet rescue dog after you."

He paused for a moment, taking in my words.

"A rescue named after me?" he said, his voice filled with genuine appreciation. "Thank you. Thank you very much."

Encouraged by his positive response, I reached into my purse and pulled out a picture of my fluff ball then handed it to the famous actor.

He looked at the picture and a small tear formed in the corner of his eye. Handing it back to me, he turned to walk away. I turned too, headed in the direction of the other Susan but didn't get too far before Alec grabbed my shoulder.

"No, really," he said. "Thank you. This means so much to me."

Here I was, in the middle of the glitz and glamour of a Hollywood event, engaging in a casual conversation with a celebrated actor about my favorite topic: Baldwin. That's when it struck me that I had something in common with all these people—my love of animals. Like me, they believed in the inherent value of all living beings, advocating for their rights and well-being. These were my people.

The rest of the evening passed in a whirlwind of excitement. The music of Paul McCartney filled the air, and I felt a newfound sense of liberation wash over me.

Afterward, I turned my thoughts toward those who genuinely knew and valued me. My childhood friend Kat, who had stood by my side through every twist and turn, offering unwavering support. Angel, who consistently recognized my true value and never failed to remind me of it when we were together. Jack, who had proven to be an excellent friend in his own right. Dad, whose love and belief in me remained steadfast, even in the face of the hardships he bravely fought. And Jason, the dedicated caretaker who had witnessed my commitment to my family member firsthand.

Above all, I considered my loyal companion, my dog Baldwin, who loved me unconditionally. Baldwin had taught me the profound strength of unconditional love and acceptance. He saw me for who I truly was—a person deserving of love, kindness, and self-compassion.

In that moment of profound clarity, I vowed to extend to myself the same love, care, and kindness that Baldwin demonstrated. I realized I no longer needed to relentlessly seek validation and approval from others. I had my own network of unwavering support—people who, day in and day out, reminded me of my inherent worth.

The Hollywood party became a turning point for me. I knew I had everything I needed within me to lead a fulfilling and authentic life. From that moment forward, I vowed to live my life unapologetically. It was time to honor and celebrate the person that Baldwin loved.

The very next morning, as Baldwin stirred awake, the weight of resentment crept back into my thoughts.

"Here we go again," I sighed to my canine sidekick. "I thought last night's epiphany would finally put an end to this roller coaster of emotions."

But as the sun rose on a new day, I realized that reprogramming my brain was not going to come easily. Healing and letting go would be an ongoing process. It wasn't something that could be achieved overnight or with a single realization.

Baldwin excitedly fetched his frisbee, seemingly urging me to snap out of my mental struggle. Perhaps he understood more than I gave him credit for, knowing that sometimes the best way to get out of my head was to embrace the present moment. I needed to follow his lead and embark on the day with a fresh perspective. We ventured outside together where I allowed the morning breeze to carry away my anxiety.

After a quick round of frisbee, we returned indoors and made our way to my office. Baldwin settled comfortably beneath my desk, and I grabbed a pen and some paper to pour out my frustrations, anger, and sadness. I meticulously chronicled all the instances in which I believed my sacrifices and contributions had been disregarded or underappreciated. Once I'd poured my thoughts onto the paper, I read through what I'd written. It became clear to me that holding on to resentment and focusing on the perceived unfairness would only keep me stuck in a negative cycle.

Instead of seeking validation from others, I'd choose to see my actions as acts of love and compassion toward Dad, driven by my own values and the desire to support someone I cared about deeply.

I decided that moving forward, whenever resentment resurfaced, I'd gently redirect my thoughts toward gratitude. In time, the pool of resentment I felt began to shrink, replaced by a sense of peace and acceptance. Mine wasn't a linear journey, but I knew that I had the power to choose how I responded in any moment.

Baldwin came out of his hiding spot under my desk and wagged his tail, sensing a shift in my energy. It was as if he understood the significance of that moment. I reached down to pet him, my sage in dog form.

"Everything starts with forgiveness," I murmured out loud to Baldwin. He barked in agreement. "You know all about forgiveness, don't you, boy? I can learn a lot from you."

That's when it struck me. "Oh my God, my need to be loved is overshadowing everything I do and say, especially with my family. It's hard to be honest and truthful when you put everyone else's needs above your own."

I realized that every time Will told me to do something, like pay the bills, I'd jump to it because I didn't want to create any conflict. But my actions were creating conflict within myself. I thought I'd learned the lesson that I couldn't change someone else when I broke up with Jack—that I had the power to change only myself. But now I saw how my unhealthy, pleasing behavior infiltrated every aspect of my life.

I furiously began writing again.

"I have no control over Will and Erin," I wrote, my right hand moving at a hummingbird's speed, "but there are many things I can control. Things like my diet and exercise."

The moment I made a conscious decision to add self-care into my daily routine, Baldwin burst into an epic case of the zoomies, darting around my office. It was as if he could read my mind.

"Exactly," I said. "It's time I joined a gym. And those unhealthy snacks have got to go. Maybe I'll become a vegetarian."

With forgiveness as my guide, I knew there were other steps to take on this journey of letting go and learning to love myself. I had the power to choose how I reacted to others. And that knowledge, along with the love of my fluff ball, was enough.

21

The Peace Puppy

After a span of several days, a brilliant idea dawned on me—an ingenious way to remind myself of the importance of embracing serenity, regardless of the circumstances. And, unsurprisingly, it all centered on Baldwin.

"You know what?" I grinned. "I'm going to transform you into my very own serenity prayer by painting a peace sign on you."

With this notion in mind, Baldwin joined me on a trip to the craft store. There, I bought a sheet of plastic to create a stencil of a large peace sign that would be impossible to miss. Our next stop was the beauty supply store, where I picked up a can of environmentally friendly, non-toxic green hair spray.

We got home and I went to work. Once the giant peace sign stencil was ready, I took Baldwin outside for his transformation. He stood motionless, patient and cooperating, while I carefully sprayed peace signs on both sides of his body.

The Peace Puppy (photograph by Erin L. Waggoner, https://pawprintspictures.com/).

167

The Peace Puppy

Before my eyes, Baldwin had turned into the Peace Puppy. As destiny would have it, the timing couldn't have been more fitting. Will and I had a pivotal meeting scheduled later that day to discuss Dad's financial future and, more important, to reconcile our differences following our recent argument.

Now, with Baldwin proudly showcasing his peace signs, we headed out to meet Will at my local Starbucks—a neutral space where I felt safe. Arriving a bit early, I bought a macchiato and secured an outdoor table beneath the shade of a patio umbrella.

Baldwin wagged his stump of a tail as Will approached. Will ignored the fluff ball's wiggles (I don't know how) and settled into the chair across from me, swiftly delving into the matter at hand.

"You really need to stop spending Dad's money," he urged, his tone carrying a blend of concern and exasperation.

I was about to answer when Baldwin saddled up next to him and lifted his paw. Will's demeanor softened when he noticed Baldwin's adornments.

"Did you do that?" he questioned.

I shook my head yes. "I painted the peace signs on him as a way to remind us to find peace with each other."

"I see," he said. "Peace, it's a good thing."

"And Baldwin makes a perfect Peace Puppy, don't you think?"

"The Peace Puppy," Will repeated.

"A gentle reminder that peace and love should be at the center of our communications."

"Not so gentle," he said with a grin, "but I hear you. I just want you to understand that we've got to stop withdrawing money from Dad's investments to cover his outstanding debts."

"But it's his money, Will. Shouldn't he have the freedom to use it?"

"Come on, Sue," Will retorted. "Every time we make withdrawals from his investments, he gets hit with substantial taxes."

I pondered Will's words for a moment and had a sudden realization: his anger wasn't directed at me; it stemmed from his deep concern for Dad's well-being.

"Who knows how long Dad will be around," he expressed, his voice tinged with worry. "His finances need to last, and I'm just worried about his future."

Before any further conversation could unfold, Will's cell phone rang. After answering, he abruptly stood up, motioning that the call was urgent. He waved goodbye, then turned and made his way to the parking lot.

21. The Peace Puppy

Even though our conversation had been brief, I valued Will's honesty, and I made a mental note to consider his concerns moving forward. Back in the car, with Baldwin riding shotgun, my attention shifted to my own finances.

"Given that I don't have rent to worry about," I mused aloud, "I can allocate some of my personal funds for Dad's needs. Besides, I'm already covering Jason's car and insurance expenses."

It all made sense to me. Now that I wasn't seeking validation, I could learn from my brother's perspective.

On the way home, the Peace Puppy and I made a frisbee stop at our local park. I opened the passenger door and Baldwin darted toward a group of special needs children gathered on the playground. Their spirited squeals filled the air, especially when they caught sight of the Peace Puppy.

"Don't touch strange dogs," a woman standing by cautioned the children.

"It's okay," I reassured her, catching my breath after chasing after Baldwin. "He's a therapy dog and visits kids in the hospital."

One adorable curly-haired girl in red-rimmed glasses made her best effort to pry the frisbee out of Baldwin's mouth. Watching her tug and pull reminded me of the time I accidentally injured my eye. A surge of adrenaline coursed through me—I needed to intervene and prevent a similar mishap.

Before I could do anything, a ginger-haired boy headed our way to offer his assistance. Little Ryan with his dimples and freckles displayed the characteristic avoidance of eye contact often seen in individuals on the autism spectrum. He stood above Baldwin and began swirling his hands above the fluff ball's head.

"Let it go," Ryan said firmly, his hands moving in a magician-like manner, as if he were about to conjure a rabbit from a hat.

Responding to Ryan's cues, Baldwin released the frisbee, took a step back, and patiently waited for Ryan to toss it. In an instant, Baldwin leaped into the air, catching the disc before returning to the group. Once again, he clutched the frisbee with determination, unwilling to let go until little Ryan saved the day with his magic act.

I stood in amazement. Baldwin never dropped the frisbee like that for me. I couldn't help but feel a little jealous as I watched the boy effortlessly command Baldwin's cooperation. How was he able to get my dog to cooperate so easily? I'd spent countless hours trying to train Baldwin, and yet here was a stranger who got the message across without a problem.

169

The Peace Puppy

I approached the boy, curious to know his secret. "Are you a dog trainer?"

The boy smiled, his eyes twinkling. "No," he said, "but I speak dog."

"I see. Maybe you can share your secret with me?"

"No secret," Ryan told me. "You just have to think like a dog."

Our conversation ended when Baldwin brought the frisbee back to the group.

"Ryan" The other kids called out, gathering around him and my boy. Ryan became a hero that day, just by getting my fluff ball to let go. And the irony went deeper than that. Perhaps Ryan was using calming techniques that had been used on him in the past. What I had initially perceived as a flaw in Baldwin had transformed into an asset.

Although I still had a lot to learn, Ryan opened my eyes to the endless possibilities of connecting with dogs. It wasn't just about following a set of instructions or commands; it was about forging a genuine connection. And, of course, thinking like a dog.

22

You Can Teach an
Old Dog a New Trick

On Father's Day, I stood in the doorway of the den, observing Dad as he ate his breakfast. Over the past year and a half, I'd come to rely on Dad's presence, and the thought of not having him around was a weighty contemplation. There was a certain fulfillment in being indispensable in his life—in someone's life—and I cherished the feeling of being needed.

Kat came over, a bouquet of sunflowers in her hands, and a hint of sorrow in her eyes. Just like me, she understood the profound emotions tied to grief. And on this day, the second Father's Day since her dad passed, those emotions were especially poignant.

"Happy Father's Day," Kat announced, handing the flowers to Dad.

"Ah, Kat, thanks for thinking of me," he replied. "How's your dad doing on this fine summer day?" He'd forgotten that her dad died shortly before Mom.

"Good," Kat answered, her eyes welling.

Out of Dad's earshot, Kat confided, "I can't explain it, but this Father's Day feels even harder than the holidays."

"I felt the same way on Mother's Day," I confessed. "I understand how tough it is to concentrate when memories keep pulling you back to the past. Don't push yourself too hard today."

Will arrived around dinner time to honor Dad. The two of us exchanged a knowing glance, sharing an unspoken understanding of the significance of this day. I grabbed the presents I'd bought on behalf of both of us and we headed to the den to surprise Dad.

"Happy Father's Day!" we chimed in unison.

Dad's eyes lit up with a excitement as he unwrapped the first package, a pair of walkie-talkies.

"For you and Jason," I explained.

Will put one in Dad's hand and took the other with him to the kitchen. "Breaker, breaker, Happy Father's Day," we heard Will say loud and clear.

Dad fumbled with his, pushing the volume button instead of the one for speaking. "Ten-four, good buddy," he said.

Will came back in and tried his best to show Dad how to properly use it. "You push this, then speak here," he demonstrated.

Dad put the walkie-talkie to his mouth and pushed the volume button again.

"Not that button," Will said, frustrated.

Baldwin tried his best to break the tension. He brought his favorite teddy bear over to Will, shaking it vigorously in an attempt to get Will to play. When that didn't work, Baldwin rolled over on his back, displaying his desire for a peaceful interaction. But Will didn't pick up on my boy's not so subtle hints.

"Look, Will, Baldwin wants some attention."

"Okay," Will said, "come over here."

Baldwin did as he was asked, and Will did as Baldwin asked. Will played tug with Baldwin. And the two tugged so hard that the poor teddy bear lost one of his arms.

"Oh no," Will said holding the arm out to me.

"Looks like it's time for a new teddy bear," I said.

Dad laughed when he opened the final gift—a pair of socks that proudly proclaimed him to be the "World's Greatest Father."

"Thank you both," Dad smiled. "In my eyes, you're the world's greatest son and daughter."

"Well, this world's greatest trio better get going," I said. "Will and I made dinner reservations at a fancy place in Sherman Oaks that you're going to love."

With Will's assistance, Dad stood up and we headed to the car. Our destination: a charming restaurant renowned for its unique twist—every waiter showcased their musical talents by singing in between taking orders.

We arrived just as one of the waiter's finished a solo. I watched as Dad's took in the scene.

"The waiters sing here?"

"Yup," I answered. "We figured you'd like that."

The maître d' seated us in the middle of the restaurant where we would see all the action.

It was difficult to have a conversation over the music, but Dad relished every song. In that moment. As we collectively embraced this special day, I sensed a flicker of hope for healing. Perhaps not the exact kind of healing we longed for, but a mending of our hearts—one smile, one laugh, and one serenade at a time.

August approached, signaling Dad's birthday. How would I top his present from last year? To make matters worse, I found myself without the energy to make any plans to celebrate the occasion. The sweltering heat of another Valley summer made me lethargic, my only solace the relief provided by central air conditioning.

I worried again about my black dog overheating, so I put our usual activities, such as agility practice and long walks, on hold during the scorching summer months.

In contrast, Dad embraced the heat. Warmth helped relax his muscles, alleviating some of his discomfort. But it did little to help his memory or mood.

"I want to go home," Dad announced one afternoon.

"Not again," I said under my breath. "Jason, he wants to go home now."

Jason entered the room, maneuvering Dad's rollator as he approached. "Ready, sir?"

Jason helped Dad toward the back door. I thought a short stroll around the yard would do the trick, as usual. But this time, Dad resisted, firmly applying the brakes to his rollator.

"No," he insisted, his voice filled with determination. "I want to go home."

Jason encouraged him to move forward, but Dad stubbornly refused to budge. Frustration mounting, Dad pushed Jason's hands away and headed back to his red chair.

"I want to go home to Kansas City, where I grew up."

I took a deep breath, preparing myself for another imaginary journey conjured up from Dad's childhood. He and Jason often talked about traveling together, but this time, his requested destination held a different significance—it was, after all, the place of his birth.

"Okay," I replied, mustering a calm tone.

I settled back on the couch across from him while Jason respectfully bowed his head before making his way back to the garage.

"You're feeling a bit nostalgic?"

"My childhood friends are having a reunion back in my old neighborhood."

"A reunion?" I repeated. "In Kansas City?"

"Yes," he confirmed. "Dan Dalter told me about it."

I knew the name, although, to my knowledge, I'd never met the man. Dad still engaged in lengthy phone conversations with Dan but I had no idea that he still lived where the two of them grew up.

"We'll stay with my old pal Julia," Dad continued.

His matter-of-fact attitude intrigued me. "Sounds like you've got it all planned out. When's this reunion happening?"

"Next month," he replied. "You, Jason and I will go."

I realized that this wasn't another one of his hallucinations. This was real. I thought about the idea for a moment. I'd read that Parkinson's disease can lead to social isolation due to its physical challenges. Reuniting with old friends and spending time in a familiar environment could provide valuable social interaction for Dad. And anyway, the idea of meeting his childhood buddies and hearing the old stories sounded interesting to me.

"Well, then, I need to start planning a trip."

Dad left me little time to coordinate the details, especially the intricacies involved in traveling with a man who hallucinated regularly and could barely walk. There was no time to wait. First, I called Dan Dalter to get all the details.

Dan confirmed the information. "The old gang's looking forward to seeing him—and you."

Although I'd visited Dad's hometown during my early childhood, my memories of that place were faint, limited to the enchanting sight of fireflies lighting up on warm summer nights.

Leaving Baldwin behind would be difficult but I'd ask Jack to stay at the Northridge house and keep him and Molly the Collie company. Besides, Kat would be there during the day to work.

While the logistics of the trip were falling into place, I couldn't help but feel a touch of uneasiness. But this was an opportunity of a lifetime and perhaps the last trip Dad would take ever.

The night before our departure, I packed for both Dad and me, all the while under the watchful gaze of Baldwin. His brown, soulful eyes tugged at my heartstrings. It was as if he were wordlessly imploring, "Please, don't go."

I got the car packed that night, so we'd have less to do in the morning. Since I'm not a morning person, as I've shared before, I didn't want to leave any details to chance.

That evening, I set out to shower Baldwin with a little more attention than usual, if that was even possible. As soon as the sun went down, we went on an extra-long walk that seemed to stretch on endlessly and I played frisbee with him in the backyard until he got tired. By the end of the night, it became evident that my bond with him had evolved into something truly remarkable. I preferred spending my time with that black fluff ball more than with any human.

"I'm going to miss you too," I told him. Exhausted from the evening's endless fun, Baldwin laid down and fell asleep.

Before the break of dawn, my alarm went off.

I jumped out of bed. "We're leaving in a half hour," I yelled to Jason and Dad.

Then I knelt in front of my beloved fluff ball and pressed my forehead against his, our noses touching.

"I'll be back soon," I whispered. "Molly will be here with you, and Jack is coming later today to stay while I'm gone. You won't be alone."

Baldwin huffed, his face turning away from mine. To distract him, I handed him a bully stick that I had hidden in my room just for that purpose.. The pathetic look on his face disappeared as he tore into his chew. With a final pat on his head, I made my way to the car with Dad and Jason. It was time to begin our journey to the Midwest.

On our way to LAX, Dad turned to me, his eyes filled with childlike wonder. "We're really doing this," he said, his excitement palpable.

"Let the adventure begin," I told him.

"I can't wait to see my old friends."

"Only a few hours until you're reunited with Julia. She's picking us up at the airport."

"Will Dan Dalter be there too?"

"He's going to meet us later at Julia's house."

"Who's picking us up at the airport, then?"

"Your old pal Julia," I reminded him gently. "We're staying with her, remember?"

Dad continued to ask questions that I'd already answered . It felt like he'd asked them a million times. But instead of getting upset and irritated about having to repeat myself, I tried my best to remain positive. Repetition had become a part of my life by then, and I knew I needed to embrace it with patience and understanding.

At the airport, I pulled into the loading zone and left Dad and Jason seated on a bench in front of American Airlines while I parked.

Before I pulled away, Dad asked, "Why are we at the airport?"

"We're going to Kansas City, remember?"

I parked the car and quickly returned to the location where I'd left Dad and Jason. As we stepped into the bustling airport, my immediate goal was to find assistance.

"Ready?"

Jason nodded as he helped Dad to his feet.

"Let's go," Dad exclaimed.

Prior to our arrival, I'd made a phone call to the airline, which had instructed me to inform airport staff of Dad's need for an electric cart to reach the gate promptly.

Once inside, I flagged down an airport employee. "Excuse me, can you help us get to our gate?"

Within moments, an airline staff member arrived with an electric cart. We wasted no time and swiftly settled into the seats on the cart. Our driver skillfully guided us through the busy airport, making a brief stop to offload our luggage.

We proceeded through the security line quickly. Dad was exempted from the usual process of removing his shoes or placing loose change in a bowl and placing items on the conveyor belt. Instead, we were escorted to the front of the line and permitted to pass through security with him and his rollator.

Afterward, we got back on the electric cart. The airport passed in a blur as the driver swiftly took us to our gate.

The whole time, Dad kept asking, "Where are we going?" I was starting to lose my patience with his constant repetitive questions, butI did my best to let it go with visions of the Peace Puppy dancing in my head.

While we sat in the busy departure lounge, I felt a sense of relief. We'd successfully navigated the hustle and bustle of LAX without incident, propelling us closer to the next part of our adventure.

When the announcement came for early boarding, Dad, Jason, and I made our way to the gate. Waiting for us were two handsome flight attendants, ready to assist Dad to his seat.

"Welcome," they greeted us in unison. With a gentle demeanor, they positioned themselves on either side of Dad.

Confusion crossed Dad's face. "What are you doing?"

"They're here to help you to your seat," I explained.

The men practically picked Dad up off his feet guiding him through the boarding corridor and down the narrow aisle inside the plane. Sandwiched between them, Dad safely reached his seat without issues.

Once we were airborne, Dad dozed off, his snoring breaking the otherwise tranquil atmosphere of the cabin. Jason quickly fell asleep too, and I took a moment to breathe deeply, relieved that the first leg of our journey was now behind us. At least he's not bombarding me with questions, I thought.

Dad and Jason woke up as we were landing.

22. *You Can Teach an Old Dog a New Trick*

"Are we there yet?" Dad asked.

I grabbed his arm. "We're here."

After everyone on the plane disembarked at the Kansas City International Airport, two more attendants helped Dad get off the plane. At the gate, Dad's rollator waited, alongside an electric cart to transport us to the baggage claim area.

We swiftly navigated through the airport again, making excellent time, and arrived at baggage claim before our luggage. We weren't there for long before a striking woman in her seventies approached us, warmly embracing Dad.

"Hello, Dick," she greeted him with a smile.

"Julia! You haven't changed a bit," Dad remarked. Then, unexpectedly, he planted a wet kiss on Julia's lips, holding the contact for a bit longer than expected.

It occurred to me that maybe I should've given his childhood friends a heads-up about his deteriorating condition. I feared his exuberant greeting after more than five decades wasn't what she expected. And who knew how he'd be with the rest of the group? But if they were all like Julia, I didn't have to worry.

Julia emanated compassion—her gray hair and wrinkled hands were in juxtaposition to her Adidas tracksuit with the iconic black and white stripes. She appeared not only kindhearted but also understanding. I would soon discover that people from the Midwest are, in general, incredibly friendly.

"Sorry about this," Julia apologized, gesturing to her gym outfit. "I just got back from my workout."

I glanced down at my white blouse, now covered in my morning coffee.

"Turbulence," I said. "Definitely not a good idea to wear white on a plane."

"You can freshen up once we get home," Julia reassured me.

On the way out of the building, I caught a glimpse of myself in one of the airport's floor-to-ceiling windows and sighed. My usually straight hair was already a frizzy mess, thanks to the humidity—and we hadn't even left the building yet.

We followed Julia to her new shiny red Prius. Jason helped Dad into the passenger seat while I struggled to fit our luggage into the trunk. Jason and I squeezed into the back seat next to Dad's rollator.

We made our way to the highway, passing the airport's spectacular 60-foot-high waterfall sculpture illuminated by red, blue, and yellow neon lights.

The Peace Puppy

"That fountain certainly makes a statement," I commented.

"That's just one of the more than 200 fountains here in Kansas City," Julia enlightened us. "Didn't your daddy ever tell you Kansas City is known as the City of Fountains?"

"Nope. I've only heard it referred to as Cowtown, and Dad has a rather amusing story about falling into a pile of cow dung—"

"I've never heard that story," Julia said, grinning mischievously at Dad.

"There's a lot you don't know about me," he winked.

Once we hit the highway, it became apparent that we were no longer in California. The landscape unfolded before us, with vast stretches of flatland contrasting with the lush, rolling green hills in the background.

Julia informed us, "We'll be at my place in about forty-five minutes. I hope you're hungry."

"I have to use the restroom," Dad announced.

I sighed in exasperation. "Why didn't you use the airport restroom?"

"I didn't have to go then."

"No problem," Julia reassured us. "We'll make a quick stop at the next gas station."

When the car came to a halt, Dad looked around and asked, "Where are we?"

"We're in Kansas City, remember? For your neighborhood reunion?"

Upon arriving at Julia's, we were greeted in her driveway by a man who I assumed was the one and only Dan Dalter. He had a kind face and stood a little taller than Dad, with a belly resembling that of the Buddha.

"Dick," the man said, embracing Dad warmly. "And you must be Suzie. I haven't seen you since you were a wee tot."

I extended my hand for a handshake, but the man pulled me into a warm embrace.

"I'm Dan Dalter," he introduced himself to me.

"I've heard so much about you."

"All good, I hope," he chuckled.

Dan then greeted Jason with a firm handshake.

"I'll take care of the luggage," Jason volunteered as Julia opened the trunk.

Entering Julia's living room, we were greeted by an abundance of house plants thriving in the natural light that streamed through her many windows. A tall floor lamp with a green shade stood in the corner, adding a touch of elegance to the room where curtains gently swayed in the breeze.

Dad settled into a comfortable-looking wooden rocking chair positioned near a brick fireplace. Portraits of family members adorned the walls, alongside paintings of angels that appeared to be surveying the room with a sense of ownership.

Julia asked, "Would you like some lemonade? I just made some fresh this morning."

"That sounds delicious," I said. "Let me help."

I followed her to the kitchen, where a pitcher of lemonade beaded with frost sat on the counter.

"How long have you lived here?" I asked, placing the pitcher and some tall glasses on a tray.

"This is my family home." She pulled a fruit platter out of the refrigerator. "I grew up here."

"I'm living at my family home. It's very comforting, isn't it?"

"Oh yes, I wouldn't live anywhere else."

I followed Julia back into the living room, where Dad and Dan were engrossed in conversation. Jason had already dozed off seated in a cozy chair in the corner.

I positioned the pitcher of lemonade on the coffee table, and when Julia added the fruit platter beside it, a momentary panic gripped me. I worried that Baldwin might reach for the watermelon, but then I reminded myself that he wasn't with us.

One sip of the lemonade transported me to another world. The flavor was incredibly sweet and juicy, with pulp dancing on my tastebuds.

"Julia, this is delicious," I commented.

"The lemons are from my tree."

Julia stood in the center of the room filled with all her childhood freinds and lifted her glass.

"Let's raise a toast. To the old neighborhood," she proclaimed, and we clinked our glasses together. "And to Dick being here to celebrate with us."

"To Dick," Dan chimed in.

Dan then pulled me aside. "Thank you for bringing him here," he expressed sincerely. "I understand that caring for your daddy can't be easy. I want you to know that your efforts are truly appreciated."

"Oh, Dan," I said, "you have no idea how much I needed to hear that."

"It's the truth," he affirmed. "And I must say, Julia was especially thrilled to have her first love back in the neighborhood."

I shook my head in disbelief. "Wait. Julia and Dad? Are you serious?"

23

Tall Tails

I'd always believed that Mom was Dad's one and only love. But after learning there was someone before her, I was eager to hear all the details. I couldn't wait to take Julia aside for a private chat, but on my way to grab her, my phone rang. Stepping outside to answer the call, I was greeted by the sweet fragrance of honeysuckle, while a white squirrel scurried away from Julia's bird feeder.

"Hi, Dudan, where are the dog bowls?" Jack asked.

"They're right there on the counter. You can't miss them," I replied, envisioning Baldwin's stump enthusiastically wagging and Molly with her patient demeanor as they anticipated their evening meal.

"Oh," Jack responded. "I see now. But where's the food?"

"Also on the counter, in the grocery bag marked 'dog food.' I used a black Sharpie to label it."

"This bag?" he inquired. I heard him rustle a bag open.

"Yes, that's the one," I confirmed, since it was the only bag I left on the counter. "Inside, you'll find individual baggies of food for each dog, so all you have to do is empty the contents."

"Thanks. How was your flight?"

"Great! We were given the VIP treatment thanks to my calls to the airline ahead of time. But here's something interesting—I just found out that Dad used to date the woman who invited us to stay with her."

"That old dog," Jack chuckled. "I knew he wasn't as innocent as he made himself out to be."

"Well, I know they never had sex."

"How do you know?"

"He told me all about the first time he had sex. And it was with Mom. I know I told you about it."

"I guess I forgot," he said. "And anyway, your dad's sex life isn't something I want to know about."

"Me neither," I said. "But I'm definitely curious about Dad's romance with Julia."

180

"Baldwin just ran into the kitchen with his frisbee, so I guess I need to feed him, then go outside and play."

Who says dogs can't talk? Well, you guys have fun and give my boy a big kiss for me." After we hung up, my curiosity about Dad's past only grew stronger. I reentered the living room and headed straight for the person who held the answers.

"Hey, Julia," I began. "Did you and my dad ever date?"

Julia looked up, surprised. "Yes, your daddy and I were involved romantically. In fact, he was the love of my life. We even discussed getting married one day. Did he tell you?"

"No." I gestured toward Dan. "I got the scoop from someone else."

Julia nodded and said, "Dan never did know how to keep a secret."

"What was my Dad like back then?"

"Oh, your daddy was quite something." She pushed a strand of hair back in place. "He was smart—got straight As in school—and was so handsome. All the girls liked him. But his real love was music. I'm still surprised he didn't become a professional singer with that voice of his."

Although I found it difficult to envision Dad as a ladies' man, I was well aware of his deep passion for music.

"He was the leader of the Sometimers Dixieland Band," I told her.

Dad played trumpet and sang in the Sometimers Dixieland Band.

The Peace Puppy

"They were called that because sometimes they were good and sometimes they were bad."

She smiled. "Sounds like your daddy."

"He always said he sacrificed his musical career for his family."

"That's just the kind of man he is," Julia said. She took my hand in
hers. "Come with me."

I followed her into her bedroom and was met with an abundance
of plants there too. There were ferns carefully arranged on her window-
sills, ivy hanging from macramé planters, and planted succulents on
almost every surface.

Her old-fashioned headboard, intricately carved with cherubs, was
the centerpiece of the room. A vintage, deep yellow velvet bedspread
added a bit of elegance to the space. I wondered about the brown paper
bag that sat in the middle of the bed.

"Have a seat," she motioned for me to sit next to her on the bed. "I
never married," she confessed.

I nodded in understanding. "Me neither." I already felt a sense of
connection growing between us.

Julia's eyes met mine. "I've always believed it's better to be alone
than settle for the wrong person. And after your daddy, they were all
wrong."

Her words struck a chord in me. "I totally get that. But it's not
always easy being single, right?"

Julia nodded. "Luckily, I have a wonderful family and group of
friends who love me."

"You never had kids?"

"No," she replied, touching a fern on her nightstand. "My plants are
my children. Some have been with me for more than thirty years."

"You've got quite the green thumb."

She reached over and took my hand in hers. "Yes, that's what everyone says, but I often wonder what would have happened if your daddy
and I got married."

"Why didn't you?"

"You know, life gets in the way," she explained, pulling the bag onto
her lap. "We were so young. I stayed here to take care of my daddy, just
like you're doing. Dick moved to New York for a job. I'm sure you know
that's where he met your mother."

A pang of realization swept over me as I connected the dots. "You
could've been my mom."

"I could have," she acknowledged. "Your daddy and I had dreams of building a family together. I even waited for him to return after World War II."

My mind raced, recalling fragments of a conversation I'd had with Dad. Hadn't he mentioned a girl back home who waited for him while he served in the navy?

"So you were his sweetheart back home during the war?"

"Yes, I was his girl," Julia confirmed. From the bag she retrieved a delicate string of pearls, glistening in the soft light. "And he bought these home for me." With great care, she draped the pearls around my neck. "I want you to have them."

I ran my fingers over the necklace, in awe the elegant beauty of the pearls. But this was more than just a string of pearls—it represented a tangible symbol of the love story between Dad and Julia.

"These are beautiful," I said.

Julia reached back into the bag and pulled out a stunning black silk kimono.

"I want you to have this, too." Julia placed it over my shoulders. I ran my fingers across the silky fabric covered with colorful embroidery.

"It's beautiful. Are you sure?"

"I'm certain. I've been praying for the opportunity to give them to you."

I looked at her, smiling at me. It was as if she wanted to pass on a part of their shared history. The beautiful string of pearls and the colorful kimono felt like a connection to their past.

"Thank you," I whispered, my voice cracking. "I'll take good care of them."

"I know you will, just like you take good care of your daddy. I looked after my daddy in his last years right in this house." She looked around the room. "So I know how difficult it can be. You're a good girl." She kissed my cheek.

"I have to admit, my decision to oversee Dad's care was driven by a sense of selfishness on my part. I wanted to make up for all the trouble I'd caused during my teenage years."

"Oh, my dear, trouble is a part of growing up. Hormones running wild, navigating the complexities of life—it's a universal experience. Even your daddy caused his fair share of trouble," she reassured me.

"He did?"

"Yes, he did. But let me tell you something," Julia continued. "Your daddy loves you more than you can imagine, and he appreciates everything you're doing for him. Your presence, your care—those are the greatest gifts you can offer him. Never doubt the significance of your actions, my dear. You are making a difference in his life, just as he has made a difference in yours. Don't you ever forget that."

Julia enveloped me in an embrace. "Find solace in the knowledge that you are exactly where you need to be."

I felt a weight lift off my shoulders as her words sank in. I couldn't contain my tears. "I don't know why I'm so emotional. We just met but I feel like I've known you forever."

"Sometimes, the heart recognizes kindred spirits even in the briefest of encounters," Julia said. "We may have just met, but our connection runs deep. We share a bond through your daddy and the love we both hold for him."

With gratitude in my heart, I leaned into Julia's embrace, allowing her comforting presence to soothe me. Tears streamed down my face, but they were not sad tears—they were tears of release and healing. Just knowing that I'd found a confidant in Julia—someone who understood the complexities of love, family, and sacrifice—made me feel at peace.

"Even when everything around you feels like it's falling apart, God's love and mercy will not fail you. Never forget that."

Our moment of solace was interrupted by roaring laughter from the other room.

"We'd better get back to the party," she said, reaching into her pocket to retrieve a handkerchief. She gently wiped away my tears. "You go and clean up, then join us."

In the bathroom, I splashed cold water on my face. Taking a deep breath, I composed myself before returning to the living room. Dad motioned for me to pull up a chair next to him. And when I did, he immediately noticed my new pearl necklace.

"Where'd those come from?"

"You gave them to Julia when you returned from the war," I replied. "And she just gave them to me."

Dad's brows furrowed slightly as he tried to recall the memory.

Julia interjected. "Dick, why don't you sing us a song?"

"Yeah, Dad, sing 'Trees.'"

At the mention of his favorite song, a spark of recognition ignited in Dad's eyes. Dad straightened his posture, then filled the room with song, his perfect tenor voice infused with strength and clarity that wasn't there moments before.

"I think that I shall never see a poem as lovely as a tree."

I closed my eyes. Dad's voice breathed life into the familiar lyrics, momentarily eclipsing the ravages of Parkinson's. As the last note hung in the air, everyone clapped. Dad's Parkinson's mask disappeared for a moment as he reveled in the attention.

Dan came over and took a seat next to me. "I want to have a little heart-to-heart with you," he began. "You probably don't know, but I'm a caregiver too. My wife has diabetes. I know firsthand about caring for a loved one."

Finally, someone who could relate to my experiences.

Dan continued. "We must always be careful that the health of the caregiver is given prime consideration. I want to make sure you're taking care of yourself."

"You don't have to worry about me," I reassured him, feeling a rush of relief. The simple act of validating the struggles I faced meant the world to me.

Leaning in closer, Dan spoke with sincerity. "What most people don't consider is that the health and emotional well-being of a caregiver declines in greater proportion than that of the person they're caring for."

I nodded. "I've learned that the hard way."

"Don't do what your mother did and neglect yourself. Your daddy wouldn't want that. Promise me you won't make the same mistake."

"I promise."

The party carried on, and when nightfall descended, Julia signaled for me to return with her to the kitchen. She opened the refrigerator to unveil a homemade birthday cake. While we added the candles to the cake, I noticed a magnet on her fridge.

"People plan, God laughs," I read out loud. "I like that."

"Me too. It reminds me of Proverbs 3:5–6: 'Trust in the Lord with all your heart, and do not lean on your own understanding. In all your ways, acknowledge him, and he will make straight your paths.'"

Julia passed me a lighter, and I carefully lit each candle. Together, we returned to the living room, where a chorus of voices erupted into song.

"Happy birthday to you!"

"You remembered," Dad remarked before clapping his hands in Julia's direction.

"Make a wish," she encouraged him.

Dad looked around the room at his friends. "You're all here. What more could I wish for?"

The party ended and I headed to my room where the lingering scent of honeysuckle greeted me. Its delicate fragrance carried a profound message that night, reminding me of the complicated nature of love. Like the blooming flowers on a honeysuckle vine, love can be fragile and unpredictable, taking unexpected turns along the way. I reflected on the support I felt since arriving in Kansas City and came to the conclusion that love can enrich our lives in the most surprising ways.

24

Downward Dog

During our week-long stay in Kansas City, Jason and I made it a habit to explore Julia's neighborhood every evening. Just like me, Jason found the fireflies fascinating.

"Look at them," Jason exclaimed. "They're miniature lightshows."

"It's as if they carry a secret message from the stars themselves."

Julia took us to the Harry S. Truman Presidential Library and Museum. After we walked through the halls and perused the exhibits, we went outside to see the final resting place of the 33rd president. He had his loyal companion, a Scottie dog named Fala, buried right next to him. I could totally relate to an American president who chose to have his faithful dog buried by his side. But it did make me miss Baldwin.

On one particularly hot and humid afternoon, we all piled into Julia's car and made our way to the cemetery where my grandparents had been laid to rest.

The grandeur of the cemetery was accentuated by the majestic oak trees that dotted the sprawling, park-like landscape, casting some much-appreciated shade on the grounds. The towering oaks served as steadfast guardians of Gramps and Granny's eternal rest.

We strolled along the well-tended pathways, and when we reached the actual gravesite, I placed a bouquet of yellow roses on their adjacent burial markers. Dad and I stood there together, surrounded by the beauty of nature and the echoes of the past.

I confided in Julia, expressing my regret at not having the opportunity to truly know Gramps.

"After he passed, Dad made the decision to move Granny to a senior home in Northridge. During my twenties, I spent a lot of time with her."

Julia nodded empathetically. "Your granny had a nurturing presence that extended beyond her own family," she shared. "She was like a mother figure to all of us kids in the neighborhood."

Was she talking about my Granny? The woman I remembered was a broom-toting sourpuss. But now, the source of Granny's disdain toward

The Peace Puppy

Mom became perfectly clear. She harbored resentment toward Mom, a stranger, because she wanted her son to marry sweet Julia.

Standing there in front of Granny's grave, I vividly recalled an incident when the old bat went to great lengths to express her disapproval. In classic Granny style, during a summer visit to California when I was young, she called Dad at his office to tell him that Mom had a man over. It turned out to be nothing more than the washing machine repairman.

I had to give Mom credit for her remarkable compassion. Despite the disappointing relationship with her mother-in-law, Mom still took on the responsibility of caring for Granny during her final years. Mom rose above Granny's vindictive behavior and attempts to undermine her marriage.

Our trip to Dad's hometown came to a close and we found ourselves boarding the red eye for our journey back home. Coincidentally, we took off on the eve of Dad's actual birthday. I approached a friendly flight attendant and let her know about the birthday boy, hoping to make this celebration even more special.

Much to my surprise, in the wee hours of the morning as we neared LAX, an announcement rang out through the cabin inviting all passengers to join in singing happy birthday to Dad.

The unexpected burst of cheerful voices filling the plane was truly heartwarming. Passengers who were strangers joined together to create a collective chorus, sharing in the celebration of a life.

But it was the radiant smile on Dad's face that truly took my breath away. Despite his Parkinson's mask, the sheer joy and surprise that lit up his features made every sacrifice I'd made to move back home and care for him, feel immeasurably worthwhile.

The party continued after we landed. As passengers exited the plane, strangers passed us and offered birthday wishes to Dad, leaving behind a trail of kindness. We were the last to get off, and when we did, I felt an intense sense of gratitude, not only for the precious memories we made during our time in Kansas City but also for the power of simple gestures and genuine acts of kindness demonstrated by strangers.

Back at home, Baldwin couldn't contain his excitement when I entered the back door. In a single leap, he propelled himself into my arms, showering me with sloppy dog kisses.

"I missed you too, boy," I said. "Where's Molly?"

I headed to my room to wake up Jack. When he heard me, Jack

rolled over still asleep, which was not surprising since he was not a morning person, just like me.

While Jack got ready for the day, I continued my search for Molly the Collie. I knew Molly suffered some serious health conditions. Her incontinence never completely went away, and her mobility issues had significantly increased since we last took her to the vet.

Concern filled my heart as I searched for her in all her favorite places—the couch, Dad's bed, a comfy dog bed I'd bought her. She was nowhere in the house.

I headed outside and there in the backyard, under the shade of a blooming crepe myrtle, I found her lying there in the dirt. When she saw me coming, Molly mustered a feeble attempt to wag her tail.

"Poor Molly," I said. "Come on, girl. It's cookie time."

Her efforts to rise were in vain, mirroring the final struggles of my pound mutt Blondie, who'd passed away a few years prior at the age of nineteen. I still felt terrible about her last days, fearing that I let my heart lead the way instead of my head when it came time to say goodbye. I should have put her down a lot sooner than I did.

"I'll stay here with Baldwin," Jack said, wiping the sleep from his eyes.

I nodded in agreement, feeling a lump in my throat.

"Jason, you help Dad and I'll get Molly."

Once we got to the car, "I'm not going to let you suffer like I did Blondie," I whispered. "And I'm afraid it may be time to say goodbye."

Even though we were all exhausted from our trip, I gathered Dad, Jason, and even Jack, conveying the urgency of getting Molly to the vet. Jason helped me lift all sixty-five pounds of her into the backseat of my SUV.

I looked at Dad in the passenger seat. "The most compassionate thing we can do for Molly now is to let her go."

"Wait," Dad said, "put her down? Are you sure? She's been a part of our family for so long."

"Molly the Collie is a good dog," Jason added from the backseat where he sat holding Molly's head in his lap.

"I remember rescuing her from the pound," I said, my neck muscles tightening. "She was just a tiny puppy, barely made a sound."

Dad nodded. "That little white pup with the brown spots. We fell in love with her instantly."

"And she loved you too," I replied. "Who knows what would have happened to her if I didn't go to the pound that day."

Dad asked, "Is she in pain?"

The Peace Puppy

"You know, dogs hide their suffering, but I think it's safe to say yes, she is in pain. She's lost control of her bladder and now her back legs have given out."

"I ... I don't understand," Dad said. "Why is this happening?"

I looked at Molly in my rearview mirror, her breathing now shallow and labored.

"It's the circle of life, Dad." I fought back tears, thinking about the imminent loss of our sweet dog. The idea of losing Molly was terrible enough, but it also made me consider how I'd feel when Dad finally passed—and it didn't feel good. "You don't want her to suffer, do you?"

"No," Dad said. "She's been such a good dog."

I called from the car just as we pulled into the parking lot of the veterinarian's office. Before I even parked, that same vet tech met us holding a stretcher, ready to transport Molly the Collie inside. Jason assisted while I guided Dad into a private room where a blanket was laid out on the floor for Molly.

With heavy hearts and tear-filled eyes, we gathered around Molly. Dad sat on the seat of his rollator, while Jason and I knelt beside her on the floor.

The tall and lanky veterinarian entered and explained the process. "Molly's final moments will be peaceful and dignified."

Before he left the room, Dad asked, "Can't we do something to help her?"

"I can see how difficult this decision is for you," the vet said, "and I want you to know that I understand. It's never easy to say goodbye."

I nodded. "She's had a good life. You don't want to let her suffer in the end."

The veterinarian continued, "I want you to take your time in making this decision. It's important to consider your dog's quality of life and the discomfort she's experiencing."

After he excused himself, I noticed a distressing sign of Molly's declining health—foam began to form around her mouth.

"Dad," I whispered, my voice trembling, "I think it's time."

"Your mom always gave her fresh turkey. It had to be fresh."

"Well, then, I'm sure Mom will be there waiting on the other side with turkey for her."

After what felt like hours, the veterinarian returned.

"Are you ready to move forward?"

Dad nodded, reaching out for a final pet.

"Go be with Mom," I whispered softly as the veterinarian administered a sedative.

"This will ensure that she feels no pain or distress. She's just going to peacefully drift into a deep sleep."

No words were exchanged when the final injection was administered, but a heavy ache settled in my heart. We stayed in that room with Molly the Collie, providing comfort even after her breathing gradually ceased. She left the room filled with her love.

The journey home, and home itself, felt empty without her presence, but the legacy of her love would forever be etched in our hearts.

That Monday evening, just as I was preparing Baldwin's dinner, the phone rang.

"Hello?"

It was Angel, her voice filled with excitement. "Darling, I'm coming to town tomorrow. Percy's landed herself a real gig," she boasted. "She's headlining at the Roxy tomorrow night." Percy was Angel's struggling-musician daughter. Her other daughter, Pressley, worked behind the scenes in Hollywood.

The significance of this accomplishment didn't escape me. Headlining at a renowned venue like the Roxy was a remarkable achievement.

"Headlining? Looks like you've got another star in the family."

"My little musician," she gushed. "I am beyond proud of her."

"I don't blame you."

"Percy's hard work is finally paying off," Angel added.

"Is Bede coming?"

"No, he's headed back to Jamaica. I'll meet up with him later."

"Oh, too bad. But at least I'll see him at Thanksgiving. That's only a few months away."

I hung up and finished preparing Baldwin's dinner, reflecting on the conversation I'd just had with Angel. The thought of my own family relationships, which had been tenuous and distant for some time, weighed heavy on my mind.

That's when I recalled the epiphany I'd had after the big Hollywood party. Instead of allowing myself to dwell on the past, I made a conscious decision to shift my focus toward gratitude. How fortunate was I to be invited to witness Percy's first step on her way to making her mark in the music industry? And there was more to be grateful for—Angel's visit. As I bent down to give Baldwin his dinner, I was reminded of one more thing I needed to be grateful for—my fluff ball of a dog, Baldwin.

25

Ruff Skies Ahead

To this day, I still vividly remember my dream from that night. It centered on Angel and seemed so real that it blurred the lines between the waking world and the realm of sleep.

In the dream, Angel orchestrated a grand gesture to liberate me from my everyday responsibilities by sending a stretch limo to pick up me and Baldwin and whisk us away.

We drove for quite a while, through bucolic rolling hills and red-wood forests, along the coast and on mountaintops. Finally, the limo dropped us off at a beautiful adobe compound that Angel had constructed, complete with a room for me.

The sight was nothing short of breathtaking—a horseshoe-shaped Spanish structure stood against a backdrop of snow-capped mountains, while colorful wildflowers grew everywhere. The sun was setting when we got out of the car, painting the sky with shades of buttery yellow, crimson, amethyst, aqua and green.

While Angel herself was absent from the scene, her presence lingered in the air. It was as if her essence guided me to the special room that she'd created just for me. With Baldwin faithfully following, I ascended the stairs and found the door, my hand trembling as I turned the knob.

Natural light filled the space, casting a glow that highlighted the room's centerpiece—the bed. Positioned in the center of the room, it beckoned with an irresistible allure. I touched the Ralph Lauren floral comforter, noting that it was crafted from the finest cotton. Without hesitation, Baldwin leaped onto the bed and rolled over, his feet kicking in the air.

I laughed, then looked around. "She decorated in my favorite colors," I said, noticing the soothing pale blues mixed with warm earthy browns.

After his playful wiggling subsided, Baldwin circled his designated spot on the bed, settling down with a contented sigh. I looked up to a remarkable sight—a ceiling made entirely of glass.

"How'd she know?" I questioned. "I've always wanted to drift off to sleep counting the stars."

I was startled awake by the sound of a neighbor's noisy rooster with his distinctive crow.

I rubbed my eyes, my mind stuck in a hazy fog. I rolled over and remembered my dream—every single detail came back to me. Oh, how I wished I could've stayed in the sanctuary of Angel's oasis. When Baldwin entered my room with his frisbee in his month, I reluctantly got out of bed.

"It's eight already?" Baldwin looked up and circled the room with that disc in his mouth. "OK, I get it. Frisbee time."

At the mention of the f-word, Baldwin herded me to the backyard.

Mindlessly tossing the frisbee into the crisp morning air gave me the space I needed to consider the meaning of my dream. Perhaps it was a message from my subconscious, urging me to pay attention to something important. On the other hand, it could be a simple reminder of the plans I had for that evening. I was looking forward to seeing my dear friend, and my excitement might have manifested in a dream. Whatever it meant, I needed my morning coffee.

I stumbled back inside through the den in search of my keys, my mind still in a cloud. Not even the blaring voices of Dad's always-on CNN could penetrate the fog.

A chilling video of a plane crashing into the World Trade Center caught my attention. The horrific scene unfolded before my eyes, prompting me to gasp, my hand instinctively rising to cover my mouth in shock and disbelief.

I looked over at Dad. An unfamiliar smile came across Dad's Parkinson's mask as if he were watching a lighthearted episode of his all-time favorite program, *The Benny Hill Show*. His expression seemed detached from the gravity of the situation, as though real-world events failed to register.

I contemplated the disparity between our reactions. Dad's demeanor hinted at a disconnect, a manifestation of his illness leaving behind a distorted lens through which he viewed the world.

"I'm so glad I don't know anyone who's flying today," I told Dad.

"Me neither," Dad responded with that silly grin still on his face.

The truth was I did know someone who was flying that day. Angel.

Her flight left from Boston that morning. A wall of denial replaced the fog in my brain. I needed to keep Angel safe, at least in my mind.

I grabbed my purse and keys, Baldwin hopped in the car, and we headed to Starbucks for my morning caffeine fix. My favorite barista had my drink ready by the time I reached the front of the line.

He asked, "Did you hear what happened?"

"You mean the plane crash?"

"Not one crash," he said. "Two planes deliberately flew into the World Trade Center. They're talking terrorism."

His words struck me like a dagger, puncturing the bubble of denial I'd created to shield myself from the harsh reality.

"Shit. Shit," I muttered through gritted teeth. "Not Angel. She couldn't have been on one of those planes."

My words were a desperate plea to the universe. The mere thought of Angel being on one of the ill-fated flights was unbearable.

I pulled in the driveway and, with a sense of urgency, and as soon as I put the car in park, Baldwin and I sprinted into the house. The blaring sound of CNN greeted us as we burst into the den; its relentless coverage of the unfolding events filled the room.

That's when Dad's voice pierced through the chaotic noise.

"I want to go home," he bellowed.

I tried to steady myself, torn between the tv and Dad's demand.

"Not now, Dad," I pleaded.

"Yes, now. I've been waiting for you all morning."

"Shh," I urged, my focus fixed on the television screen. "I need to hear where the planes originated from."

For the first time since I had moved back home, Dad's crazy demands faded into the background, replaced by a somber realization. Like a chilling echo, the newscaster's voice revealed the origin of the first plane—Boston. My heart sank. The world around me spun out of control.

"No, no, no," I screamed.

I knew in my core that Angel had boarded that plane. With weakened knees, I reached out to Dad for support.

"Angel was on that plane," I cried.

My legs gave way, and I slowly sank to the floor. Baldwin came over and positioned himself across my lap, just like he did with that little cancer patient on his first therapy dog visit.

Then I remembered the dream, so vivid and real. I flashed on a Bible verse, John 14:2: "In my Father's house, there are many rooms. I shall prepare a place for you." Had Angel shown me a slice of heaven?

Angel. My rock, my north star, my person for the last two decades. The mere thought of a world without her sent a shiver down my spine.

Driven by a mixture of hope and desperation, I made my way to Angel's home in the Hollywood Hills. When I arrived, I found myself part of a somber gathering, a collective of Angel's family and friends.

Together, we formed a vigil, hoping for Angel's presence to manifest before us. Maybe, just maybe, she hadn't boarded that flight. Perhaps she was caught in a twist of fate, stranded at the airport. Or maybe she was still safe at her home in Cape Cod. But any hope we had was dashed when the airline called that evening to deliver the bad news.

We all knew the truth when Pressley, Angel's daughter, screamed and dropped the phone. Angel would not be coming home.

My dear friend perished that morning on American Airlines flight 11 along with the other passengers and crew members when the jet crashed into the North Tower of the World Trade Center. She occupied seat A in row 19. I would never see her again.

The events of September 11 left an indelible mark on the world. Thousands of lives were lost. For me, the heartache was particularly acute—I lost a dear friend.

In the years since 9/11, I've learned to cherish my memories of Angel. I remember the time we spent exploring New York City together, lighting candles inside every church, the sound of her laughter and the warmth of her hugs. And I remember her unwavering optimism and belief in the goodness of people and, of course, her love of dogs.

A few weeks after the tragedy, Jack announced his plans to head to New York and volunteer at the crash site.

"Keep an eye out for Angel's gold ring," I told him, "the one with the cross on it."

To this day, I can't fathom why that specific piece of jewelry popped into my head. Angel dripped in jewelry from head to toe with rings on almost every finger. I could have told Jack to search for any number of rings or even bracelets or necklaces, yet that gold cross ring held a symbolic significance in my mind.

Jack returned not long after he left. His mission to volunteer didn't pan out, and he ended up coming home with firsthand accounts of the distressing aftermath of 9/11. As Jack described it, the atmosphere, heavy with dust and the pungent odor of devastation, was made even worse by the echoing sound of emergency sirens. The absence of the Twin Towers, once a defining feature of the city's iconic skyline, created a haunting void that altered the visual landscape.

The Peace Puppy

Months later, Jack called to tell me about an article in *People*. "The story is about all the items they discovered at ground zero," he explained. "You'll never believe what they found."

I wasted no time getting a copy for myself. And to my astonishment, among the prominently displayed items was the very ring I'd asked Jack to find.

"What do you think it means?" I asked Jack.

"I don't know but it's definitely a message to you from Angel."

After the terrorist attack, American flags popped up everywhere. According to the U.S. Census Bureau, Americans spent more than fifty million dollars on American flags in the United States that year. (The previous year, the figure was around seventy-five thousand dollars.) There were flags flying everywhere and each one reminded me of the last time I saw Angel when she accompanied Baldwin and me on a therapy dog visit to the children at LA-County USC. After 9/11, I dragged around an eight-by-ten picture taken that day of Angel holding three flags, a gigantic smile on her face.

A few days later, when I parked my car on Ventura Boulevard, a glimmer of red, white, and blue caught my eye. There it was, a tiny American flag, like the ones Angel held in that picture. It seemed as if it was waiting for me there in the gutter, a subtle reminder of Angel's presence.

I reached down, picked up the flag, brushed it off and held it in front of me. "I see you, Angel."

To my surprise, I found another small American flag on my front lawn when I pulled into my driveway. I picked that one up too, then looked up to the heavens and said, "I hear you, my friend."

Days passed, and I tried my best to get back into life's steady rhythm. Driving along the 405 freeway lost in my own thoughts, a third flag flew across my windshield. It was a fleeting moment, but its significance was not lost on me. Angel had three flags in her hand in that picture.

"That was you, right?" I held tight to the steering wheel. "I get it, Angel. You're flagging me down. Message received."

26

Paws for Concern

It was impossible to grieve over the loss of Angel due to my never-ending responsibilities. But I had to keep going. Dad needed me. And my business needed me too. Kat and I found ourselves busier than ever and our constantly growing list of clients deserved my best efforts.

Among the notable additions was the prestigious Camelback Inn, a renowned luxury resort nestled in the Sonoran Desert in Paradise Valley, Arizona. I couldn't wait to take travel writers there and experience the resort's indulgent amenities. And I didn't have to wait long. Another media FAM was on the horizon.

Lucky for me, Kat's unwavering support extended beyond professional matters. As usual, she stepped into the role of overseeing Dad's care when I was away on business. And this time, I was headed to my first meeting at Camelback Inn for the day. The meeting went well and when I returned Kat eagerly approached me with a story.

"Your dad," she began, a smile lighting up her face, "he spent the entire afternoon in the company of—wait for it—George Washington, Cleopatra, and Albert Einstein."

"Where did that hallucination come from?"

Kat shrugged. "I have no idea. But when I went in to check on him, I found him sitting in his red chair clapping. Apparently, his new 'friends' had just finished a tap dance performance."

"George Washington tap dancing?"

"Yup," Kat said nodding her head. "With his good buddies Cleo and Albert. All wearing top hats."

"Well, I've got to hand it to him. This one's a doozy. At least he didn't try to grab anyone's boobs like he did with that massage therapist."

Kat laughed and added, "And no demonic squirrels either."

It seemed that, once again, Parkinson's had taken Dad on another trip. I was happy that his latest illusion brought him a little bit of happiness, even if the experience existed solely in his mind.

The Peace Puppy

While I found Dad's hallucinations sad, I knew I had to accept things the way they were. Besides, I had to immerse myself in the task of organizing yet another media FAM.

I'd secured eight highly regarded travel writers to join me at Camelback Inn, including freelancers who contributed to well-known publications like *Travel + Leisure* magazine and the *LA Times*.

Kat and I crafted an itinerary that surpassed all expectations. These fortunate journalists from across the United States were in for the opportunity of a lifetime. After landing at Phoenix Sky Harbor International Airport, these celebrated writers would immerse themselves in the wonders of Camelback Inn.

They'd savor the culinary delights offered by Camelback Inn's fabulous restaurants, meet the executive chef and master sommelier, and indulge in luxurious spa treatments at the world-renowned spa.

We carved out time for them to enjoy the resort's amenities, including multiple swimming pools, a fitness center, tennis courts, a world-class golf course and more. Additionally, guided hikes, golf and tennis lessons, and relaxing poolside yoga sessions were all on the itinerary.

The week before the trip, I called all the journalists to book their spa treatments.

One of them asked, "Does the spa offer those fish pedicures?"

"I'm sorry, fish pedicure?"

"Yes," she said. "They're all the rage. You soak your feet with flesh-eating fish. They say it's a great way to soften calluses and increase circulation."

"Sounds interesting but Camelback doesn't have anything like that. They do have a bindi ayurvedic herbal body nourishment treatment that I think you'd like. No fish involved but your whole body will be exfoliated. Would you like to try that?"

"I guess so," she answered. "I was really hoping to try something new."

As I hung up, Kat answered an incoming call, and I overheard her discussing spa treatments with another reporter.

I heard her say, "No, the resort doesn't offer snake massages." She finished the call, then turned to me and asked, "What's with all these peculiar questions about spa treatments?"

"You know how the media is, always eager to experience something unique."

"I guess it's their job to read up on the topic and know about the latest treatments," she added.

"Exactly, but who'd want a snake massage? Not me. I hate snakes."

"Me too," Kat agreed. "Along with sharks and alligators. I'm surprised no one has created a spa treatment incorporating shark teeth."

The much-anticipated day finally arrived, and I found myself packed and ready to go. Baldwin made his best attempt to accompany me on the trip, seated on top of my suitcase on the morning that I had to leave. I managed to divert his attention with a yummy bully stick. Yes, once again, a bully stick to the rescue! I was so glad I found these treats, even though they smelled nasty. Unlike a rawhide, these treats were safe to give unsupervised without the risk of choking. Large pieces of rawhide can get stuck in the esophagus or other parts of the digestive tract. They can even get stuck in a dog's throat and cause them to suffocate.

With Baldwin content and occupied, I proceeded to drive myself to Burbank airport, where I entrusted my car to the valet service.

After checking in and successfully passing through security, I made my way to the designated gate. I sat there waiting to board when I heard my name being called on the airport intercom system. I approached an attendant to find out what was going on.

The attendant responded matter-of-factly, as if this was a common occurrence, saying, "You probably forgot to leave your keys with the valet."

I looked and found my keys still in my purse. Acknowledging my oversight, I ran back to the airport entrance and promptly handed them over to the valet.

Having resolved that issue, I went through the boarding process once again. Following the standard security procedures that I'd just completed moments ago, I once again removed my shoes and placed them in the designated bin. I positioned my laptop and other personal items on the conveyor belt for X-ray screening. And this time, I was selected for an additional body search.

Feeling flustered and anxious, I urgently pleaded with the security agent, "Can you please hurry? I don't want to miss my flight."

The Peace Puppy

It seemed that my request fell on deaf ears since my question was met with silence. The security agent, undoubtedly accustomed to similar requests, proceeded with her protocol, using a handheld wand to check me before conducting a thorough pat-down with her hands.

Throughout the process, I kept a close eye on my watch. Each passing second brought me closer to departure time, leaving little margin for delay. She finally completed her security screening, and I ran all the way back to my gate. Fortunately, I arrived just in time.

When the plane took off, my thoughts turned to Angel. I imagined her in the air without a care in the world. Her youngest daughter was performing later that night. Little did she know that the very flight she was on would be hijacked by five terrorists.

It's believed that the terrorists forcefully took control of Flight 11's cockpit, holding the passengers and crew members captive in the back of the economy cabin. There are reports that some individuals on board managed to use their cell phones to make calls, reaching out to their loved ones and authorities. Unfortunately, Angel didn't have a cell phone.

Did Angel witness the flight attendant that was reportedly stabbed? She certainly followed the hijackers' demands and moved to the rear of the aircraft.

I'd heard the terrible news that there was an infant onboard. Knowing Angel's affection for babies, I envisioned her, in her final moments, comforting that baby, a testament to her loving nature even in the face of unimaginable circumstances.

When the plane touched down, I gathered my thoughts and mentally prepared for the interactions with the media. The ride to the resort was quick and when I reached my destination, I was immediately captivated by the stunning Southwestern architectural style which blended harmoniously with the desert. The sprawling property, nestled against the backdrop of Camelback Mountain, showcased a timeless charm.

Stepping into my room, I felt a profound sense of awe. The floor to ceiling window in front of me framed the Sonoran Desert stretched out in all its grandeur—as far as the eye could see.

Towering cacti stood proudly; their unique shapes added to the allure of the scene. Wildflowers speckled the terrain, painting the desert floor with splashes of color. The sunlight danced on the landscape, casting mesmerizing shadows that accentuated the contours of the desert. Majestic rock formations emerged seemingly out of nowhere.

26. Paws for Concern

As much as I longed to stay in the comfort of my room looking out that window, the time came for me to meet the important media guests I'd invited. But I had something to do before joining the group at the resort's Lincoln Steakhouse for dinner. I needed to call home and check on Baldwin and Dad.

Jason answered and said, "Baldwin is fine. But your dad is at the hospital."

My heart sank. "What? Dad's in the hospital again? Why didn't you call me immediately?"

Jason hesitated for a moment before responding, "Will told me not to call you."

I ended the call with Jason and immediately dialed Will's number. "Why is Dad in the hospital?"

"It's nothing," he said dismissively. "I'm taking care of it."

I pressed further. "But why is he there? What happened?"

"He just has a little urinary tract infection. I'm sure he'll be back home before your trip ends."

"Please keep me in the loop. I'm worried about him."

"Don't worry; he's fine."

Something about the situation didn't sit right with me. Why would a urinary tract infection require a trip to the hospital? I couldn't shake the feeling that there was more to the story.

Despite my worries, I had to get to the fancy dinner stat. Putting my concerns aside, I pasted on my smile and headed to the restaurant.

At the Lincoln Steakhouse, I was greeted by Laura, a freelance travel writer I'd never met before. Laura, a rather sizeable woman, was waiting at the upscale restaurant wearing a terry cloth robe, her hair dripping like she'd just gotten out of the shower.

"I just had the most amazing massage," she said, showing no sign of apology for her attire.

"I'm so glad to hear that," I said. "Please, sit wherever you want."

I turned back toward the door and was pleasantly surprised to see my friend Susan approach. Susan, the journalist who took me to the party at Paramount Studios, had put great effort into her appearance for the first night's dinner, showcasing her impeccable sense of style.

Dressed in a stunning dress that accentuated her figure, Susan looked effortlessly chic. The garment hugged her body in all the right places.

"Here's my party pal!"

The Peace Puppy

"Hey, nice to see you," she said. "Let's sit together."

"Sounds like a plan to me."

The rest of the travel journalists showed up within minutes, ready to devour a delicious five-course meal. I sat back, content that the FAM was already off to a good start. Did I count my blessings too soon?

27

Peace, Love and Belly Rubs

There's usually at least one journalist on a FAM who creates problems for everyone else, especially me. Rarely have I seen a group of travel writers forge real bonds on a familiarization trip, but this particular group defied the odds. Even Laura with her questionable attire turned out to be a complete delight.

I was surprised to see the writers continue their revelry after the welcome dinner ended. Even the renowned executive chef, a true artist in his own right, joined the afterparty.

As the night progressed, I found myself appreciating the company of every member of this group of travel writers, just like I did in the old days before Mom died. Yet I couldn't shake my worries about Dad. Why was he in the hospital? The thought tugged at me, threatening to dampen the evening. I stayed, though, telling myself there was nothing I could do at that hour anyway. In the wee hours of the morning, we all said our goodbyes and headed to our rooms.

I woke up the next morning with a slight pang in my head reminding me of the previous night's indulgence. I'd woken up later than I wanted and I found myself nursing a bit of a hangover. I'd wanted to call the hospital before meeting the media. But now I didn't have time.

Breakfast was being served at Rita's Cantina, the restaurant's spacious outdoor patio. On my way there, a gentle breeze caressed my face. I had a feeling this was going to be an excellent day.

Stepping into the restaurant, I was greeted by warm sunlight casting its golden rays on the well-appointed tables. It was a sight to behold. But what truly took me by surprise was the presence of every single media person. Yes, they were all there waiting for me to arrive. Now this was a rare (and much appreciated) occurrence on a FAM trip, where at least one journalist showed up late or even missed meals or events, requiring me to track them down.

The Peace Puppy

When it comes to a media trip, the property covers all expenses in order to give journalists a firsthand experience and the journalists will hopefully provide positive coverage afterward. For its time and money, a property expects to receive publicity. It's always frustrating when journalists don't show up at a function and cause concern for those who are paying the bill.

However, this group seemed to understand the value of their presence, which made my job easier. I couldn't have asked for a better group of professionals to work with, especially when I understood the topic of conversation that morning—dogs.

"Now I know why you're such a remarkable group," I said. "You're all dog lovers."

The comment was met with laughter and nods of agreement.

The other Susan pulled out a picture of her blue merle Australian Shepherd.

"This is my boy Calvin," she told the group.

Laura took a look and commented, "Of course you have a beautiful dog like that, with your long legs and blue eyes. The two of you could walk the catwalk together."

"That should be the dog walk," another journalist chimed in.

One writer added, "I love my dog so much, I think she's my child."

"I get that," I said half seriously. "I believe I did give birth to Baldwin."

Susan asked, "There's something special about dogs, isn't there? They have this amazing ability to bring people together. It's no wonder they hold such a special place in our hearts."

Everyone nodded, continuing to share their own stories about their dogs. The topic filled the room with a collective warmth and shared appreciation for the incredible bond between humans and dogs.

After breakfast, the itinerary called for some free time to explore the property until we met again for lunch. I told them I had some work to do and bid my adieu. The work—to call the hospital about Dad.

"Good morning, Northridge Hospital," a friendly voice answered.

"I'm calling about my dad," I stated, my voice filled with apprehension.

"Room number, please."

"I'm sorry, I don't have his room number. He was admitted yesterday. His name is Dick Hartzler. Can you look it up for me?"

"Yes, yes, just a moment, please." The person placed me on hold.

Every ticking moment intensified my guilt. Here I was relishing the luxuries of a top-tier resort while Dad languished in the hospital.

Finally, the person returned and informed me, "Looks like he's in the ICU. There are no phones in the rooms on that floor."

My heart sank at the mention of the intensive care unit.

"The ICU? Why is he in the ICU?" I asked, my voice trembling.

"That, I cannot tell you. Do you want to be connected to the nurse's station?"

"Yes, please."

I waited anxiously as the call was transferred. As soon as a new voice greeted me, I introduced myself, expressing my concerns about Dad.

"He was admitted with a urinary tract infection," she explained. "I don't know much more than that. Would you like for me to leave a message for his doctor to call you?"

"Yes, as soon as possible, please."

I took a moment to process the information I'd received and consider what to do next. Should I leave the FAM and head home? Could this time be the end? Was there anything I could do back home that I couldn't do from here? My mind was swimming. I put my head in my hands and decided the first step would be to call Kat.

"Hartzler Public Relations," Kat answered.

"Do you know why my dad's in the ICU again?"

"I was wondering where everyone was when I arrived this morning. Why's he in the ICU?"

"I was hoping you would know. Will told me he was taken to the hospital yesterday but said it wasn't anything serious."

Kat's voice softened. "Oh, Sue, not again. I'm so sorry to hear that. What are you going to do?"

I paused, contemplating the best course of action. "That's a good question. Should I leave? I mean, my presence alone wouldn't necessarily change the course of his treatment. But I feel like I should be there as his advocate."

Kat acknowledged the validity of my point and raised an important consideration. "True, but if you do leave, who would be the point person for the media? It might be hard to find a suitable replacement at such short notice."

Her words struck a chord in me. I understood that leaving the FAM trip abruptly could create a logistical nightmare and affect any resulting media coverage. The responsibility of overseeing the journalists and maintaining the flow of communication with the resort would be left unattended.

Taking a deep breath, I contemplated the options. "Maybe you could come and take over?" I asked.

Kat thought for a moment. "Of course, I can do that for you. I'll catch the next flight."

My phone beeped, letting me know I had another call. "Thanks, Kat. I think the doctor's on the other line."

Sure enough, it was the doctor. "Your dad's condition has deteriorated," he told me. "I'm afraid his UTI has turned into sepsis."

"What's sepsis"

"Sepsis is a critical medical emergency wherein the body's immune system responds excessively to an infection, posing a life-threatening situation."

"So, you're saying my Dad could die?"

"I'm saying it is a real possibility."

"I'm in Arizona for work."

"Well, I suggest you get here as soon as you can."

I hung up, updated my return flight, and let the relevant parties at the resort know about the change. Then I packed my things and called the concierge to gather my luggage. I'd say my goodbyes to the group at lunch.

I headed to the spa restaurant with a pit in my stomach. I wouldn't get a chance to try the healthy alternatives served poolside but, then again, I wasn't hungry.

Once everyone was seated, I gently tapped my water glass with a spoon to get everyone's attention.

Clearing my throat, I began, "Thank you all for being on time again. I have something important to share with you."

I looked around the table at my new friends; their expressions ranged from curiosity to concern.

I steadied myself and continued. "I've just received news about my dad and I'm sorry to say I have to leave." My news was met with gasps.

"I want to express my sincere appreciation for each and every one of you. Your professionalism, understanding, and friendship mean the world to me. My associate Kat will be your point person. She's catching a flight as I speak. You're going to love her, I promise."

I raised my glass for a toast. "Here's to the best travel writers on the planet—and fellow dog lovers!"

Before leaving, I exchanged hugs, handshakes, and words of encouragement, soaking in the group's support. The journey back home held many unknowns, but I knew I needed to be there for Dad. Oh, and there was a silver lining—I'd get to hug Baldwin.

When I changed my ticket at the last minute, it meant I was on stand-by. I sat in front of the gate, twirling my hair and biting my fingernails. At the eleventh hour, I managed to secure a seat. Maybe he'd make it through this. As the plane soared through the skies, my mind fixated on Dad. I had to laugh to myself when the Energizer Bunny came to mind. He keeps going and going.

Once the plane touched down, I swiftly retrieved my car from the valet, setting a record for speed. Rather than heading home, I steered directly toward the hospital. But I didn't get very far due to the rush hour traffic.

It took me well over two hours to reach the hospital, something that should have taken no more than half an hour. I parked my car and stepped out, my mind a jumbled mess. Few things are as agonizing as being trapped in traffic when a potential life-or-death situation awaits you at your intended arrival point.

The cool evening breeze gave me chills after being in the desert. I made my way to the ICU where Dad was once again unconscious, surrounded by a labyrinth of machines that served as his lifeline. The beeping and whirring sounds filled the air, a constant reminder of his fragile state.

I met with the doctor on call that night. In his crisp white coat, he delivered news that shook me to the core.

"How'd my dad get so sick?" I asked. "I thought he had a UTI."

The doctor sighed. "He did have a urinary tract infection, but unfortunately, it has triggered a chain reaction in his body. He's in septic shock. The infection has spread into his bloodstream." He touched my shoulder. "It's a severe and life-threatening condition."

"Is he going to die?"

"I'd say you need to get his affairs in order."

I stood there stunned. He couldn't be talking about the Energizer Bunny.

"But whatever you do, don't bring your brother back here. He caused quite a commotion yesterday when he came to check on your dad."

"What happened?"

"I don't know how it started but the situation escalated to the point where security was called."

"Poor Will," I muttered. "You can't blame him for losing it. That's his dad."

The doctor confided in me that the incident left the entire ICU staff on edge, fearing the repercussions like a nasty lawsuit. The very notion of honoring Dad's DNR (do not resuscitate) order had suddenly become a delicate matter, entangled with legal uncertainties.

"I understand."

I was well aware that Will struggled to convey his emotions, a fact I'd closely observed after Mom's passing. When I contemplated his emotions in the face of the inevitable loss of our dad, I couldn't help but imagine the storm of emotions raging within him. I understood the reality—he was struggling to say goodbye.

I watched the doctor walk away and pulled up a chair next to Dad's bed. It was going to be a long night.

28

Keep Calm
and Love Your Dog

"Listen, Dad," I told him, "I know you're holding on for your son. But you don't have to do that any longer. It's true, he's having a hard time, but I promise I will look after him for you. You have my word."

After his last hospital stay, I'd jotted down some sentiments I wanted to convey before Dad departed from this world. Ever since then, I'd carried that folded piece of paper in my purse, praying that I wouldn't have to use it anytime soon. But in the hushed ambiance of the hospital that night, I knew the time had come.

I retrieved the crumpled paper from my purse. Clutching it tightly in my trembling hands, I steeled myself for the emotional challenge of sharing my most intimate thoughts with him, realizing that this might indeed be the last opportunity to do so.

I gazed down at my notes and, with a quivering voice, began to read aloud. "I want you to know that you've been an incredible father, but now it's time to go with Mom. She's patiently awaiting your arrival in heaven, just as Siesta and Molly the Collie, and all the other dogs you loved, are. They'll all be wagging their tails to greet you."

Tears flowed down my cheeks, landing on Dad's hospital gown. I watched them mingle with the worn fabric, bearing witness to my profound love and sorrow.

I took his hand in mine and noticed it was swollen and black and blue from numerous blood draws. "Dad, I want you to know that I will carry your legacy with me always. Your kindness, compassion, and unwavering spirit will always inspire me."

I leaned in and placed a gentle kiss on Dad's hand, a silent plea for connection, as if etching my devotion onto his skin.

"It's okay to leave this earth. You've fought a good fight, but now it's time for you to find peace with Mom. Know that you will never be

209

forgotten and that the impact you've made on my life, and the lives of those around you, will live on."

His body remained motionless and fragile, his presence overshadowed by the symphony of beeping monitors and the rhythmic hum of machines. Each beep and whir echoed through the sterile space.

"Thank you, Dad, for being the greatest father I could have ever asked for. Rest now. Until we meet again."

I put my head on his chest, releasing a torrent of tears. When I looked up, his nurse had entered the room. She was stunningly beautiful with her long, sleek black hair pulled back into a ponytail, accentuating her gracefully contoured cheekbones and porcelain complexion. I noticed the name tag on her light blue scrubs—Cinderella. For a fleeting moment, I questioned my own reality.

"Cinderella," I said shaking my head in disbelief. "Is that really your name?"

With a gentle smile, she responded, "Yes, it is."

Immediately regretting my initial reaction, I apologized. "I'm sorry, I didn't mean to be rude."

"No worries," she replied, shifting her attention to Dad's vitals. "I get asked about my name all the time. And I assure you, there are no evil stepsisters in my life."

"How about a fairy godmother?"

Her laughter momentarily lightened my spirit. Here I sat, in the solemn presence of Dad's possible death, engaged in conversation with a nurse named Cinderella. It was as if the boundaries between reality and imagination had blurred, casting an otherworldly glow over the moment. I wondered if this encounter held a deeper meaning or if it was merely a coincidence. Maybe Mom had something to do with it. It would be just like her to add a little levity to the situation.

By the time nine o'clock rolled around, the exhaustion of a long and eventful day began to take its toll on me. From an early morning media breakfast to a final deathbed conversation, my body and mind were weary. I was about to leave when suddenly Dad forcefully pulled his hand away from mine.

In that moment, I felt a flicker of hope, the possibility of the return of the Energizer Bunny. However, my elation turned into concern when he pointed toward the door, a desperate plea for help that reverberated with a haunting urgency.

With a pounding heart, I rushed to the nursing station in search of

Cinderella. She sat in front of a computer. Just another day in the life of a nurse.

Panic and fear fueled my words as I pleaded, "Can you give him something to ease his pain?"

Cinderella responded, "I just administered morphine."

"Well, it's not working. Can you give him more?"

"I'll ask the doctor."

The weight of the situation pressed on me when I reentered his room, the air now thick with hopelessness. Dad's condition had worsened considerably in the little time it took for me to travel to and from the nurses' station. His breath now resembled a haunting death rattle, and each labored inhalation sent my heart pounding with dread.

"They wouldn't let a dog suffer like this," I whispered.

He kept pointing at the door. In a moment of overwhelming anguish, I grabbed a pillow and a flicker of an unthinkable act crossed my mind.

"I'm not going to let you suffer." I hugged the pillow tightly, then hesitated, my hands trembling. "I could end up in jail." I released my grip on the pillow, letting it fall to the floor, and I backed out of Dad's room.

I quickly made my way down the corridor of the ICU. Once inside the safe cocoon of the elevator, I did my best to steady my racing heart. I pressed the button for the ground floor and noticed the soft hum of the elevator's machinery. It was oddly soothing, a brief respite from the emotional turmoil I'd just experienced.

The elevator chimed softly, signaling my arrival on the ground floor. Exiting the hospital doors, I tried to outrun the sterile hospital smell that clung to me. Inside the sanctuary of my car, I allowed myself to scream.

"I'm not ready!" I hit the steering wheel, "I'm not ready!" The road stretched out before me; the passing scenery blurred by my tears. I needed Baldwin—my ultimate comfort. I craved him now more than ever.

I pulled into the driveway without fully registering the drive. Entering the back door, I saw him—my Baldwin.

Sensing my distress, the fluff ball greeted me in his own unique way. With his stump of a tail wagging and a mischievous glint in his eyes, he bounded toward me. I knelt to embrace him, his warmth and unconditional love wrapping around me like a soothing balm. He wiggled in my arms, desperate to take away my worries.

"Okay, okay, boy," I said, letting him bathe me with his sweet puppy kisses.

I drifted off to sleep with Baldwin, his comforting presence beside me providing a sense of security that I sorely needed. His gentle snores harmonized with the steady rhythm of my breath.

In the realm of dreams, I found myself standing in the backyard of our family home, bathed in a warm, ethereal light. Before me, my little cupcake of a mom stood with an air of unwavering confidence, her hands placed firmly on her hips.

"Now, Susan, stop worrying. I'm taking care of everything, including your Dad's suffering."

In that moment, it was as if Mom's spirit had connected with mine, bridging the gap between the living and the dead. The phone's piercing ring brought me out of my slumber. I hastily reached for the receiver, bracing myself for what could only be bad news at three in the morning.

I brought the phone to my ear and uttered a hesitant "Hello?"

"Your father is struggling to breathe. Should we perform any heroic measures?"

"No," I replied, my voice resolute and steady. "He signed a DNR order."

It was a choice he'd made, a choice that I'd promised to honor. I knew that by adhering to his wishes, I was relinquishing any chance of prolonging his life. But I also knew it meant an end to his suffering.

I placed the phone back on its cradle, then looked over at Baldwin. He sat on my bed looking at me, a silent pillar of support. I found myself torn between two paths. Should I return to the hospital? Or should I stay here, safe with Baldwin?

The answer was clear. I needed to be with Dad, holding his hand for the last time. So, on that cold January morning, I made my way back to the hospital.

I entered Dad's room and saw him, his once commanding presence now reduced to a frail form, his face pallid and devoid of its former vitality. The sound of his breathing, once steady and rhythmic, still carried a gurgling undertone that I'd witnessed before.

I had no more words to share. At that moment, I hoped my presence would be a silent affirmation of love and support to help him on his final journey. I pulled up a chair and took his hand in mine.

"Give Mom a kiss from me," I murmured into his ear, then waited for his breath to fade away.

29

Unleash the Hounds

When I got home, I gathered my fluff ball into my arms.

"He's gone," I cried.

The sight of Baldwin reminded me of what Dad said the last time he came home from the hospital—how being greeted by my fluff ball and Molly the Collie was the best part of coming home. But there would be no homecoming for Dad this time. Still, I figured he'd be smiling in heaven, reunited with Molly, Siesta and even Pepper, the Dalmatian who surely was in heaven by now after living out his life at that farm.

For the next week, Erin, Will and I worked together to plan a celebration of life for our dad and take care of all the tasks that come along with the death of a family member.

At the service, I found myself surrounded by my family of friends while Erin, Will and their families supported one another. I didn't experience the same level of anxiety I'd felt during Mom's funeral, yet it's worth noting that her passing was a sudden blow to all of us, while Dad's departure appeared to be an act of mercy.

As I had done for Mom, I wrote a eulogy to deliver at Dad's service. When it was my turn, I stepped up to the lectern.

"Today, we gather here to honor the life and legacy of a remarkable man, my beloved father." My voice quivered, and I paused briefly, trying to hold back my tears.

"As you all know, he was a good man. And now my heart aches. I can't believe he's gone. But at the same time, I'm filled with an overwhelming sense of gratitude, thankful for the profound impact he had on my life."

I looked around the church at the familiar faces, a congregation of souls that had journeyed alongside Dad.

"My dad was more than just a father to me; he was my guiding light, my unwavering support, even through his final days battling with Parkinson's. He was the one who taught me to never give up, to believe in myself, and to chase my dreams. His love and encouragement were constant, driving me forward even when life seemed insurmountable."

Clearing my throat, I continued, "Beyond his role as an elder in this church and his stature as a respected professional engineer and community leader, it's well known that he had a remarkable sense of humor. April Fools' Day was one of his favorite occasions, and I lost count of the times he managed to trick me.

One year when I was about eight years old, he burst into my room, exclaiming that our family dog Siesta had miraculously given birth. I knew Siesta couldn't have puppies. She was spayed. But I fell for it. On another occasion, he convinced me that a family of goats had taken up residence in our backyard, a claim that proved to be entirely false, much to my disappointment."

In that instant, I started to cry.

"I don't know why his sense of humor is hitting me so hard," I said through my tears.

The room fell silent. I tried my best to regain composure. But I couldn't. That's when Kat came to my aid. Quickly making her way to the lectern, she draped her arm around me and took hold of my notes, proceeding on my behalf.

"From the simple joys of family vacations to the quiet moments we shared, each memory is a cherished treasure that I hold close to my heart—or close to her heart," Kat said, looking over at me. "His wisdom was a wellspring of guidance and inspiration, his kindness, integrity, and unwavering moral compass served as examples for me and all who were privileged to know him."

Kat stopped reading for a moment to add a piece of her own commentary, "I can attest to that. Dick Hartzler was one of the kindest men I ever knew."

She looked down at my notes and continued. "But it was his unconditional love that truly defined him as a father. Dad's love knew no bounds. It was a love that embraced me in moments of triumph and provided solace during my darkest days. It was a love that saw past my flaws (except when he tried to tutor me in math) and believed in my potential. I hope to carry his love, his values, and his wisdom with me throughout the rest of my life."

Somehow, I got myself together and motioned to Kat that I wanted to continue. She nodded and handed back my notes but stayed by my side.

"He often recounted a favorite story about me—a memory that still makes me smile. One day when I was about five, Dad and I passed a dog in front of a store and according to him, I dropped his hand and went over to pet it. 'Don't pet strange dogs, Suzie,' he told me. Undeterred, I knelt before the dog and said, 'Hello, my name is Suzie.'"

I looked at Will and Erin in the front row. The three of us, now orphans. Sure, we were all adults, with real-life responsibilities. But the three of us were now going through an incredibly painful stage of our lives, one that each of us would have come to terms with in our own way.

"One certainty is that when he arrives at the gates of heaven, introductions will not be necessary. God and his angels will recognize him by name. Mom will be there too, welcoming him with open arms. And back here on earth, his love will forever be alive in our hearts. Thank you for being an incredible dad, for the love, the laughter, and the memories. Farewell, dear father. May you rest in peace."

During the reception, a woman from the church approached me. I barely knew her. "It was so moving when your sister stood up to help you through your eulogy," she said.

I thought about telling her Kat was not my sister but decided against it. After all, Kat was my chosen sister.

The woman went on to say, "You're such a good girl. I truly wish I had a daughter like you."

Those words struck me with a mix of surprise and comfort, reminding me of the initial motivation that drove me to take on the responsibility of overseeing Dad's care—a desire to be seen as a "good girl" in the eyes of my family.

I'd hoped that by shouldering the responsibility of caring for Dad, I could prove my worth. In the process, I learned that my worth as a "good girl" could not be solely defined by the perception of others. I came to the conclusion that my true value was in the love, compassion, and dedication I'd shown Dad, regardless of the recognition I received. At least, that's what Baldwin would say if he could talk.

In the end, I understood that being a "good girl" was about finding fulfillment in knowing that I'd done what I believed to be right.

And with that understanding, I learned to embrace my life, feeling a fresh wellspring of gratitude for myself—a sentiment my chosen family, including Baldwin, had always held.

Afterword

In the absence of Dad, the family home felt empty. I missed his blaring CNN—I missed his humor—I missed his crazy hallucinations—I missed him. No more Jason, no more Molly the Collie either.

For the last three years, my life had revolved around being there for Dad, providing him with the care and support he needed. I'd built a purpose around well-being. So, when he passed away, it felt as though the foundation of my world shattered to bits.

Grief encompassed not only the loss of Dad but also the loss of my identity. It was a profound adjustment, one that required me to redefine my sense of self and find new meaning in life. I couldn't have done it without the love of Baldwin.

As time passed, and with the help of my family of friends and my boy Baldwin, I gradually learned to navigate life again. I discovered new paths and interests, found strength within myself, was surrounded by the love and support of those who genuinely cared, those who believed I was a good girl after all.

As for Mom's secret, unfortunately, that went with her to her grave. Over the years, I've asked relatives and her friends if they knew, but no one could shed light on the big secret. I've since come to terms with the not knowing. As a wise therapist once told me, I had only one night to find out what she hid while she had forty-two years to share her truth.

I continue on my journey to let go, something Baldwin brought to my attention so many years ago. Letting go is not an easy task and one that is never fully complete. My mantra now is let go and let go and let go. Sometimes I have to let go a hundred times or more a day.

The key to letting go starts with redirecting my focus to the present moment, another lesson I learned from Baldwin. The future is merely a creation of my imagination—it lacks actuality. The past only survives in recollections—and memories can be distorted. Only the current moment is authentic.

Afterword

Fear overcomes me from time to time when I consider the possibility of fighting my own battle with Parkinson's. I think about what Dr. Tapper told me about the disease being part genetic and part environmental. When I go down that rabbit hole, convincing myself that I have it, I reach out to Will, who talks me off the ledge.

I continue my volunteer work as the leader of a therapy dog team with my current pack, Seven and Paige Turner, two beautiful Australian Shepherds. Following in the pawsteps of Baldwin, they share their special kind of love with high school students at a nearby school. Witnessing the joy they bring to the kids they meet never ceases to amaze me.

The character Kat in this book is actually a combination of two dear friends, Kim and Cathy. I've known Kim since the fifth grade. She is a tremendous support and major part of my family of friends. Kim is the very definition of a "friend in need" and is always there for me when times get rough. Plus, she asked me to be her daughter's godmother and she gifted me my younger Australian Shepherd, Paige Turner. (The name is a combination of my goddaughter's middle name and a drag queen.)

Although we no longer work together, Cathy, whom I've known since the first grade, remains a significant presence in my life too. She left my growing business to marry a dog trainer! And I was there on their first date—Cathy and I donning kitty ears at an upscale restaurant. She is the mother of my other godchild and, of course, a treasured member of my family of friends.

After the strange occurrences I experienced following the deaths of Mom and Angel, I stayed on high alert after Dad passed, hoping for a similar connection with him from beyond. But I didn't notice anything out of the ordinary. After months, I began to think that maybe I would never receive a message from him.

In my quest for reassurance, I purchased white candles, their flames dancing with flickering hope. But, alas, there was only silence. I released balloons, wrote and burned heartfelt notes, smudged his red chair with white sage—I even created an altar next to his cherished TV. Still, I found no spiritual connection with Dad. The universe seemed resolute in its silence, withholding the confirmation and comfort I desperately craved.

While I yearned for a message from Dad in heaven, pennies started appearing everywhere. At the most unexpected moments, I stumbled upon one. They revealed themselves in the folds of my laundry, on sidewalks and in parking lots. Whether I found them when stepping out of my car at the gas station or on my walks with Baldwin, these small copper coins appeared as if deliberately placed in my path.

I found so many pennies that I finally picked one up, gazed up at heaven and asked, "What's with all the pennies?"

Suddenly, it struck me—I remembered the countless times Dad scattered pennies and spare change along the sidewalk on my route to grade school. He'd told me it was his way of bringing a bit of happiness to the lives of children, a way to brighten their day.

I grasped the meaning behind all the pennies from Dad—they were and are "pennies from heaven." Through these pennies, he reached out to me, reminding me to spread kindness, just as he'd done during his time on Earth.

Pennies have become tokens of love, reminders of Dad's selflessness, and a call to continue his legacy of making a positive difference in the lives of others. And so, my ritual to honor Dad was born.

I gather all the pennies I find throughout the year, and on Dad's birthday, I scatter them in front of a local elementary school. Scattering coins serves as a heartfelt tribute, spreading the love that Dad always gave so selflessly.

The pennies are a reminder of his love. And in the grand scheme of things, love is truly what matters. When I think about love, I think of Baldwin, the little fluff ball who embodied pure love in its most genuine form. I would have never been able to care for Dad without that fluff ball by my side.

But Baldwin's not alone. Dogs have an innate ability to love unconditionally, without judgment or reservation. They offer us their whole hearts, showering us with affection, loyalty, and devotion. Their love is not tainted by the complexities of human emotions or conditional expectations. It flows freely and effortlessly, creating an unbreakable bond between them and their human companions.

Dogs have an uncanny ability to sense our emotions, providing solace and companionship when we need it most. They offer a listening ear without interruption, a warm snuggle when we're feeling down, and a playful spirit when we need a little levity.

There's a good reason dog is God spelled backward. In the eyes of our four-legged family members and the Creator, we are perfectly imperfect and deserving of boundless affection. Dogs teach us valuable lessons about forgiveness, resilience, and the importance of living in the moment. Their simple presence reminds us of the power of love and its ability to heal, soothe, and lift our souls.

Afterword

Dogs serve as a constant reminder that love is the purest and most potent force in the universe. They teach us to cherish the connections we have with others, to embrace empathy and compassion, and to appreciate the simple joys that life has to offer.

In a world that can sometimes feel chaotic and uncertain, dogs remind us of what truly matters—to cherish and nurture the relationships we have and to embrace the beauty of the present moment. In the end, it's only love that counts—along with dogs, of course.

Appendix

Resources

Parkinson's Foundation
FL: 200 SE 1st Street, Ste 800, Miami, FL 33131, USA
NY: 1359 Broadway, Ste 1509, New York, NY 10018, USA
Helpline: 1-800-4PD-INFO (473-4636)

The Michael J. Fox Foundation for Parkinson's Research
Grand Central Station
P.O. Box 4777
New York, NY 10163-4777
212-509-0995

Caregiver Action Network
1150 Connecticut Ave, NW, Suite 501
Washington, DC
202-454-3970

Family Caregiver Alliance
235 Montgomery Street, Suite 930
San Francisco, CA 94104
800-445-8106

Terms and Places

CPAP

A CPAP (Continuous Positive Airway Pressure) machine is used primarily to treat obstructive sleep apnea by delivering a continuous flow of air to keep the airways open during sleep. It consists of a mask that fits over the nose and mouth, connected to a machine that generates and regulates air pressure. CPAP therapy helps improve sleep quality and reduces daytime fatigue for individuals with sleep apnea.

Appendix

Grunge

Grunge fashion emerged in the late 1980s and early 1990s, featuring flannel shirts, ripped jeans, and unkempt appearances that symbolized a rejection of mainstream trends and a desire for authenticity. The genre's popularity surged globally in the early 1990s, influencing fashion, culture, and music well beyond its Seattle roots, though its commercial success eventually waned by the mid-1990s

Northridge

Northridge is a neighborhood in the San Fernando Valley region of the City of Los Angeles. Home to California State University, Northridge, the area can trace its history back to the Togvan people and later to Spanish explorers. Northridge Hospital, ranked by Healthgrades as one of America's 50 Best Hospitals, is a 394-bed not-for-profit hospital. It holds a special place in my heart. During my teenage years, I volunteered as a candy striper there. When I split my head open in high school, I joked to the doctor in the ER that I was thinking of doing some sewing that day.

1959 Nuclear Disaster at the Santa Susana Field Laboratory In the mid-1940s, high in the hills above the farthest end of the west San Fernando Valley, Atomics International dedicated 2,850 acres of land to test rockets intended for space exploration and for nuclear reactors designed for energy production. Over the years, Santa Susana hosted sensitive projects, which in turn left their toxic legacies, including one of America's worst nuclear meltdowns.

Parkinson's Disease

Parkinson's disease is a chronic neurological condition marked by the progressive loss of nerve cells in the brain that produce dopamine, a key neurotransmitter for movement and coordination. As dopamine levels decline, individuals may experience movement issues such as tremors, severe rigidity, and shuffling gait, as in Dad's case. Parkinson's disease dementia is a complication of Parkinson's disease characterized by cognitive decline and changes in thinking, memory, and behavior. It affects some but not all people with the condition, typically developing later in the disease.

PETA

The international animal rights organization PETA, or People for the Ethical Treatment of Animals, promotes vegetarianism, veganism, and ethical treatment of animals through protests, legal actions, and public awareness campaigns.

Reiki

Reiki is a holistic healing technique that originated in Japan. Practitioners use their hands to channel universal life force energy to promote relaxation, reduce stress, and facilitate physical, emotional, and spiritual healing. It is based on the belief that energy can be transferred through touch, balancing the body's energy centers and promoting overall well-being.

Relationship Cycling

Relationship cycling refers to the pattern where individuals repeatedly break up and reconcile with their partners. It often reflects unresolved issues or conflicts within the relationship and/or participants, leading to a cycle of separation and reunion.

Reward-Based Dog Training

In reward-based training, dogs are taught using motivators like treats or play, and these rewards are withheld when the dog misbehaves. Hint: it works with people, too!

Roger Wagner Chorale

The Roger Wagner Chorale was quite the sensation in its prime. Under the direction of conductor Roger Wagner, the group became famous for their renditions of timeless classics and contemporary choral pieces.

Sherwood Forest

A community in Northridge often referred to as Sherwood Forest due to the large estates and small ranches within its boundaries.

Spago

On January 16, 1982, the groundbreaking restaurant created by renowned chef Wolfgang Puck welcomed its first patrons. It immediately became a sensation, transforming the culinary world from its location on the Los Angeles Sunset Strip. Spago became known as the place where business magnates and Hollywood celebrities indulged in drugs and engaged in sex in the restroom, all while hard-pressed line cooks hustled to serve the restaurant's signature dishes.

Appendix

Stages of Grief

The 5 stages of grief, as proposed by Elisabeth Kübler-Ross, are denial, anger, bargaining, depression, and acceptance. These stages represent a framework for understanding the emotional process individuals may go through when facing significant loss or trauma, though not everyone experiences them linearly or sequentially. They serve as a guide for acknowledging and navigating the complex emotions of grief and mourning.

The Yangtze or Yangzi River

The Yangtze is the longest river in Eurasia, the third longest river in the world, and the longest river to flow entirely within one country.

Index